The War Against Naturalism

In the Contemporary American Theatre

Robert J. Andreach

D1571158

UNIVERSITY PRESS OF AMERICA,® INC.
Lanham • Boulder • New York • Toronto • Plymouth, UK

Copyright © 2008 by
University Press of America,® Inc.
4501 Forbes Boulevard
Suite 200
Lanham, Maryland 20706
UPA Acquisitions Department (301) 459-3366

PO Box 317
Oxford
OX2 9RU, UK

Library of Congress Control Number: 2007932869
ISBN-13: 978-0-7618-3864-7 (paperback : alk. paper)
ISBN-10: 0-7618-3864-3 (paperback : alk. paper)

For Kevin, Jason, and Thelma; George
and Elaine; and Jim (in memoriam) and Mary

Contents

Acknowledgments

I wish to thank Akadémiai Kiadó for permission to reprint, in rewritten form, Robert J. Andreach, "Richard Foreman's *Paradise Hotel* and Georges Feydeau's Farces," *Neohelicon* 30.2 (2003) 119–32, and Robert J. Andreach, "Aeschylus' *Eumenides*: Providing Entrance to Mac Wellman's Theatre," *Neohelicon* 33.1 (2006) 179–90, @ Akadémiai Kiadó.

I also wish to thank a former colleague, Professor John Stibravy, for sharing resources and Professor Colby H. Kullman of the University of Mississippi for sharing his experiences with the contemporary American theatre.

Finally, I wish to thank Ms. Patty Shannon of The Wordstation, Avon, New Jersey, for preparing the manuscript; Ms. Joanne P. Foeller of Timely Publication Services, Dunkirk, New York, for preparing the index; and Ms. Patti D. Belcher of University Press of America for assisting in the production process.

Introduction: The War at the Close of the 20th Century

Tracing the development of his interest in playwrighting through *The House of Blue Leaves*, John Guare concludes the preface to a volume of his early plays with the realization he had in the late 1960s that

> what the playwright does with the icon of naturalism, the kitchen sink, is the story of twentieth-century playwrighting. Does the playwright elect to keep that kitchen sink to soothe the audience? Does the playwright dismantle the kitchen sink and take the audience into dangerous terrain? How the playwright resolves the tension between surface reality and inner reality, how the playwright restores the theater to its true nature as a place of poetry, song, joy, a place of darkness where the bright truth is told, that war against the kitchen sink is ultimately the history of our theater.[1]

The "dangerous terrain" may be imagination, dreams, the unconscious: a force beneath the surface in conflict with the surface. But I want to extend the closing sentence so that it is an approach to the contemporary American theatre. I do not mean the war against just the sink but the war against the naturalistic play, the symbol of which is the kitchen sink with running water. I argue that to generate the "tension between surface reality and inner reality" that creates the war, the surface reality that must be in the play is some element of the naturalistic play.

Marvin Carlson's encyclopedic *Theories of the Theatre* is a good starting point for isolating the elements that distinguish the naturalistic play from other types of plays. A naturalistic play emphasizes surface, material reality: how the characters actually live accomplished through the accumulation of details from their everyday, commonplace existence in a milieu that is presented with such scientific objectivity that the audience is an observer of the life depicted rather than an imaginative participant in it.[2] Although Carlson

1

discusses the scientific determinism of Émile Zola, whose *Thérèse Raquin* many consider to be the quintessential naturalistic play, William W. Demastes summarizes Zola's position more concisely because he is not surveying the history of Western theatre as Carlson is:

> Identifying the fundamental difference between [George Henry] Lewes and Zola basically identifies the difference between realism in general and what has been specifically coined naturalism. Realism, according to Lewes's presentation, assumes that close study and creative reenactment of real life will guarantee accuracy and "truth" in art. It is an approach to drama whose flexibility theoretically can succeed at reflecting any of a variety of outlooks or perspectives on, and philosophies of, existence. Zola goes a bold step further, using realism in a specific and limited manner to present his adopted philosophy of scientific determinism, one founded on a belief in some basic rationality governing the universe that can be tapped and used to predict human events and behavior when applied to prior knowledge of genetic and social antecedents. . . . Zola's naturalism . . . has managed to fuse both realist technique and its own adopted assumptions into one, gathering and presenting common experience, but assuming precision in observation and deriving a sense of "inevitability" that Lewes's realism nowhere presumed.[3]

To the starting point, we can add the following: Since the universe is rationally governed, the playwright, who like the scientist is an experimenter, sets in motion the characters and the forces such as heredity and environment that determine their behavior, forces that they can neither fully understand nor control, so that the audience can observe the inevitable outcome.

We can test the validity of these elements by analyzing their presence in Tracy Letts' *Bug*, a work that premiered in London in 1996, played in Chicago in 2001, and had a very successful run in 2004 in New York's Off-Broadway, where I saw it performed. In the prologue a woman, Agnes, stands in the open doorway of a motel room, smoking and staring into space. The motel is on the outskirts of Oklahoma City, the sounds those of radio music from another motel room and the drone of traffic on a nearby highway. This is her milieu: a disheveled room with her waitress apron on the floor, a rumpled bed, an air conditioner that works only after she bangs on it with her fist, full and empty wine bottles, dirty dishes that she collects and puts in the bathroom sink with running water, and cocaine that a lesbian friend and co-worker, R.C., freebases in scene 1 and that she and another character, Peter, smoke off and on throughout the two-act play in the single-set motel room.

The costumes are appropriate for the situation: shirt and jeans, cutoffs and tank top, bathrobe, and occasionally none at all. The language is coarse. Believing the caller on the telephone that rings periodically in the prologue to be her ex-husband, Agnes calls him a "son of a bitch," hangs up on him with "Fuck you," and tells him, "Fuck off, all right? I don't need this shit."[4] His language is scatological. In act 2 he asks R.C. whether she remembers the time when her sexual partner had an urgent call of nature and "took a crap off the balcony at Mickey's place 'n hit that police car?" (33)

Agnes is trapped in the milieu. She lives in the motel in an attempt to escape her ex-husband, Jerry, but though he denies being the caller, the phone calls suggest that he has tracked her and is not intimidated by her threat to alert the police: "If they can trace it [the particular phone call] to you, you're busted, you're in direct, y' know, whatever" (8). Presumably she means a court order theoretically protecting her. Just released from prison after serving a sentence for armed robbery, he slaps her, knocking her to the floor. She is not alone in feeling besieged. When scene 1 opens, Agnes, smoking the freebase, and R.C., cutting the cocaine, are talking about a man, who the audience assumes is Jerry, until the dialogue indicates another man, who enters the room from the bathroom after the scene is well underway. He is Peter, whom R.C. picked up in the course of the evening and who stays in the room after R.C. leaves. At first he seems to be slow—certainly odd in his affectless statements that suggest he inhabits another plane of existence. It is in act 2, however, that he articulates one of the naturalistic play's distinguishing elements if "forces" is substituted for "people" in the following exchange:

Peter: People can do things to you, things you don't even know about.

Agnes: What kind of things?

Peter: They try to control you. They try to force you to act a certain way. They can drive you crazy too. . . . I shouldn't talk about it. I don't know if it's safe or not (21).

In scene 3 he elaborates after he and Agnes in a scene that is funny and disturbing tear the bed apart searching for the bug that bit him. Stationed in the Syrian Desert during the Gulf War, he and other members of his outfit were subjected to tests by doctors that made them sick. He was brought home to an army hospital where the testing intensified and where he was kept for he thinks four years until he managed to go AWOL. "Those fucking doctors were experimenting on me. . . . They're after me. These people don't fuck around, Agnes" (29), he concludes his narrative. Act 1 ends with the two hugging, Agnes noticing something in his hair, and both aware of the sound of a helicopter, first heard in scene 2, now getting louder.

Act 1 of *Bug* is thoroughly naturalistic, so much so that were the critics alive who attacked Zola, they could reapply their criticism. The work investigates the "'crude and gross.'" As for Jerry, he is a mere animal "with nothing human about" him. "Synonymous with scatology," the work stimulates "interest in the vulgar and obscene." It is "exclusively interested in the baser side of man," ignoring "the interior, the invisible, the spiritual" in human nature.[5] The final point would be the critics' weakest argument, for Agnes suffers guilt for having lost her child years earlier. As she relates the event, she left him unattended for a moment while shopping in a grocery store, and when she returned, he was gone, having wandered off or been kidnapped; years of searching failed to recover him. Peter believes that humans have a "center" that should be kept "sacred, in some sense, on some level" (26), but convinced of conspiracies against victims like himself, he is wary of revealing the center until he is sure of the other person.

Act 2 is naturalistic and something else. Peter has cluttered Agnes' disheveled room with her lost son's "*kiddie chemistry set*," and all the contents of the foot locker in which it was stored, and "*weapons of a bug war*" (30) such as sprays, fly strips, and flyswatter because he has come to believe that the room is infested. As the act opens, he is conducting an experiment with a captured bug in a petri dish containing a few drops of his blood in an attempt to determine the rationality governing the universe because he has come to believe that the bugs are evidence of the presence of the forces attempting to control him; they are evidence of the conspiracy. R.C. introduces the something else. She and Agnes enter during the experiment; unknown to Peter, they have been to a dermatologist. As Peter pressures Agnes into agreeing with his perception, the co-worker interrupts to argue that "there ain't no bugs in the microscope, on your skin, *in* your skin. In the room. *There ain't no fuckin' bugs.*" Since the dermatologist, who prescribed an ointment for Agnes, said her wounds were "'self-inflicted,'" R.C. takes the argument to its logical conclusion. Confronting Peter, she claims that Agnes "done this to herself, just like you. Or you done it to her" (37). From her perspective, the bugs are a delusion and Peter is a person in need of "serious medical attention" (38). She urges her friend to leave the motel and stay with her for a while.

Agnes is caught between the two. Confused by the dermatologist's diagnosis and the fact that hers is the only room in the motel that has bugs, she does not know what to believe. She does not want to alienate her one friend, nor does she want to antagonize the one person who has brought love and companionship into her lonely motel existence. When she shows Peter the prescription ointment, he throws it into the bathroom, accusing her of disloyalty: "They got to you. Goddamnit, if you're part of this —." No, she protests; she only wants "some kind of explanation" (36). She will get that in the final two scenes. This scene ends with Peter's collapse following what appears to be a violent bug attack and her decision not to leave with R.C. but to stay and care for him.

If Peter is right, the bugs not only exist but they have infested the room, and they are evidence of forces that control people. He is trying to understand how and why. In other words, there is a rationality, evil though it may be. If R.C. is right, the bugs do not exist, Peter is mentally ill, and the conspiracy is not merely a theory but a delusion. As for a rationality governing the universe, there may or may not be one. The final two scenes dramatize both possibilities, which up to a point are both plausible.

Lying in bed with Agnes, the couple swatting bugs, Peter gets the insight that a sac of bugs was implanted in him, an unwitting guinea pig, as an experiment to test his reaction before being used as a weapon of war, for example. The arrival of a Doctor Sweet supports the contention. Initially professing to be a consultant who wants to help Agnes' companion, "diagnosed as a delusional paranoid with schizophrenic tendencies" (44), he reverses his position and admits to being part of the experiment in which Peter is the "project" (46) on whom a mistake was made and who must be brought in. Peter kills him—or it, since to the guinea pig, Sweet is a programmed machine. The pace becomes feverish with the room barricaded and the two inhabitants, he goading and she complying, constructing an explanation, a conspiracy theory that accounts for the events, even those such as the son's disappearance that happened years earlier. Its crowning piece is her insight that she too has been part of the experiment with the queen bug having been implanted in her waiting for him to come to the motel with the sac of drones in him so that their intercourse would release an army of bugs. Convinced they are right, they throw gasoline around the room and in the closing image strike a match. In an act of self-immolation, they sacrifice themselves to stop the bugs from spreading. It is their sole way to escape the forces controlling them and all of life under the dominant culture's power.

The explanation that Agnes seeks may be a paranoid delusional lunacy constructed by two crackheads, one of whom is a desperately lonely woman who will do or say anything so as not to lose her man as she lost her son, or there may be a conspiracy. To substantiate his contention, Peter cites instances where the government experimented on American citizens as unwitting guinea pigs. If, however, one's interpretation is R.C.'s interpretation, the something else that she introduces is a parody of a naturalistic play with act 2 performed so over the top that it is an effort for the spectator not to howl with laughter. Furthermore, that *Bug* has elements of other types of plays in it—play noir, the equivalent to film noir, for example—suggests that it may not be a pure naturalistic play. In act-1's scene 1, Peter emerges from the bathroom in the middle of the conversation Agnes and R.C. are having about the stranger the latter picked up earlier in the evening. Scene 2 opens with Agnes waking up in bed and the sound of someone showering in the bathroom. The audience and Agnes assume the someone is Peter, but when the figure emerges, he is Jerry, who entered the motel with Peter out shopping and his ex-wife asleep. He can be a menacing figure.

Yet *Bug* also contains elements of a naturalistic play not emphasized. In September of 2004, Kate Buddeke replaced Shannon Cochran in the role of Agnes in the New York production, a change reviewed in an article entitled "Stepping into a Battle for Survival." The title implies the Darwinian struggle fundamental to naturalism while the closing lines imply its pessimistic determinism: "What the two Agneses have in common is that it's hard not to like them, and to hope that just this once, they will come out triumphant against evil and ex-husbands and bug bites. Yet you somehow know from that first moment, watching her watch the cars pass by, that even before the infestation, Agnes is outnumbered."[6]

Whether performed as a naturalistic play or a parody of it, as waging war against it or having fun with it, *Bug* is thoroughly enjoyable theatre but with the element of controlling forces the issue so dominating act 2 that the audience can overlook the other elements. To correct this sort of imbalance, Edwin Wilson reminds his audience that *naturalism* as a term referring to a theatre championed by 19th-century writers such as Zola—a theatre in which characters are products of heredity and environment—is a special use:

> Aside from this special use, the term *naturalism* is used more broadly for attempts to put on stage as exact a copy of life as possible, down to the smallest detail. In a naturalistic stage set of a kitchen, for instance, a performer can actually cook a meal on the stove—the toaster makes toast, the water tap produces water, and the light in the refrigerator goes on when the door opens. Characters speak and act as if they had been caught unobserved by a camera and tape recorder. In this sense, naturalism is supposed to resemble an undoctored documentary film. Naturalism is sometimes called *slice-of-life* drama, as if a section had been taken from life and transferred to the stage.[7]

If we think of the elements as divided between philosophical issues and production issues, the division follows from the second basic document in naturalistic theatre, Zola's *Thérèse Raquin* with its preface being the first document: August Strindberg's *Miss Julie* with its preface. In the preface's first half, Strindberg addresses the forces making characters who they are; in the second half, the unnatural conventions in scenic and lighting designs, for example, and in the actors playing "directly at" the audience rather than "for the audience."[8]

Thus the critic must be mindful of the shades of meaning when using the term. It can be used to describe Beth Henley's theatre, for instance, but only in certain ways. The dominant culture in her plays is patriarchal whose members perceive women and other marginal characters naturalistically. They perceive them as animals. When a man in *The Wake of Jamey Foster* makes an advance on his sister-in-law's sister by lifting her chin, she protests that she is not a horse. "You are a horse! A goddamn horse!"[9] he answers her, backing her against a chair. They perceive them as governed by disorders they cannot control. A brother in *Control Freaks* does not hit his sister but not because he loves her or respects women. He does not hit her because she has "woman problems" like "PMS disease" and cannot help herself.[10] They perceive them as driven by need as opposed to intelligence or judgment. In a bar in *L-Play*, one man advises another man, who wants "to get laid," to buy the woman a trinket; women, he argues, are so desperate for signs of affection that they can easily be maneuvered into bed.[11] The plays are not philosophically naturalistic, however, because the outsiders discover spiritual qualities and faculties in themselves that the patriarchal culture denies them. They discover love and imagination that enable them not only to create art but more importantly to create their own lives. Henleyan heroines and heroes are characters who overcome the culture's naturalistic perception of them and the attendant self-deprecation.

As a mode of production, the term does apply to Henley's plays but only those of the 1980s. The first full-length play of that decade, *Crimes of the Heart*, opens on the play's single set, a kitchen with refrigerator, table, counter—what an audience expects to see in a kitchen. At this point the mode is realistic. Midway through act 1, one of the sisters, Babe, decides to make lemonade. To do so, she has to collect the ingredients, cut the lemons, pour in the sugar, stir the ice cubes, and so on. *Crimes* becomes naturalistic, the mode supported by Henley's reminiscence in the introduction of her delight when the prop master designed a "fake cake with a smaller real section allowing the sisters to cut, eat, and smear cake every night."[12] The setting of *The Wake of Jamey Foster*, also of the 1980s, specifies twenty-four items for the interior of the house in which the action takes place with some of the items plural: books, wreaths, and drill-team outfits, among others. The mode of production is important in discussing Henley's theatre because it is not naturalistic in the 1990s. In the second decade, she experiments with light and sound to set a scene.

Plays in which characters through self-discovery overcome a naturalistic perception of them as less than fully human and/or an attendant self-deprecating perception are not included in the study. Cheryl L. West's *Jar the Floor* therefore is not included, although its naturalistic setting with most of the action taking place in the well-decorated kitchen and living room of a woman's home would qualify it for inclusion. Performance art is not included because the war is against the naturalistic play, and performance art succeeds precisely because it does not resemble a play. Neither are plays included which bear no resemblance to a naturalistic play. To be included, a play must have a surface reality indicated no matter how oblique or tenuous it is because the key passage extended from the Guare quotation opening this introduction has to do with the "tension between surface reality and inner reality." The two realities are required to create a tension and a war.

The book is a study of a variety of models in which contemporary American playwrights combat the naturalistic play, and the models are examined according to categories beginning with the total play and then moving through such categories as setting, language, and character behavior, trying to keep them separate while knowing they cannot be. Characters do not use language in a vacuum; they speak while acting or behaving in a stage setting. Nevertheless, the book will try to keep the categories separate. Finally, some of the playwrights whose plays are examined as models express their attitudes toward the naturalistic play in their non-dramatic writings. Their comments should help to dispel any lingering confusion at the outset in recognizing the type of play under attack.

NOTES

1. John Guare, preface, *The War Against the Kitchen Sink* (Lyme, NH: Smith and Kraus, 1996), xii.

2. Marvin Carlson, *Theories of the Theatre: A Historical and Critical Survey, from the Greeks to the Present*, exp. ed. (Ithaca: Cornell UP, 1993), 230 passim.

3. William W. Demastes, *Beyond Naturalism: A New Realism in American Theatre*, Contributions in Drama and Theatre Studies 27 (New York: Greenwood, 1988), 15–16. Demastes' book is also important for studying playwrights who precede those in this book. For Carlson's analysis of Zola's position, see *Theories of the Theatre*, 274–82.

4. Tracy Letts, *Bug* (New York: Dramatists Play Service, 2005), 7–8. Hereafter to be cited parenthetically.

5. Carlson, 285–86.

6. Ada Calhoun, "Stepping into a Battle for Survival," *New York Times*, 26 Sept. 2004, sec. 2, 5.

7. Edwin Wilson, *The Theater Experience*, 3rd ed. (New York: McGraw, 1985), 259.

8. August Strindberg, "Preface to Miss Julie," trans. E.M. Sprinchorn, in *Dramatic Theory and Criticism: Greeks to Grotowski*, ed. Bernard F. Dukore (New York: Holt, 1974), 573.

9. Beth Henley, *The Wake of Jamey Foster*, in *Collected Plays Volume I: 1980–1989* (Lyme, NH: Smith and Kraus, 2000), 124.

10. Beth Henley, *Control Freaks*, in *Collected Plays Volume II: 1990–1999* (Lyme, NH: Smith and Kraus, 2000), 138.

11. Beth Henley, *L-Play*, in *Collected Plays Volume II: 1990–1999*, 219.

12. Beth Henley, introduction, *Collected Plays Volume I: 1980–1989*, ix.

Chapter One

The War in the Total Play and in Setting: Ludlam and Eno; Johnson, Lindsay-Abaire, Lucas, and Groff

The Ridiculous Theatrical Company's *The Artificial Jungle* is a good place to begin the total play because one of the sources for the play's plot is Zola's *Thérèse Raquin*, and the Company's founder, Charles Ludlam, expressed his attitude toward naturalism more than once in notebooks and papers collected and edited after his death in 1987, as in these lines: "The theatre has been held in a kind of death grip during the last seventy years of naturalism. It has evolved into pornography—a peephole on life."[1] Here he is referring to naturalism as a slice-of-life drama in which the cast perform as if unobserved behind an invisible fourth wall. For playwright, director, and actor Ludlam, theatre should be theatrical; cast and audience should be interactive bodies, drawing energy from each other. Elsewhere he refers to naturalism as a mode of production or a conception of humankind. Either way it is "shallow" (17), being "less than you are" (17), a "limited exercise in style" (95), and a "stereotyped way of saying that the conditions of your life determined who you were," a conception the members of his Company "rejected" (235). In summary, whereas naturalism is exclusive, the Ridiculous Theatrical Company is inclusive, reviving discarded theatre traditions and conventions, and whereas naturalism is constrictive, the Company is expansive with outlandish costumes, heightened language, and exaggerated acting styles—all consistent with the ridiculous treatment of the subject matter. For Ludlam, the "ability to recognize opposites in ourselves is the basis of art, definitely of drama" (165). Opposites in the human being are the male and female principles in a conflict that ranges from awareness of both but with only one acted on to collision when both are active. The goal is to achieve some kind of harmony until the next inevitable eruption, for the absence of conflict is death. The fundamental human drama is the fundamental stage drama. In practical terms "forcing together two things that don't usually mix" is one of the playwright's

The War in the Total Play and in Setting   11

tactics: "I love to put two literary or theatrical forms on collision course, even when they don't seem to go together, and even when I can't figure out what their relationship is" (99).

The two forms he puts together in *The Artificial Jungle* are Zola's *Thérèse Raquin* and James M. Cain's *The Postman Always Rings Twice*. The setting for Zola's play is the residence of the Raquin family: Madame, son Camille, and daughter-in-law Thérèse. "*It is lofty, dark and dilapidated . . . cluttered up with cardboard boxes of haberdashery,*"[2] sold below in the family's shop to which a flight of stairs leads. The novel *Thérèse Raquin*, from which Zola made the dramatization, has a much fuller description of the grubby shop beginning, "In one window there were some odd bits of clothing. . . ."[3] *The Artificial Jungle* is more faithful to the novel in that it is set in the shop, but it is immediately a takeoff on Zola's work. The audience is seated as if in the back of the shop looking at the family—Mrs. Nurdiger, son Chester, and daughter-in-law Roxanne—in the front of the shop and beyond them to the street. Moreover, the business is a pet shop with caged rodents for clientele such as the lady who buys a "weekly rat for her boa constrictor"[4] and as a centerpiece a tank of piranhas fed periodically by the family. The treatment is ridiculous, but at the same time, it captures the Darwinian struggle in the natural world.

A stranger's arrival in the shop activates the struggle for survival in the human world. Cain's roman noir opens with a drifter, Frank Chambers, having been thrown off a hay truck entering a California roadside sandwich joint, where the owner, Nick, offers him a job as mechanic in the adjacent filling station. He accepts only after he sees Nick's wife, Cora. In what seems no more than a twenty-four-hour period, he asks her, "'How come you married this Greek, anyway?'"[5] advises him to have a new sign made for the business after the old one comes down during a windstorm, and with Nick gone into town, locks the door so that he and Cora will not be disturbed. "'Bite me! Bite me!'" she urges him to kiss her. He does with the result that the blood is running down her neck as he carries "her upstairs" (11). In act 1 of *The Artificial Jungle*, Zackary, identified in the cast listing as a "*drifter and a smoothie*" (879), enters the shop, accepts a job offer, and with Chester out of the shop whispers in Roxanne's ear, "Why did you marry this guy, anyway?" (883) He too proposes a new sign for the business but has to wait until act 2 for a kiss, urged by Roxanne: "Now kiss me, Zack. Kiss me till I bleed" (890).

Ludlam's play continues to appropriate passages and details from the other two works but always ridiculously. In the roman noir, Cora confides in Frank that she cannot tolerate living with her husband any longer. "'There's one way'" they can be together, she says, to which he replies, "'They hang you for that'" (16). The comparable dialogue in the play even includes a line Thérèse says when the conversation in the group that meets every Thursday evening for dominoes in the naturalistic play turns on getting away with murder: "What no one knows, doesn't exist" (41). "Let's do it," Roxanne says to Zack, prompting his reply, "You can fry for that," to which she replies, "No one will know but you and me. . . . And what no one knows does not exist" (890). It takes two attempts for Frank and Cora to kill Nick, the second attempt in his car rigged to look like an accident. Killing Chester takes two attempts also, although the second requires adjustment before it is successful. Roxanne's plan is to poison her husband and then have Zack and her dump the body in the piranha tank, where the fish will destroy the evidence. The two conspirators have to adjust the killing to smothering, Zack applying a pillow, when they realize that the poison is lethal to piranhas. Act 2 ends with a dead Chester dumped into the tank.

In the 19th-century play, Laurent, Camille's boyhood friend and Thérèse's lover, kills her husband, but the desire that brought the two together is now blighted. On their wedding night, Laurent tries to persuade Thérèse that they can be happy until he sees Camille's portrait that he painted and that hangs on the bedroom wall. "*Recoiling in terror*" (71), he believes the dead man is alive and in the room with them. By act 4 the strain of living together pretending to be a happily married couple is unbearable. "He is living with us—he sits on my chair—he is next to me at the table" (90), Laurent raves to his co-conspirator. In the 20th-century play, the dead Chester actually appears in scenes until he rises from behind the domino table "*and sits in his chair*" (905), giving Ludlam, who played the role in the premiere run, an opportunity to display his comic versatility; Everett Quinton, who played Zackary, an opportunity to scream and rave; and Black-Eyed Susan, who played Roxanne, an opportunity to try to calm her lover. The repeated appearances at different places onstage gave them the opportunity to actualize the Ridiculous Theatrical Company's style, as stated in production playbills, of synthesizing "wit, parody, vaudeville farce, melodrama and satire, giving reckless immediacy to classical stagecraft." Each Company member was virtuosic in revealing himself/herself as performer, the role or roles he/she was playing, and the multiple facets of a role while all of these constituents were on a collision course and without blurring them.[6] By varying the direction of his gaze onstage and at the audience and the emotion it conveyed, Ludlam was Charles Ludlam, nerdy Chester, and wrathful Nurdiger. But, the critic can argue, he could have achieved the same style without the naturalistic play; he could have paired *The Postman Always Rings Twice* with some other work.

Yes, he could have, but by reimagining *Thérèse Raquin* in ridiculous theatre, he revived interest in Zola's play, just as he awakened interest in the genre of play noir, theatre's counterpart to Cain's roman noir, itself the source of an outstanding film noir. Most important for this study, however, is that *The Artificial Jungle* dramatizes a defining objection to naturalism, an objection that will be repeated in subsequent models. In his preface to the novel

Thérèse Raquin, Zola states his aim as trying "to explain the mysterious attraction that can spring up between two different temperaments," and a page later, he characterizes the writing of the novel as a "giving" of himself "up entirely to precise analysis of the mechanism of the human being."[7] Ludlam's theatre's policy is "to give the irrational free play and to mine this source" (115). The final image of *The Artificial Jungle* is that of a mystery, that which defies precise analysis.

In the Zola novel and play, Madame Raquin suffers a stroke upon discovering that Laurent and Thérèse murdered her son. She tries to communicate with her eyes to the group that gathers for the Thursday domino games, but the guests misread her signals. The novel ends with the conspirators dead from poison they drank on the floor by her feet while her eyes "crushed them with brooding hate" (256). The play ends with her "*slowly sitting*," for she summoned enough strength to stand, while exulting: "Dead! dead!" (93) Just before he dies from the poison, Ludlam's Zackary bitterly complains to the "stars, the thousand unseeing eyes that look back" on the world, that they reveal an "indifference" to humankind's plight. The universe is "senseless and ultimately stupid" (905). His speech can be interpreted as naturalistic in that there is or was a rationality governing existence, but it cannot be used to predict human behavior because it has retreated, leaving humans victims of impulses they cannot control. Yet even if interpreted this way, the speech's central image collides with the play's closing image. The stage lights "*fade except for two tiny points of light on* Mother Nurdiger*'s eyes*" (905). The contrast between Zackary's "unseeing eyes" and Chester's mother's seeing "*eyes*" is unavoidable. Furthermore, intensifying the mystery in the eyes seeing the scene, eyes that are not indifferent to her son's death, was the giving of the role not only to a male but to an actor whose height alone made him a great stage presence seated or standing: Ethyl Eichelberger.

This closing image illustrates Ludlam's belief that one of theatre's functions at the end of the era naturalism dominated is the recovery of its "magical and religious basis," a basis naturalism rejects. "I don't think everything can be explained" (137), he continues before concluding this section of his edited autobiography: "The Ridiculous is not only a wonderful form of entertainment but a lens through which we gladly contemplate the mystery of existence" (142). The Company's founder saw his theatre as an "instrument for social change" (35) by making audiences more tolerant of other possibilities for living. Hence the cross-dressing in productions as an instance of addressing the multiple, conflicting impulses within the human being, male and female sexual determinants being obvious ones.

A Ludlam criticism of naturalism, quoted above, is that it is a "peephole on life" in which the cast perform as if unobserved behind an invisible fourth wall. Will Eno's criticism is essentially the same. Because a naturalistic set is complete, "down to the last electrical outlet," this kind of theatre "makes no use of the audience's imagination. There's nothing to do, except sit there until you leave." He then gives an example of something happening in a "desperately naturalistic play" that will awaken the audience: the disconnection between the onstage actor turning on a light switch and the offstage manager turning on the light a "second early or late."[8] Disconnection, or the contrast between what is expected and what occurs, therefore is a way of getting the audience to engage in the action, and as Eno writes in a note to *The Flu Season*, the "audience is meant to participate . . . and not just watch. . . ."[9]

Disconnection from theatrical convention or dramatic structure is immediately apparent in Eno's play because the first two speakers are Prologue and Epilogue, the latter the only one aware of both of them. Their disconnection is apparent when Prologue introduces the play as "'The Snow Romance'" and Epilogue corrects the title to "'The Flu Season'" (19). Yet the fact that he makes the correction and goes on to agree with Prologue in the description of the time and place establishes their connection. The two speakers have different perspectives on the action—one the original conception and the other the revision—but they are in the same play. If *The Flu Season* eliminated narrative, it might be an absurdist play, a surrealist play, or performance art. It is none of these. Rather, it experiments with narrative though not ridiculously as Ludlam does. Prologue and Epilogue appear not only before the first scene, for example, but at the end of scenes to comment on the action they have been observing.

At the end of act-1's seventh scene, Prologue comments, "Our love story has progressed." Epilogue agrees while cautioning, "Maybe there's more to it" (39). To appreciate Eno's experiment, we will first examine the creating of the love story and hold off on the "more to it." The play's setting is naturalistic: a "mental health institution" (17) with characters whose generic designations imply they are clinical subjects in a Zolaesque sense rather than individuals, for a character named Doctor enters and approaches a character, seated in darkness, named Man. Doctor's language is disconcerting in that it is a mixture of formal and informal—"Licking our wounds with our wounded tongue. . .?" he asks (21)—although the audience might conclude that his manner is intended to relax a new patient apprehensive about the institution's procedures. Once the interview begins, however, a noninstitutional undercurrent makes itself felt. Doctor and Man and then Nurse and Woman, the latter a patient, build the dialogue on the repetition with minute variations of their own and one another's verbal images, as Doctor did with "wounds" and "wounded." When Man protests that he cannot engage in the exchange his interviewer would like him to because the mind does not work "quickly," Doctor "quickly" asks him a question (22). When Woman uses the idiomatic expression "totally out of the blue," Nurse repeats it (23). At one point while Doctor asks Man a torturous question about multiple personalities, the patient, holding his breath, turns "*blue*" (22). The scene's language ranges from silly—Man trying to speak while holding his breath—to overly "elegiac" (25)—Nurse's judgment on Woman's lament for her situation.

Since the first scene's surface is a mental institution, *The Flu Season* is naturalistic; in the 2004 Rude Mechanicals Theater Company production, David Korins' scenic design was hospital white with a minimum of furniture. Since the scene's language and behavior reveal an undercurrent or subsurface, the play is also taking place on another level of reality. Man indicates one possibility when he says, to Doctor's expectation that he will answer directly and pointedly, "The mind doesn't work this way" (22). The other level can be within the mind because in the next scene, Man says about his failed attempt to impress Woman with his conversational skills, "This is how the mind works" (26). As they stood by a pay phone, he waiting for a call, she wanting to make one, she invited him to converse, but his attempt was so disjointed that she left.

It may be difficult trying to grasp how the action may be taking place within the mind, but Prologue's declaration that the play is a "chronicle of love and no love, of interiors and exteriors" (19) establishes contrast as a structural device with some of the contrasts obvious. Prologue's appearance before the first scene to speak on behalf of the play's initial conception is the conventional place for his speech. Epilogue's appearance with him to speak on behalf of the revision violates convention, although the relationship between the speakers is traditional in that Prologue is unaware of Epilogue's presence whereas the latter is not only aware of the former, he corrects the play's original title. Doctor and Man and Nurse and Woman form contrasts in appearance and roles in the institution. The interviews establish another contrast. When Doctor enters the darkened room in which Man sits and turns on a light switch, light and darkness describe the amount of brightness needed in order for the eye to see. As they converse, seeing comes to mean mental illumination: understanding. Seated across from his interviewer, Man wonders how Doctor can write upside down. When the latter turns the paper around so that the former can visually see that the writing is not upside down for him, the writer, Man understands: "Oh, right. I get so used to seeing things from my own perspective." Doctor responds, "I see" (23).

This first scene enables the audience to understand the second scene. Man and Woman stand by a pay phone. He will not allow her to make a call because he is waiting for an incoming call; she will not allow him to wait undisturbed because she wants to make a call. Each acts only from his or her perspective, the condition that puts them in the institution. They are discon-nected—"separated" (32) is the term he later uses—from normal relation-ships and interactions; they are disconnected from normal feelings toward and responses to other persons, although Man knows he is disconnected. Picking up on his word "conversation," Woman invites him to "make some conversation," but his attempt is so disjointed that she walks away, leaving him in a state of self-rebuke: "Ice cream, you scream. This is how the mind works. Poorly. Around. On the ruin of the last thought. I'm glad we had this little chat. Et cetera. 'Social architecture.' I'm an idiot. She has nice hair. My last ruined thought" (26).

The passage is important for a few reasons. Revealing Man's awareness of his problem of ruining interpersonal possibilities and his frustration with his problem, it implies he is receptive to change, just as Prologue reveals Woman's awareness and frustration and implies she too is receptive. As Pro-logue contrasts the two patients, he characterizes her reaction to the aborted scene: "She is walking back and forth somewhere, ingoing, unverbal, biting her nails, rethinking the last scene" (26). The passage continues to develop dual perspectives, though not in this instance between characters. Man's awareness—"This is how the mind works"—is the interior level of reality, within him, contrasted with the exterior level, within the institution. The au-dience, however, may be aware that what Man calls mind, the audience calls emotions and may also be aware that Man does not because he is discon-nected from his. He perceives his problem as mental; others perceive it as emotional. Finally, the passage's language is more naturalistic than that of many naturalistic plays. A criticism that we will encounter later of language purporting to be naturalistic is that it is too coherent, too rational, for natural expression. Man's language moves in the "fits and starts" in which Eno in the back-cover blurb describes *The Flu Season*: "The play revels in ambivalence, lives in fits and starts, and derives a flailing energy from its doubts about it-self."

Although "fits and starts" describe both the movement of the play's lan-guage and its actions, the description does not apply equally to all the lan-guage and actions. Scene 3 is a split stage, on either side of which the patient is on a couch and the therapist is in a chair. Another similarity is that each mini-scene opens with the patient recalling the preceding scene at the pay phone, presumably because they are undergoing analysis, but the therapist takes over and reveals his/her perspective and verbal patterns. Speaking first, Nurse narrates an experience years earlier when, traveling by train to meet her lover whom she hoped to marry but who rejected her, she saw a horse stand-ing in "frozen marsh water" (27). Speaking next, Doctor narrates an experi-ence he had standing "ankles-deep in a brook . . . thinking of the shape of a horse and trying to picture the cloud that might best represent it" (28) when a woman passed by who declined his overtures for months until she finally accepted an invitation to be with him for a time. Man's language at the pay phone is disjointed in the sense that it juxtaposes unrelated images: haircut, social architecture, and ice cream. Nurse's and Doctor's language is disjointed in that it also juxtaposes unrelated images, but it is different from Man's disjointedness in that the two speakers' awareness of themselves as having the experience, as being at the experience's center, gives their narratives a coherence lacking in Man's attempted conversation. Having a greater awareness of themselves means that they are less frustrated by their failures. More accepting of themselves, they nevertheless inhabit the exterior institution and the interior mind or emotions. Therapists, they are trained to work in the exterior institution helping patients enter their interior selves to understand their problems. Speaking from within their interior selves, they too reveal potentially isolating perspectives. Nurse cuts off Woman's attempt at conversation by claiming they have no "more time, for today" (29), and Doctor interrupts Man's attempt because he wants to record some notes.

Yet Doctor and Nurse share images in their disjointed narratives. The horse is an example. So too is Doctor's admiration for the body of the woman he saw while he was standing in the water: her "clavicles, and so on, down the bones of her body." When Nurse next speaks, she refers to her perception as "looking out, from a body of bones" (28). All four characters have been repeating one another's images beginning in the first scene because the four are telling a common story, the "love story" that in the back-cover blurb Eno acknowledges *The Flu Season* "tries to be."

The commentary by Prologue and Epilogue, whom the play calls "narrators" (18), supports the creating of the love story and the naturalistic surface in which it is taking place, while at the same time they fuel the impinging subsurface that threatens to collapse the surface and the story it attempts to contain. At the end of scene 2, Epilogue says, "In a little while, we begin to depart from reality" for the following reason: "If we could control life, it wouldn't be life. If we could control our likeness of it, it wouldn't be a likeness" (27). The reason is a classic criticism of the naturalistic play, the type of play purporting to be a faithful representation, or slice, of life. In an interview Eno gave the same reason in more colloquial language: "'I really have that sort of snotty, sullen teenager's reaction to a very naturalistic play. . . . Who are these people and why are they talking to each other? That's not a living room.'"[10] In this criticism life is too amorphous, elusive, and unruly to be contained within the ruled surface of a naturalistic play. Nevertheless the two narrators continue to support the naturalistic surface of *The Flu Season* as a vehicle for a love story. In scene 6 Prologue asks, "Have life and the whole world already been written—been foreseen, foretold, long been forborne? Is the ending of the story already in your bones?" Epilogue's answer, "Maybe. Probably. You know what's what," recalls the Zolaesque scientific experiment of setting a problem and working out its inevitable solution. Yet by adding the hope of a "surprise" (36–37), he undercuts the foreseen, foretold ending.

Act 1, scene 7, which follows, dramatizes a surprise. Woman enters wishing Man a happy birthday. That the day is not his birthday is beside the point. The surprise is in her "gracious" and "mysterious" act because not knowing each other, they have "hardly talked" (37). They begin talking, though, to each other about their personal lives and feelings, even to putting their fingers in each other's mouth as they feed each other imaginary cake. They are falling in love, and love is doing what it always does: disposing the lovers to empathize with each other and to extend themselves to each other and respond to each other's giving of the self. The falling has been in fits and starts to be sure, but it is taking place, not only weakening their isolated perspectives so that they can better understand each other but also weakening Doctor's and Nurse's perspectives, for they too are becoming attracted to each other. Since scene 8, which ends for Man and Woman with their "*exit, him carrying her*" (44), seems to be the inevitable ending to a love story, the birthday surprise does not undercut the naturalistic play, but it is not the sole surprise. A second surprise, which occurs in act 2, is the "more to it," withheld until the creating of the love story was completed, that collapses *The Flu Season* as a naturalistic play.

As act 1 ends, the disconnections are ending. The characters are becoming connected to their emotions and to one another, as the narratives have been connecting into a common story. Scene 8, act-1's penultimate scene, contains the strongest statement, by Epilogue, of the connections forming a naturalistic play: "What is between the man and woman is starting to seem inevitable, as with the rock and the bird [beside each other in ancient Chinese writing]." When, however, he asks, "Will they be beside themselves forever?" his answer not only acknowledges the impinging subsurface, it reveals its imminent breakthrough: "All will painfully make itself painfully clear" (45).

If there is one question that does not yield a corresponding opposite possibility, Epilogue asks it midway through act 1: "Is the main action of the play a man with a pencil in his hand, sitting at a desk in the morning, trying to come up with a word for sunset?" (33) The answer is an unequivocal Yes because the play's primary thrust is trying to create theatre. The setting is a mental health institution; it is also a "theatre, as each narrator makes clear" (17). In the interview in which Eno faults the naturalistic play from a sullen teenager's perspective, he repeats the criticism of it as a false representation of life when he gives the connection that links his various plays: "'In general terms there's a strong form that gets established quickly which eventually proves too weak to contain the feelings that develop within that form so that there is always—in some way of saying it—an effort to put on a brave face that ultimately fails.'"[11] The strong naturalistic form fails because its ruled surface cannot contain unruly subsurface feelings. In *The Flu Season*, the unruly feelings surface in act 2.

Act 1 ends on an ominous note; act 2 opens on one. After Prologue sets the time, Epilogue asks, "What if you were writing a play and your feelings changed? You didn't even know how you felt anymore, or what you thought" (49). Since the lovers were beginning to understand their feelings as act 1 progressed, what Epilogue says implies that act 2 will unravel act 1, and it does. As Man and Woman talk in the first of their scenes together, he suddenly turns on her, "Forget I said I'm sick of you and your body and sick of our story" (50). In their next scene together, as she tries to get him interested in a name for their baby she is carrying, he announces that he is "in love with someone else" (52). His announcement is the surprise that collapses the naturalistic play, the "more to it" than simply creating a love story, the unruly subsurface that breaks through the surface ruled not only by a purported fidelity to everyday life but the way in which the everyday life is represented onstage. Man's announcement signals disconnection: character from character, plot from conventional dramaturgy, and *The Flu Season* from the naturalistic play.

Ludlam's *The Artificial Jungle* treats the naturalistic play ridiculously, but it honors conventional dramaturgy by dramatizing the two narratives that collide. After the play's opening dialogue, Zackary, inspired by drifter Frank in Cain's *The Postman Always Rings Twice*, enters the family pet shop inspired by the family haberdashery shop in Zola's *Thérèse Raquin*, and from that point on, the collision fuels the plot. Granted that act 1 of *The Flu Season* has an undercurrent that swells as the act proceeds, Man's announcement is a genuine surprise because there was no hint of his involvement with another woman and the involvement was never dramatized. It is reported as an offstage action. Were it not for the consequences to Woman, abortion and death, one might think Eno is trying to treat his material ridiculously. He is not.

To Man's announcement, Woman asks, "How could you do this?" He replies, "This? Is that how you would denote my million million feelings: 'this'? Or do I mean 'connote'?" (53) In this exchange *The Flu Season* is dramatizing the failure of the naturalistic play to accommodate more than a simplistic "this": a single strand of feeling. Man is saying that there is more to his inner life than a single strand. His feelings are multiple and changing, and more often than not, he is disconnected from a coherent network of feelings. "I'm so sorry," he confesses after Woman dies. "I thought I loved her.

Then I thought I didn't love her. That was the end, I thought. Then everything kept ending" (62–63). Doctor, Nurse, and Epilogue disagree about the ending. The two therapists "soldier on." Prologue's dismissing the audience with, "The End. Good night," is followed by Epilogue's rejoinder, "There is no end. Good night" (65–66). His closing lines collapse resolution.

The second thing the play is doing is trying to find a form that can contain in dynamic relationship the ruled surface and the unruly subsurface, which is why the setting is a "theatre" as well as a "mental health institution" (17). Feelings such as Man's "million million feelings" constitute an unruly subsurface. Playwright Eric Overmyer breaks down a ruled—prescribed or regulated—surface that by itself forms a naturalistic play. Such plays "are rooted in reductive, mechanistic psychology; have a linear and boringly predictable narrative; and are infested with characters who are the sum of their exposition and are described and circumscribed in terms of their jobs, family histories, ethnicity, age, sex, and current dilemma. . . . The characters of the American naturalistic play have pat and explicable motives, and are much less interesting than anyone knows in 'real life.'"[12]

As Epilogue admits, the play fails in its attempt to create a new form, collapsing into a "pile of words" (65). The hope for a new type of play remains, however. In his opening speech, this narrator talks about the time spent on the revising and the misgivings about putting on a play before it is ready. "There's always a different word, some other title, something better the language might cough up" (19). Plays are meant to be performed, though. Love is four connected letters until actualized in performance. So long as there is life therefore, the attempt is worth the effort, for life "is a word game" (61).

This is where *The Flu Season* succeeds: as a game of finding words to incarnate emotions and "metaphors for simple things" (33). The play has puns, aphorisms, literary allusions, dictionary entry, foreign languages, repeated images, disjointed images, erotic images, interrupted narratives, speaking while holding one's breath, talking with a face swollen by bee stings, and deliciously crazy dialogue such as the instance of the tender overture that normally leads lovers into snuggling:

Man: Are you thinking what I'm thinking?

Woman: Are you thinking about when I burned my hand one year on New Year's Eve?

Man: No.

Woman: Then no (41).

Occurring late in act 1, the dialogue reveals that for all their progress, the two are still disconnected, still patients in a mental health institution, the condition that persists in Man's self-absorbed reply to Woman's painful questioning him about his hurting her: when he wonders whether the verb he wants is denote or connote. Yet it is the word game that engages the audience, for the spectator tests the words and the ways in which they are spoken and responded to against his/her experience of a love story. Thus it is the onstage disconnection that engages the audience to participate in the creating of a love story by connecting verbal and visual images with committed emotions.

Although the play's language engages the audience, this study does not pursue it because of the study's strategy. All of the plays examined are multidimensional, yet the book arranges them by the category in which the war they wage against the naturalistic play is best understood. In the drama's total conception, Ludlam's theatre gives the first defining objection by exposing naturalism's elimination of mystery, which presupposes a reality in or beneath the surface reality that the surface reality does not accommodate. Eno's theatre gives the second defining objection by exposing naturalism's inadequacy for the task of dramatizing the unruly subsurface. So long as the second level of reality is contained within Man's mind as in act 1, the naturalistic play can acknowledge its existence, yet it is unable to dramatize the level simultaneously with his love story with Woman when the level emerges as his love story with the other woman. *The Flu Season* relegates the second story to a reported offstage action because actualizing the second story in the stage's surface reality requires a second naturalistic play.

From the total play, we move to the category that gives the audience its first impression of the theatrical experience to see whether this category can actualize the two levels of reality. The setting of Cindy Lou Johnson's *Brilliant Traces*, stated in the playbill, is "in the state of Alaska, in the middle of nowhere," but I doubt that many in the audience believe the statement once the play starts. I did not when I saw it performed in the spring of 1989 at New York's Cherry Lane Theatre. A line in the script reads, "The lighting in this play need not be concerned with the realistic environment, so much as the psychic or spiritual landscape of the players."[13] I do not remember the lighting in the opening scene; my memory of that scene is that it establishes the setting as the two characters' psychic or spiritual landscape.

The stage is the darkened interior of a cabin that although sparsely furnished has a telltale sink that makes the set look naturalistic until the play begins with pounding on the door and a female voice calling for help. Receiving no answer, she pushes the door opens, enters, and addresses the figure shrouded in a blanket who rises from the cot. "*She is wearing a wedding gown and veil. Also silver satin slippers"* (7). That she has been walking for over an hour in a howling blizzard is preposterous in naturalistic theatre but not in non-naturalistic theatre. The setting is a metaphor for withdrawal from society: an inability to commit to life or another person because of painful events that have broken the self-esteem of the two, the runaway female and the shrouded male, who are repressing the painful events that drove them into isolation. Yet as Rosannah and Henry gradually disclose the events, they gravitate toward each other, and the audience forgets that the stage is a metaphor. The two become more recognizable as recluses, and although the stage has not physically changed, it becomes a more realistic-naturalistic place, no doubt abetted by a lighting design that softens the harshness as the two become more responsive to each other. The closing image has Henry catching a falling Rosannah. Though she is *"still terrorized"* (48), revealing the repressed subsurface has lessened the tension between it and the surface reality so that the implication is that the two will be able to commit.

Incidentally, in the summer preceding the *Brilliant Traces* production, I saw Joan Cusack, who was Rosannah to Kevin Anderson's Henry, in a bona fide naturalistic play at New York's La Mama Annex. For *Road* by British playwright Jim Cartwright, the theater was converted into a representation of a small Lancashire town where the inhabitants suffer their dead-end lives unaltered by sexual adventures or drinking bouts. *Road* was a sensation when it premiered in London, so much so that in addition to the La Mama production, I saw on public television a BBC production filmed in an industrial town somewhere in the United Kingdom that had seen better days.

The playbill for David Lindsay-Abaire's *Fuddy Meers* has no statement about the set; in the script, which does, the playwright indicates the dual nature of the heroine's, Claire's, journey: "I imagine the set being representational and fluid."[14] It is not until the end of the opening scene, however, that the audience can recognize a fluid subsurface in the representational surface. Claire suffers from psychogenic amnesia. Whatever she has learned or experienced during the course of a day, she forgets as soon as she falls asleep. The consequence of her condition, her husband admits in the opening scene in which she awakens to a ringing alarm clock, is that every morning the two of them "have to start all over again" (8). "Hey, what's my name?" (9), she calls after the man who calls himself Richard, the man claiming to be her husband who leaves the bedroom to take a shower. Since she and he know that the clues to identity lie in the past, he prepared a booklet for her containing information such as her name so that she can learn about herself while recovering from her condition. The booklet is not the sole repository of information. When Claire asks Richard about amnesia being "brought on by some sort of physical or psychological trauma," he remarks that she *"never* mentioned" trauma before, leading her to surmise that "today *is* a special day" (9) because she is beginning to remember without the aid of the booklet. She has clues to her identity within her memory; her immediate task therefore is to bring the past to the present, the subsurface to the surface.

To Claire's question about the trauma that brought on her amnesia, Richard's reply is that she is not ready to receive all of the information, that she must progress slowly through the recovery. Opening the booklet, she follows the directions. As she does, the *"head of a man in a ski mask pops out from under the bed"* (9). Crawling out, he identifies himself as her brother Zachary and urges her to flee with him from her husband, who intends to kill her. She and the man whom the theatre playbill and the published script identify only as the Limping Man exit as the first scene comes to an end. Hidden under the bed and appearing after Claire begins to explore her past, he surfaces from a reality she has been repressing. Interacting with him, she perforce interacts with that which she has repressed in a quest that takes her to two levels of reality that increasingly yield self-knowledge.

The opening scene activates the quest's twofold nature. With an amnesiac mother; a foulmouthed, rebellious son Kenny, who takes money from her purse; and a husband Richard, who practices a lesson he learned in self-defense class on Kenny, a dysfunctional family such as this one is a subject of the naturalistic play. Offering no explanation as to how he got under the bed or how long he was there, the Limping Man, on the other hand, materializes as if in a dream that is more like a nightmare, for he is grotesque. He is masked, walks with a limp, speaks with a lisp—"Thachary" for Zachary— and *"has a manacle on one wrist, a bit of chain hanging down as if it's been cut"* (10). Yet Claire leaves with him. The scene gives clues, though, why she would. Since she is beginning to remember without the aid of the booklet, "today *is* a special day" (9). At one point looking into a mirror her husband hands her, she calls him "Philip." He corrects her, "Richard" (8), but since he does not pick up on the name Philip, the conversation continues. Nevertheless the implication is that someone named Philip is in her past, and seeing herself as an Other—getting outside of herself to see herself as a face in a mirror—is the fillip that brings the name to the surface. Finally, as soon as the masked head emerges from under the bed, the journey is, on one plane of experience, dream-like.

The play, however, is not a dream. Claire is not in scene 4, which takes place on a road that her husband and son are traveling in pursuit of her. When Richard realized that she was missing, he got Kenny from school and started driving until he found the information booklet that she took with her and that the Limping Man threw away. Since the photo of her mother's house is missing, Richard concludes that is where she is headed. So too are he, the son, and the policewoman he takes prisoner when she stops him for speeding. Neither is the play totally realistic. The house in the country may be the best place to remove the manacle, but having Claire there defeats the escaped convict's long-range plan. Although the mother, Gertie, has difficulty communicating verbally because she is recovering from a stroke, she can point to photos to identify the Limping Man. How can he expect Claire to run away with him given the revelations about their relationship that Gertie and the memories connected with the house are likely to release? And if the amnesiac undergoes a change of heart and decides to go, how can he expect the co-conspirator posing as a policewoman to continue to aid him? The woman, Heidi, helped him to escape from prison because of his promise to run away to Canada with her.

The play has its silliness and cartoonish characters, but following a successful run at the Manhattan Theatre Club in the fall of 1999, the production moved to Off-Broadway's Minetta Lane Theatre in the winter of 2000 with the cast largely intact, headed by J. Smith-Cameron as Claire; she had won an Obie award for her 1997 portrayal of the scam artist in Douglas Carter Beane's *As Bees in Honey Drown*. Reviewing the Manhattan Theatre Club opening, Ben Brantley wrote, "By the evening's end, what started as a feather-light sendup [of the mid-life crisis syndrome] has acquired a surprisingly touching depth."[15] I would add that its treatment of the relationship between the surface and the subsurface makes Lindsay-Abaire's play worthy of examination. A key statement in the production notes is that "Claire lives in an unsettling world where mad fun and genuine danger are wrapped around each other" (74). Neither totally oneiric nor totally realistic, *Fuddy Meers* combines Claire's journey through the surface and subsurface and thereby interacts the two levels of reality: the naturalistic and non-naturalistic forces that create identity.

In scene 1 Claire awakens to the world outside the self: the representational surface. Not knowing who she is or where she is, she defers to Richard's judgment about her likes and dislikes and his identification of the teenager taking money from her purse. She accepts the information in the booklet, and she leaves with the Limping Man because he claims to be her brother. She questions these sources outside of, or without, her, but she does not reject them. In the second scene, in the car with the man purporting to save her life, she begins to awaken within herself. In her head she hears music from her past, and she discovers a scar on her forehead. By the third scene, at her mother's house, she is so stimulated, and Gertie's speech is so jumbled, that she misses the latter's warning signals. The masked man's taking the amnesiac to the house is illogical, but we can understand why the playwright wants her there. The house functions on the play's two levels. A realistic place, it is the "*ren-*

dezvous" (19) for escaped convict Millet, the third of the three conspirators, and a symbolic state, it is Claire's mind.

In the house as place, the heroine continues the exploration begun in the first scene when a voice from a standing figure spoke to her. She recognizes the tree that her brother Zack used to climb when they were kids; she smells her late father's cologne; and she remembers not only where he kept his tools in the basement but his routine running the family's kennel. Although these experiences originate within her, they refer to the world without her. In the house as state, she continues the exploration begun in the second scene with the figure whose submerged voice spoke to her in the first scene. She smells the cologne; she remembers that when the family played croquet, she was always the blue mallet; standing in the kitchen, she can visualize the location of the tools in the basement; and she can "picture" (16) her father and scenes from her childhood. Although some of these experiences refer to the world without her, their presence within her indicates that her imagination, which is housed in the fluid subsurface, is not only developing but the development is accelerating.

One instance of the acceleration in scene 3 prepares for scene 5. When Gertie sees Claire at the kitchen window, she calls to her, "In . . . come . . . in . . . come in," an invitation that the daughter then translates for the Limping Man: "That means '*come in*' in stroke talk" (14). The translation is unnecessary because the two words, clear in themselves, are simply reversed and the older woman gestures to come in while speaking. In the kitchen, however, Claire has such difficulty understanding her mother that she wishes they had a translation book for stroke language. One striking exception is "Ina la," which she translates, "In the cellar" (16). What makes the translation so perspicacious is that the Limping Man's question to Gertie was not where the hacksaw is but whether or not she has one. And even though the older woman points downward, "Ina la" could mean anything. Yet according to the script's appended translation (67), the two sounds mean exactly what the younger woman says they mean.

When toward the end of scene 3 Claire leaves the kitchen to descend into the basement with the manacled Millet, she is penetrating her subconscious mind. When scene 5 opens, she is skipping rope and singing a "*children's song*" with him. "Isn't it fun down here?" (25), she squeals as she explores the room, attaching a memory to each of the contents she touches. Hearing noises associated with her childhood, she dons a monster mask, arms herself with a squirt gun, and adopting a "*silly monster voice*" (28) threatens to cut off Millet's hand unless he gives her the information she demands about her amnesia. Divulging information he was not supposed to, Millet sums up the significance of the house's lower level as a symbolic state: "I hate this basement! It's like truth serum!" (48)

The arrival of Richard, Kenny, and Heidi, who was supposed to prevent the other two from reaching the house but was instead taken prisoner, causes a melee in act-1's closing scene that contributes to the confusion that has reigned since the opening scene. To correct act-1's distortion, act 2 reforms the groups and slows down the action by immobilizing some of the characters. In the kitchen Claire, who learns she was a school nurse, bandages the wounded Kenny, and then Heidi attends to the Limping Man's knife wound. From Kenny, Claire learns that the Limping Man is Philip, her first husband and his father: a man who physically abused her until she turned on him in the incident that disfigured him and brought on her amnesia. She is not simply a passive recipient of this information. The stage directions have her "*sorting it out*" (52) until she takes over and recreates the incident, eliciting her son's encouragement: "She's coming back strong" (53). By the time Gertie and Richard join them, having overpowered Millet and Heidi, the erstwhile amnesiac has so accelerated the development of her historical sense that it is apace with her imagination and she is all the way back.

The setting of *Brilliant Traces* is a frozen subsurface that warms, but except for the closing scene when Henry, with a different outcome by saving the falling Rosannah, reenacts the painful event that brought him to the cabin, the two narrate the repressed events. Furthermore, since identity is not an issue, they do not confront philosophical naturalism's deterministic forces. *Fuddy Meers* is naturalistic in two senses. Because Claire wants to know who she is, her quest takes her to a discovery of the forces that determine her identity. The forces that she cannot control are those of her collective history: her parents and brother, formative years, and marriages, son, and interpersonal relationships—in short, her heredity and environment. As she discovers her historical sense, as her "vision of her world becomes clearer," Lindsay-Abaire writes in the production notes, "so too do her surroundings. For example, each time we revisit Gertie's kitchen, maybe there's a new piece of furniture, or there's a wall where there wasn't one before." The physical stage does not have to change, he explains, because scrims and projections "can easily transform a space" (74), but if furniture changes the kitchen, which of course has a sink, the mode of production becomes more detailed and consequently naturalistic.

Regardless of what happens in the kitchen, the dramatized scene in the basement where Claire relives her childhood is not philosophically naturalistic, for she is not a helpless victim. Once she discovers her identity, she takes control of her life. With Philip and Heidi subdued, her husband speaks for her as he does every morning: "You're doing okay, Claire." Now, however, she reverses the play's opening exchange: "Richard, don't tell me how I'm doing. Kenny, call the police. Gertie, you'll stay with us tonight" (60). Yet though she is in control of herself, the control is not total. She does not know how she feels about Richard, for example. She cannot reciprocate when he declares his love for her; she even slips and calls him "Philip" (62). And the audience does not see her integrating her stimulated imagination with her recovered historical sense, for she falls asleep, thereby leaving open the question of whether she has made a full recovery or will awake an amnesiac again, but the ending only enhances *Fuddy Meers*. Its accomplishment is in demonstrating that a play can actualize the subsurface, or inner, reality without forgoing the surface reality.

The funny mirrors of the title of Lindsay-Abaire's play are a funhouse image: the mirrors in which amnesiac Claire sees reality, at first distorted but gradually clarified as she penetrates the representational surface and the fluid subsurface. Craig Lucas' *Reckless* does not have a mirror (or a rabbit hole). It has a window, but many scenes are enacted before the audience recognizes the level on which the action is occurring. For good reason! The playbill has no statement about the setting or the heroine's journey, and the opening scene has the look of a naturalistic scene. On Christmas Eve a wife, Rachel, dressed in nightgown stands by the window of a darkened bedroom excitedly talking about the joy of giving the kids presents to her husband, Tom, who is lying in bed watching television. There are clues, but they come so quickly in a scene whose mood is euphoric that they are missed. The snow, she says, is so deep and so swallows all other sounds that "you feel like you've been wrapped up in the hands of a big, sweet, giant, white . . . monster. Good monster. He's going to carry us away into a dream."[16] From the television set, from which comes the room's only light other than that of the window framing Rachel, comes an announcer's voice telling of an Albanian woman who fled into Yugoslavia—the play dates from the 1980s—to give birth to a "two-headed child" (8). At this point Tom informs Rachel that he has taken out a contract on her life, regrets what he did, but since it is too late to rescind the contract, she must flee the house. At first she does not believe him. Once she is convinced, however, the scene ends with her departing through the window.

The taking out of a contract is horrendous yet plausible, as are subsequent scenes. Scene 2 has Rachel in robe and slippers at an outdoor pay phone asking friends to come get her. Since they think she is playing a joke, they hang up, stranding her and forcing her to accept a ride with a stranger. In scene 3 the two are in a car, Rachel fabricating a story to explain her situation and the driver, Lloyd, inviting her to spend Christmas with him and his girlfriend, Pooty. With minimal props the scenes are not naturalistic, but the audience does not expect them to be naturalistic. *Reckless* consists of twenty-seven scenes after scene 1 in locations such as pay phone, car, living room, and doctor's office with some as brief as a half a page or a page of script, played with

a brief intermission. Were a stage crew to dismantle a naturalistic set and secure another one between scenes, the mode of production would conflict with
the episodic structure and the evening would be rendered interminable.

Dialogue and images are tantalizing, but the scenes move so rapidly that
the spectator has no time to ponder them while they are being played. Conversations revolve around questions of whether people can know one another
or trust one another, whether the characters belong to families, and whether
they are happy or have been hurt. Rachel makes no effort to return home or
contact the police, though she asks a friend to look in on her two children.
Lloyd presents Pooty as a deaf paraplegic with whom he communicates in
sign language. She, however, is not as disabled as she appears to be. She pre-
tends to be totally disabled because Lloyd believes she is, and since she wants
him to want her, she maintains the pretense. Both she and Lloyd are run-
aways, she from a government debt and he from a bad marriage. Acting on
Pooty's advice to talk to someone about the hurt she experienced, Rachel goes
to a doctor's office in scene 9, where the pieces of the puzzle begin to align.
After she recapitulates the events of the first eight scenes, this scene ends with
the psychiatrist asking her, "When did you have this dream?" (24)

Yet the dream is not over. *Reckless* does not become a naturalistic play at
this juncture, which partly explains why the scenes continue to be symbolic.
To state what is happening another way: Rachel is not cured, for she is apparently in therapy. If she were cured, the tension would be destroyed. In
Fuddy Meers the pressure comes from within Claire to learn who she is and
from the dangerous situation she is in. In *Reckless* the pressure comes from
within Rachel to get better and from the psychiatric sessions. At least the audience should be aware that the heroine's journey is taking place on two levels. The problem, however, is trying to determine which scenes rise to the naturalistic surface and which descend to the fluid subsurface. In one scene
Lloyd, Pooty, and Rachel are contestants on a television game show "*dressed
as the solar system with cardboard and paper-mache constructions over their
heads*" (27), he as the Sun, Pooty as the Earth, and Rachel as Venus. Lloyd
wins a hundred thousand dollars, enabling him to pay back the money he stole
when he became a runaway. In another scene poisoned champagne left on the
doorstep by an embezzler to kill Rachel for stumbling upon the embezzle-
ment instead kills Pooty and husband Tom, who has sought out Rachel to
apologize for what he did. Rachel, whose name may be Eve and who may be
in therapy ever since Christmas Eve, has sessions with six different doctors,
but they are all played by the same actor. Yet as somber as some scenes are,
the play has fractured narratives, funny episodes, and absurd revelations. For
example, Rachel confides in the first doctor that her "mother was run over by
a school bus" when she was six (34), a trauma that may be the root cause of

her condition; rather than abandoning her children, specifically her son Tom Junior, she may feel abandoned, as she is throughout the play. Many scenes later, attempting to calm Rachel-Eve, hysterical after being shot at in a television studio, and to get her to understand that she can eventually be cured and have a new self, the doctor confides that she was once a bus driver who became a psychiatrist.

On the serious side, the doctor's position makes the play philosophically non-naturalistic in that one can overcome heredity and environment. Whether that position holds in the play depends on the spectator's interpretation of the play. If the dream changes for the better, the implication is that dreamer Rachel is changing—getting better—providing the spectator can distinguish between scenes that are dreams, generated by the inner reality, and scenes that are surface reality. The final scene serves as a test. In scene 28 Rachel is a doctor, a psychiatrist, and her patient is a young man named Tom, whose problem stems from the time his mother abandoned him and the family on Christmas. Encouraging him to talk about his feelings, she becomes the mother and he becomes Tom Junior. As the session ends, they agree to meet the next day and the day after that, which is Christmas. When I saw the 1988 Circle Repertory Company production, couples near me were upbeat leaving the theater because they saw Rachel as a patient who became a psychiatrist.

I do not want to continue with *Reckless* because I would repeat what I wrote about it elsewhere.[17] I ask the reader, though, to consider the closing sentences of scene 27 to be as important as the closing question of scene 9 before judging scene 28. As part of her therapy, the psychiatrist asks Rachel-Eve to do the following: "I want you to imagine someone standing there, Eve. Someone who makes people feel good about themselves and does all the things you ever wanted to do and has all the things you ever wanted to have. I want you to imagine that person standing there in that place at that exact time of day doing exactly what that person would be doing . . . Eve . . . if that person. . ." (53). The implication is that the unspoken words are "were you."

Trying to determine whether a scene is or is not imagined is not a problem in Rinne Groff's *What Then*, which ran in Off-Off-Broadway in January 2006. Neither is trying to determine what a character is imagining. The play takes place in a futuristic America suffering from environmental convulsions so warming the climate and polluting the land that although crops such as tomatoes can still be purchased, they are synthetic: odorless and tasteless. So too was Jo Winiarski's single set for the Clubbed Thumb production synthetic: a kitchen with sink and running water and a refrigerator with a light that went on when the door was opened, but the water was not potable and there were no wooden cabinets or curtains. The latter were not needed because the kitchen had no windows looking out on a landscape. It had skylights, but sunlight did not flood the kitchen; paneled lights in the walls illuminated the room.

The play opens on this surface reality with a wife, Diane, in pajamas greeting her husband, Tom, in running suit returning from his morning jog with the announcement that she has quit her job to devote her time, some fourteen hours a day, to sleeping. In dreams, she explains, she can change the world, for she becomes a landscape architect overseeing the construction of a project that will convert a nearby polluted lake into land where tomatoes can be grown naturally. He is incredulous, for he works for a corporation involved with the drainage of the lake for a purpose not specified but by implication sinister, and though he does not project any sinister vibrations, his metallic briefcase identifies him as adjusted to the surface, just as his belittling of her project, undertaken below the conscious mind, identifies him as disconnected from the subsurface realm that generates imagination and dreams. They argue. She criticizes him for reducing life to abstractions, a world in which people do not communicate naturally, which is to say emotionally, as they themselves have not done lately, but in the corporate language of acronyms. He criticizes her for escaping reality by retreating into a fantasy world. The scene ends with her recumbent on the set's centerpiece, the counter, and him leaving for his corporate commitment.

The opening scene is not imagined. It is the surface reality, the equivalent to the bedrooms in *Fuddy Meers* and *Reckless* but different too. After the metaphoric set of *Brilliant Traces*, the surface in the other two plays is naturalistic, but the threat to each play's heroine comes so quickly that the set elicits little or no audience response. The sets the audience responds to are subsequent ones, signposts on the heroines' journey to release repressed events in their personal lives, gradually revealed in the changing sets, the therapy being that by confronting the events, the two women can begin to take control of themselves and live more fulfilling lives. This is not the situation in *What Then*. Its set immediately realizes the reason for the contemporary war against the naturalistic play, judged by non-naturalistic theatre to be conventional and literal, pedestrian and artificial: the ground for which judgment becomes evident as the action develops. In *What Then* the set when the stage lights come up is artificial; its sameness is depressingly bland. Tom is literal-minded. He cannot understand what she is doing, Diane tells him, because whatever he cannot imagine does not exist. The situation is not personal. It is so epidemic that one can say that naturalism has won the war and ironically so because it has ceased to be natural. Its very pervasiveness, however, provokes its opposing force into action. Since everyone is affected by its power, others will follow Diane's rebellion.

Tom is the first to try to follow, which is why he becomes a sympathetic character. Upset by Diane's criticism that they have been drifting apart in large measure the result of his corporate commitment, he returns home when he is not supposed to be there and enters a scene that is momentarily disorienting, although clarified quickly and related, if the audience remembers, to an earlier conversation between Diane and her stepdaughter Sallie. In order to qualify for a residence removed from the encroaching pollution, one must be drug-free for a period of time. Sallie, who has a history of drug use, cannot pass the test. She needs clean blood, and she knows that father Tom, with whom she has an ugly relationship, will not agree to letting her have some of his so that she can pass the test.

Kirk Bookman's lighting design changed to indicate a dream sequence. The counter on which Diane is recumbent was lit from within; the light bathing her originated in a subsurface reality. But since she is recumbent for most of the play, the audience's attention can be drawn away from her, especially if arresting activity is taking place elsewhere in the kitchen, as it is when the cast's fourth member enters. Only later does he identify himself as Bahktiyor. He enters and silently proceeds to drain blood from Diane's arm so that it is momentarily possible to interpret the scene as her dream enacted. Tom's entrance after the blood has been taken and put in the refrigerator dispels any lingering doubt about the scene and creates one of the play's funniest scenes. In business suit he confronts the stranger who, dressed in street garb, could be a terrorist or a drug dealer. Correctly identifying him as Sallie's drug connection, he buys some because for him drugs are a portal to the subsurface that Diane inhabits when sleeping. He has the right idea in that to recover his atrophying emotional life, he has to connect with his inner reality, but his approach is misguided. The mistake, however, was the audience's gain because actor Andrew Dolan's lurching about the kitchen was a hoot, his irrepressible facial and bodily muscles betraying his efforts to control them until he collapsed on the floor.

The cast was excellent. Though she spent much of the time recumbent, Meg MacCary's Diane was the very opposite of a negligible presence, for her occasional shifting of weight or altering of position was sensuous, and when she was awake or active in a dream sequence, her smile was alluring and endearing. Merritt Wever's Sallie had a smile too, though hers emerged on a face only in control of half of herself. She was able to prevent her muscles from putting her on the floor but unable to prevent them from thrusting forward with hostility toward her father and Bahktiyor when he denied having taken the blood that she had sent him to appropriate for her test. As played by Piter Marek, he was a man of mystery who went from thief to devotee in one of the play's tenderest scenes, a scene that epitomizes the play.

Diane awakens but does not see Tom unconscious on the floor. Seeing Bahktiyor, she accepts him as a given and converses with him, telling him she is hungry and would like a cannoli in the refrigerator. As she lies prone on the counter, her head at one end, he lowers himself to a crouching position to extend the cannoli so that first she and, with the lighting changing for a dream sequence, then he can eat it. As the play progresses, Bahktiyor announces that he too is a landscape architect. He has one of the play's most pregnant lines. With Sallie's dismissal of her stepmother as a kook—or something to that effect—he disagrees: "No, she's deep." In a dream sequence, he and Diane also share a tomato grown in their reclamation project.

Diane and Bahktiyor reclaim more than tomatoes. *What Then* reclaims theatre from naturalism's dominance in actualizing only surface reality. The defining objection to naturalism that emerges from Eno's *The Flu Season* is that it cannot simultaneously actualize surface and subsurface actions or stories or narratives—that is, the two levels of reality. The naturalistic play can acknowledge the existence of an inner reality or subsurface, as it does in act 1 of *The Flu Season* when Man talks about how the mind works, but it cannot bring that reality to the surface other than naturalistically, and since it cannot, it reports the newly surfaced reality as an offstage action. Groff's play actualizes Diane's love story with Bahktiyor while actualizing her love story with Tom. Yet I do not mean to imply that *What Then* is the sole play in this section that has been emphasizing setting to make a reclamation breakthrough. By bringing two repressed stories to the surface not to dramatize them but to dramatize the effect of the narrating of them on the narrators, *Brilliant Traces* effects a change in the surface; it becomes less harsh, more conducive to human interaction. *Fuddy Meers* embeds a fluid subsurface in a representational surface while *Reckless* embeds a representational surface in a fluid subsurface.

The simultaneous second story in *What Then* is the dramatization of Diane and Bahktiyor in the fluid subsurface in which the development of tomatoes and love is natural, actualizing the inner reality in the surface reality until all four characters are changed, and the change creates a scene unlike any prior scene in the play or this chapter. Tom is learning how to respond to his and his wife's inner reality, and Diane lovingly welcomes him back into her life, for he is the love of her life. Bahktiyor becomes love's devotee. The most significant change, however, is in Sallie. In the three plays previously examined, danger is in the journey into the subsurface to release the repressed events blocking one's development as a human being. The danger is worth the facing because the goal is psychological, emotional, spiritual health. In Groff's conception the surface masks the danger. In an early conversation, Diane is supportive of her stepdaughter's desire to pass the blood test to secure better living quarters or if that is impossible to come live with her and her father, but Sallie sends Bahktiyor to steal her blood. And when the contrite thief denies having taken it, Sallie attempts to kill him by plunging a knife into his gut.

Yet she becomes a new person, and her newly discovered inner reality transforms the theatre, a transformation that is not surprising given Groff's background as a founding member of the performance company Elevator Repair Service. The scene that Sallie creates bears comparison with a similar scene in *The Flu Season*—indeed, with the entire play. Eno's narrators, Prologue and Epilogue, speak to the audience but not as actors in the drama. They are onstage commentators on the action as Shakespearean Prologues and Epilogues are except that they speak at ends of scenes. Man and Woman are the actors, and they do not speak to the audience because they are in a naturalistic play, as in the scene that bears comparison. It occurs after Man learns that Woman has died. He says to Nurse, "I'm so sorry" (62), going on to try to explain his feelings until she interrupts. In *What Then* Sallie enters the kitchen with a hand-held microphone and alternately facing Tom, Bahktiyor, and the audience as if in a cabaret sings a song beginning, "I'm sorry." The number completed, she hands the mike first to Tom and next to Bahktiyor. They have to be coaxed. They grin sheepishly at one another and the audience. They shrug off their embarrassment. And each sings, "I'm sorry," with Diane, sitting up on the counter behind them, beaming approval.

Though the cabaret scene in *What Then*, which is performance art in a naturalistic play, is evidence that the characters have become so receptive to their inner reality that they summon it to their surface reality, the environmental surface does not become benign. Not only does the tension between the inner reality and the environmental surface not disappear, particles falling through the skylights intensify the war. The falling follows a confusing scene. A telephone message arrives in what is apparently a dream scene with Diane, who was up in a sitting position for the cabaret scene, again recumbent and near death because Tom asks Sallie if she, Sallie, is a ghost. His daughter replies in the negative and then speaks the message, but I do not understand why Sallie is supposed to be Diane or why she speaks what is supposed to be a transmitted message. Jason Zinoman's review offers the tantalizing possibility that the critic should "think of Diane as Mother Earth and Tom as the Americans who neglect her."[18] The condition from which she suffers at play's end is dehydration, which mirrors the condition of the nearby polluted lake. When in the bloom of health, sensuous on the counter, she could be a Joycean goddess. After Bahktiyor comes under her influence, he too suggests more than a naturalistic character. When Sallie's knife thrusts into his gut do him no harm, she questions why he does not die. A later scene reveals that the knife has a retractable blade. Still, the play may be suggesting that as one comes under the influence of the fluid subsurface, as embodied in Diane, one develops potentials beyond the naturalistic. Perhaps Sallie begins to take on her stepmother's characteristics. As for the latter's depletion, perhaps the releasing of her energy to influence her stepdaughter and the others is at her expense. The script when published should shed some light on these conjectures.

The ending restores the tension between the characters' inner reality and the environment's surface reality. With Diane in dire straits, someone must go for help, but with the others unable to tell from the few that fell through the skylights whether the particles are snow or toxic fallout in a scene that is no longer a dream, entering the street is dangerous. After a momentary pause, Bahktiyor goes, leaving Tom and Sallie to minister to Diane as the stage lights come down. Like the absence of an invisible fourth wall, the absence of resolution is so widespread today that this study does not consider the presence of a pat resolution a defining objection to the naturalistic play. Since it is the presence of tension that matters, the next chapter pursues the tension in the categories of language and character. Without tension there is no war, and without the war plays are divided into separate types with naturalistic on the one hand and absurdist and surrealist, for example, on the other hand. In the contemporary theatre, the twain not only meet, they interpenetrate, continuing the trend begun in this chapter with dream sequences merging with waking scenes and Diane's energy flowing into Bahktiyor and the other characters, whose energy flowing into naturalism's surface reality transforms the stage.

The new type of play that blends disparate sources—historical and fictional, for example—genres and styles, tones and moods can be called a hybrid play. New dramaturgical-theatrical concepts and terms are withheld until the conclusion, however, which cites two important books published in the new century's first decade.

NOTES

1. Charles Ludlam, *Ridiculous Theatre: Scourge of Human Folly*, ed. Steven Samuels (New York: Theatre Communications Group, 1992), 255. Hereafter to be cited parenthetically.

2. Émile Zola, *Thérèse Raquin*, trans. Kathleen Boutall, in *Seeds of Modern Drama*, Laurel Masterpieces of Continental Drama 3 (New York: Dell, 1963), 19. Hereafter to be cited parenthetically.

3. Émile Zola, *Thérèse Raquin*, trans. Leonard Tancock (London: Penguin, 1962), 33. Hereafter to be cited parenthetically.

4. Charles Ludlam, *The Artificial Jungle*, in *The Complete Plays of Charles Ludlam* (New York: Perennial, 1989), 883. Hereafter to be cited parenthetically.

5. James M. Cain, *The Postman Always Rings Twice* (New York: Vintage, 1992), 7. Hereafter to be cited parenthetically.

6. For an analysis of the style in other Ludlam plays, see Robert J. Andreach, *Creating the Self in the Contemporary American Theatre* (Carbondale: Southern Illinois UP, 1998), 134–36 and *Drawing Upon the Past: Classical Theatre in the Contemporary American Theatre* (New York: Peter Lang, 2003), 49–62.

7. Émile Zola, preface to the 2nd ed., *Thérèse Raquin*, trans. Leonard Tancock (London: Penguin, 1962), 22–23.

8. "Twenty Questions," *American Theatre* 22, no. 7 (2005): 104.

9. Will Eno, *The Flu Season* (London: Oberon, 2003), 18. Hereafter to be cited parenthetically.

10. Will Eno, "Stepping into Darkness with Will Eno," interview by Jake Hooker, *The Brooklyn Rail* Sept. 2005, 44.

11. Eno, "Stepping into Darkness," 44.

12. Eric Overmyer, "The Hole in the Ozone," in *7 Different Plays*, ed. Mac Wellman (New York: Broadway Play Publishing, 1988), 448–49.

13. Cindy Lou Johnson, *Brilliant Traces* (New York: Dramatists Play Service, 1989), 5. Hereafter to be cited parenthetically.

14. David Lindsay-Abaire, *Fuddy Meers* (New York: Dramatists Play Service, 2000), 74. Hereafter to be cited parenthetically.

15. Ben Brantley, "Born Anew Every Day to Be Abused and Baffled," *New York Times*, 3 Nov. 1999, E1.

16. Craig Lucas, *Reckless* (New York: Dramatists Play Service, 1989), 7. Hereafter to be cited parenthetically.

17. Andreach, *Creating the Self in the Contemporary American Theatre*, 161–65.

18. Jason Zinoman, "In a Flight of Imagination, Escaping the Meltdown," *New York Times*, 12 Jan. 2006, E5.

Chapter Two

The War in Language and in Character: Wellman, Maxwell, and Gibson; Foreman and Groff

In 1989 Broadway Play Publishing came out with a volume of six contemporary American plays entitled *Anti-Naturalism*. In a note prefacing the volume, the publisher, Christopher Gould, declares his attitude toward the naturalistic play and the anti-naturalistic play. Joining naturalism and realism, because the "difference seems too narrow to worry about," he characterizes the "American naturalistic/realistic play" as "stuck in a dreary dead-end that is piled high in kitchen sinks and trailer parks, mired in self-indulgent autobiography." The kitchen sink has become synonymous with naturalistic theatre. A few years before his play *Bug*, which is set in a seedy motel, enjoyed successful runs in New York and other cities, Tracy Letts' play *Killer Joe* garnered attention; it is set in a seedy trailer park. Milieu, however, is only the introduction to the distinction between a naturalistic play and an anti-naturalistic play, although Gould acknowledges the power of naturalism in the works of its artists. Anti-naturalistic plays take the audience out of "this world as we know it." They "plunge the audience into a surreal world." The protagonists are "explorers across uncharted realms of the imagination." Though Gould does not use the terms, we should recognize that in his comparison, naturalistic plays are all surface reality whereas anti-naturalistic plays take their questers and audiences into an inner or subsurface reality. He also wants something in a play that he calls traditional but I associate with the naturalistic play while agreeing with him that "some form of logical development" is not unique to that type of play. We both agree why it or some other element that is traditional or naturalistic must be present. "Without some form of logical development, there is no tension to a play, and so the audience rapidly loses interest."[1]

Gould's description of what distinguishes an anti-naturalistic play recalls Overmyer's 1988 argument, from which the preceding chapter quoted, for reclaiming theatre from naturalism, for theatre's raison d'etre is staging the imagination and "language . . . story-telling, myth. . . ."[2] His play *On the Verge*, one of the six in Gould's volume, is, "at least in part, a play *about* language" and therefore a "play about the imagination, and about theatricality."[3] In these production notes, Overmyer argues for respecting the language's "rhythm and sound" (75) and against naturalizing or paraphrasing the language, methods actors use to bastardize a text. He is one of two authors in Gould's volume whom the publisher cites for expressing themselves "through the use of heightened language. To read any play by one of these two gifted writers is to revel in poetry and in an overwhelming imagination" (v-vi). Though not the other author that Gould cites, Ludlam also argued for "heightened diction" in the theatre. "The idea of having an ear for dialogue, of capturing the way people really talk, is silly. Language can do so much more than that—why not use it?" His use was "trying to layer the language so that it wasn't like everyday speech. It was almost another language, a poetic medium."[4] Yet it is a Mac Wellman play that opens this section waging war against the naturalistic play through language.

In the prefatory note to *Fnu Lnu*, Wellman gives the play's genesis as a commissioned "site-specific theater piece for the Italian Club in Ybor City, Florida" and what for him was the city's and the club's salient feature, but he is not referring to the manufacturing of hand-rolled cigars. The feature was that "many of the diverse workers (from Sicily, Galicia in northern Spain, and Cuba) were anarchists, who built their own schools, hospitals, and mutual aid societies (like the Italian Club)." The workers are not in the play as they are in Nilo Cruz's 2003 Pulitzer Prize-winning *Anna in the Tropics*, which evokes a cigar factory's working conditions in Ybor City's heyday before the manufacturing died. The contents of *Fnu Lnu* are "local legend and hearsay to create a new version of Aeschylus's *Eumenides*, a strange and wonderful drama about the origin of the polis, and of political thinking as such."[5] *Eumenides*, the third play in the *Oresteia* trilogy, is the dramatization of the mythic birth of Athenian democracy and civilization in that immortals and mortals cooperate to replace blood vengeance with a trial-by-jury system. The polis becomes a model for a political-social-economic entity in which people can live and work together: the ethos that characterized Ybor City in the late 19th and early 20th centuries, according to the prefatory note. To make the connection between the Ybor City that flourished then and a reimagined *Eumenides*, Wellman has to disconnect from naturalistic theatre.

Since the Italian Club and other sites are either vestiges of the culture that flourished when the manufacturing flourished or works created to recall the era, anyone coming into Ybor City, the cigar-manufacturing district of Tampa, to attend the production could have been aware of the naturalistic world surrounding the sites. Surrounding but not enveloping because the sites are portals to another world. In two short paragraphs, Porter Anderson, who reviewed the 1994 premiere production, contrasts the old or past Ybor City and the contemporary or present Ybor City that are the play's two worlds or realities:

> For decades there have been calls for the renovation, restoration and rejuvena-tion of the bustling Cuban-Italian-Spanish splendor of this fabled suburb, site of visits from Fidel Castro, Teddy Roosevelt and some of the roughest riders of Hispanic-Floridian lore from the late 19th and early 20th centuries—and *nada*.
>
> Well, not quite nada. A few proud restaurants have persevered in the rundown storefronts, along with a couple of party rentals in the great social clubs and old show buildings. Artists have tried to turn old Ybor into a new bohemia, but failed because rental rates have been too high. Some historic-landmark work has been done in fits and starts. A bust here. A plaque there. But all Tampa's city council members and all the old town's friends have never really been able to put Ybor City together again.[6]

Fnu Lnu has been produced since 1994. In 1997 Wellman was honored by a six-month festival of his works in four cities with *Fnu Lnu* opening the fes-tival, but even though revivals are set outside of Ybor City's two worlds, the play begins naturalistically in another sense. The prologue is the voice of a bus tour guide identifying places of interest in the contemporary Ybor City and persons associated with the sites: the Afro-Cuban Club, where the Cuban exile, José Marti, organized the Revolutionary party; Charlie Wall, a vice lord of a gambling operation in the 1920s and 1930s who had to flee Tampa in the 1940s when war broke out among rival lords and who returned in the 1950s to be murdered in 1955, one theory being that his operation was encroaching on the operations of larger organized crime in southern Florida; and the Ital-ian Club, said to be "haunted" (209). The producing company does not have to build a replica of Ybor City or the Italian Club. The stage simply becomes the Italian Club. In fact, a production works best with a minimum of natura-listic details because the play is a journey into the mind and the imagination. As in Shakespeare's plays, the poetic language stimulates seeing: imaginative participation. The play leaves the naturalistic world for the journey.

The prologue has two functions. It corresponds to the opening of *Eu-menides* in which Apollo's priestess summarizes the evolution of the Delphic oracle prior to entering the temple from which she immediately reappears so shaken that she is on all fours in a famous Aeschylean image before compos-ing herself to report what she saw: a man, Orestes, clutching a suppliant's branch and a bloody sword and ringed by sleeping Furies, female avengers who pursued him from Argos. In *Fnu Lnu* the lights come up on a man seated at a table with a microphone. Behind him at another table are seated three women, called the Figures, who must be reimagined Furies because they sing about a "man on fire / . . . / trying to become / . . . / he's on the run" (209–10). The man, who calls himself Deezo, is presumably a contemporized Orestes, although he does not appeal for help as Aeschylus' hero does before Apollo dispatches him, guarded by Hermes, to Athena, nor does he appear to be suffering the guilt his classical counterpart suffers for killing his mother. Nevertheless he is the focus of a scene that introduces the playwright's experimental theatre, which is the prologue's second function. As soon as the tour guide finishes identifying the places of interest in the naturalistic Ybor City that are portals to the non-naturalistic Ybor City, the portal that is the "haunted" Italian Club opens on the voices of the three singing Figures.

Wellman has a body of non-dramatic writings. I will, however, with one exception confine the discussion to "A Chrestomathy of 22 Answers to 22 Wholly Unaskable and Unrelated Questions Concerning Political and Poetic Theater," which prefaces the volume in which *Fnu Lnu* is collected and which sums up the other writings. "A Chrestomathy" contrasts two theatres, but before we look at the criticism of naturalistic theatre, Wellman's commending American naturalism's original intention should be noted. Originally "art on behalf of the poor, the disenfranchised," it opposed the "geezerdom" of its day, Broadway superficiality, yet "eventually mutat[ing]" into the theatre its creators despised, it ended up "sacralizing the nonevent" (7). Today geezer theatre is naturalistic theatre, which observes Aristotelian unities in a linear narrative of social conditioning that produces a univocal meaning. Because plays of this theatre are predictable, dramatizing the nonevent, they "feel more like the reanimated corpses of plays than plays proper" (8). Poetic theatre draws its energy from the chaos that undergirds surface reality; its disruption and subversion of the unities, linear narrative, and predictable motivation and resolution "confirm the presence of deep structures we do not normally perceive, because they do not function in linear time" (3). Dramatizing the event, which is unpredictable, generated as it is from the undergirding chaos, this theatre consists "of surprising texts, in surprising contexts" (9) that disperse multivocal meanings. The surprise induces awe and wonder in the audience, experiencing insights into itself—human nature—and the world in which it lives that it did not experience before. Images create the surprise. A visual image such as the one that opens Wellman's *Sincerity Forever* surprises. On a beautiful summer night on the outskirts of a town that could be anywhere in the United States, "*two girls sit in a parked car talking about things. Both are dressed in Ku Klux Klan garb.*"[7]

Yet it is verbal images—language—to which Wellman devotes space. "In fact," he writes, "a whole new vocabulary may be necessary to do justice to the 'hot,' unstable, poetic theater of our time—as well as the 'hot,' unstable theater of all time" (6). Dialogue in a naturalistic play is not realistic, he argues, going on to give instances that contradict naturalism's stable, rational language, the first instance being that "people don't always know what they mean when they say something" (9). In his plays single words in new usage such as furball and geezer and neologisms such as bodacious flapdoodle surprise as does a flow of verbal images such as the torrent of invective from the mouth of the African-American Jesus H. Christ in *Sincerity Forever*. Not surprising is the part of a language system that Wellman favored in a 1991 interview: syntax. Why? the interviewer asked the playwright, who answered, "Syntax is the flow of meaning through language. Grammar is the set of shackles that gets imposed on meaning."[8] Although the examination of Wellman's theatre will continue to use the playwright's terms, his surface reality and chaos in geezer and poetic dramaturgical structure are equivalent to the representational or fixed surface and the fluid subsurface, his grammar and syntax in linguistic structure are equivalent to the ruled surface and the unruly subsurface. Whichever terms are used, the oppositions of fixity and fluidity, above and below take us back into the opening scene of *Fnu Lnu*.

As soon as he speaks, Deezo reveals oppositions and contradictions. He does not want the audience to think of the locale as Ybor City's Italian Club but as "Deezo's Museum / of the Mind" (210). He collects found objects such as a ball of hairs for the museum, even though he does not know what the ball is good for. He says that he is the master of ceremonies just for one night while admitting that this sort "of event . . . tends to repeat itself. / Like a tape loop, infinite regress, or / something nested in an image of itself" (211), an admission that prepares for a recursive narrative rather than naturalism's linear narrative. His mental museum has no lack of pieces, but they are random pieces: ball of hairs and cigar boxes, José Marti and Fidel Castro, Charlie Wall and demons. That is, he knows of personalities associated with the old city such as the Cuban revolutionary, José Marti, and the numbers boss, Charlie Wall, and he speculates about being "in love with a DEMON" in a former life (212), but he also confesses, "I don't know what the / hell I'm talking about" (212), a superfluous remark because it follows an example of not knowing what he is talking about. Three places from which immigrants came to work in the old city are "Gargantua, Pirandello, / Fellatio" (211–12).

Yet Deezo is the play's hero, and, like most heroes, he will go on a quest. So far the direction is inward (Museum of the Mind) and the movement is circular (Like a tape loop). As this opening scene continues to unfold, it also gives the quest's remaining direction and the first part of the task or the reason for undertaking the quest. One of the Figures challenges Deezo to tell the audience about something that happened to him, in the telling of which encounter with a *"demented street person"* (213), he becomes the street person.

Another actor does not appear onstage. The actor playing Deezo speaks the lines, but his reluctance to tell reveals his fright encountering the person while his speaking the lines reveals that the voice is within himself, suppressed under his museum. The demented person or the demented part of himself does not surface apropos of nothing. The summoning conforms to the calling of the hero to the adventure. Countering the notion that such calls happen willy-nilly, Joseph Campbell writes, "They are the result of suppressed desires and conflicts. They are ripples on the surface of life, produced by unsuspected springs. And these may be very deep—as deep as the soul itself. . . . The herald or announcer of the adventure, therefore, is often dark, loathly, or terrifying, judged evil by the world."[9] A repository of information about the old Ybor City, Deezo has been questing but only superficially for collectibles, yet the questing not only awakens the suppressed depth but summons it.

The demented part of Deezo is the voice of the disorder that "A Chrestomathy" calls chaos: the "fundamental, unseen architect of all that is orderly" (4). The term the play uses for the chaos that undergirds orderly or surface reality, the disorder that interacts with order to create, is anarchy, the absence of externally imposed rules. Since the remaining direction is downward into the suppressed anarchy, the quest's directions are inward and downward in a circular movement. Since the destination is the old city, the first part of the reason for undertaking the quest or its task is recovering the old city's meaning. The demented voice gives clues to the buried Ybor City. He does not believe his mother (an allusion to Clytemnestra?) about Western values, but he knows that the old city suffered the destruction of those values, which destruction accounts for the dominance of the values that characterize the present city: drinking, guns, vandalism. These values are not new to the city. They were always there, as Deezo knows when he lists, among others, "Crime. / Loss. Public betrayal. Defection" (212). But to him they are "odd stuff" or "scary stuff" (212): the stuff of museums rather than of creativity. Hence to descend into the museum's vault, *Fnu Lnu* disconnects from naturalistic theatre's surface for poetic theatre's depth, from naturalistic theatre's stable order for poetic theatre's unstable disorder. The quest is not archaeological searching for ruins under the present Ybor City. Old, lost, buried are metaphors for the Ybor City and its positive values that flourished in the late 19th and early 20th centuries and that are given in the play's prefatory note: workers building their own schools, for instance. And the quest is multidimensional. In addition to the political dimension, the quest is linguistic and theatrical, the last-named dimension a reimagining of the *Eumenides*.

Above I suggested that Deezo's questing, although superficial, prompted the call to adventure. Another way of looking at the scene is that Deezo's questing was the call that prompted the underworld's response by sending its herald, the demented person (a contemporized Apollo?), to encounter the quester and get him started on the journey to the old city. The interpretation depends on what one makes of the demented voice's question, "You want to know why the 'Y' in Ybor?" (213) After Deezo returns to his normal self, he recounts asking passersby on the present city's Seventh Avenue that question and not only not getting an answer but confusing them with a question that made no sense to them. His questioning passersby was the call that elicited the underworld's response, which begins with the demented voice repeating the question Deezo posed. The problem is that after Deezo returns to his normal self and before he recounts asking passersby, he says, "I turned into a / stranger. A man possessed. 'Why the "Y" in / Ybor'? That's all I could focus on" (215). The tenses indicate that after the encounter he asked passersby the question the herald posed. The problem here is that after he returns to his normal self, he also says that he jumped on a bus to get away from the demented person, leaving him no time to go tramping along Seventh Avenue because the play's action continues on the bus.

Wellman is destabilizing meaning and disrupting and subverting linear narrative to uncover the old city, a metaphor for the play's anarchy and one of poetic theatre's "deep structures" (3) alluded to in "A Chrestomathy." The demented voice heralded the buried kingdom's existence, but whether Deezo asked passersby the question before or after the encounter, he asked in the wrong place, the surface of the present city, and he bolts from the depth's herald. Aeschylus' *Libation Bearers* closes with Orestes, with the Furies in pursuit, fleeing Argos for Delphi and purgation for the crime of matricide. In *Eumenides* the purged hero flees Delphi, with the Furies in pursuit, for Athens and acquittal of the crime because Apollo demanded the blood vengeance for Clytemnestra's killing of Agamemnon. In *Fnu Lnu* the Figures are on the bus with Deezo, who cannot escape them or himself.

When a passenger pronounces the words "Fnu Lnu," repeated in question form by the hero, the scene undergoes a *"catastrophic change"* and Deezo finds himself in "someplace strange" (218). He has crossed the first threshold of Campbell's schematization to the "zone of magnified power."[10] I do not mean to suggest that Wellman is slavishly following a schematization because he is not. I cite Campbell to show that as Deezo's journey progresses toward the buried kingdom, the play's fixed forms begin to dissolve. The three singing Figures become three singing Zobop sorceresses. When Aeschylus' Furies become the Eumenides, they switch from chthonic black to celebratory red. Wellman does not specify the color of the Figures' outfits until they are sorceresses, at which time they wear *"red gowns and red tricorn hats"* (218). The play's language, which began with the prologue's stable, naturalistic identifying of tourist attractions, also is dissolving into unstable, poetic im-

agery and narrative. "All I don't know is / 'why'" (220) is a statement made
by the first sorceress. The same sorceress tells a tale of two demons responsible for Florida's existence. From his station in hell, Charlie Wall, the de-
structive force, daily disintegrates the state whereas from an unknown location, Fnu Lnu, the positive force, daily restores the state—makes it new.

Aeschylus' Furies become Eumenides toward the trilogy's end when they
agree to accept the jury's acquittal of Orestes. In return for their accepting a
new concept of justice to replace the old law of blood vengeance, Athens will
honor them as Kindly Ones. Switching to red, they join in the procession celebrating Athenian democracy and civilization. If the Figures' putting on red
signals their becoming kindly, they are so in the sense that by crafting a myth
of two competing demons, which the first sorceress calls a "mystery" (220),
to explain the old city's nature, they assist Deezo in completing his task's first
part. They also assist him in the task's second part, not by crafting another
myth but by answering the question he posed—why the "Y" in Ybor?—po-
etically in metaphors:

> The letter "Y" is the fork of time.
> Time and human choice. Y is the human
> question turned upside down. Turned upside
> down to ensure human freedom (222).

Telling Deezo that he has "split off from someone else" (223), the Figures
morphed into Zobop sorceresses-cum-Eumenides send him to search for
someone who can answer the question, "and only Fnu Lnu knows that" (223).
With his identity linked to the question, Deezo finally stops trying to evade
his twofold task and instead "set[s] off to find out the truth" (223). He enters
the quest's initiation phase, which Campbell describes as a "dream landscape
of curiously fluid, ambiguous forms," where the quester "must survive a succession of trials."[11]

The first half of Campbell's description applies to Deezo's adventure; the
second half does not. Reviewing the play's premiere production, Porter Anderson likened Deezo's adventure to being hurled "through an Inferno without a Virgil."[12] The Dantean image invokes the descent, but there is a significant difference between the poem and the play. In Dante's poem the pilgrim
interacts with hell's inhabitants to a degree that reflects his attraction to or re-
pulsion for the sins being enacted on the downward spiraling circles. Deezo,
on the other hand, has minimal interaction with the inhabitants of the four
scenes that constitute the initiation. He is not being tested in four trials but is
learning about himself as "split off from someone else" (223). Encountering
the demented part of himself, he acknowledged the existence of a buried

kingdom. With the assistance of the Zobop sorceresses-cum-Eumenides, he
learned that the buried kingdom is the anarchy that flows as positive and negative forces. The second task is learning why Ybor City's anarchy bifurcates
into positive and negative forces, life and death: why the Y.

Since Deezo does not understand the sorceresses' poetic answer to the
question, he has to descend into poetic language, which is another way of saying that he has to descend into the anarchy that is the old Ybor City, where
presumably he will find Fnu Lnu while discovering why the anarchy bifurcates. Although the first of the four scenes opens with one of the sorceresses
becoming a fortune-teller who is a demon and the second scene opens with
the table at which Deezo sits with his microphone becoming a theater for performing alligators, the "curiously fluid, ambiguous forms" of Campbell's description are not visual forms because the sets do not change. The play should
not be staged naturalistically; language, with synchronized lighting and sound
effects, creates the bus on which Deezo attempts to flee the demented voice
and the descent after he leaves the bus. Verbal forms change because it is the
language that eludes being bounded. Geezer theatre is literal; poetic theatre is
metaphoric. For instance, Y is a letter in the alphabet or an ordinate in a rectilinear coordinate system in geezer theatre, the fork of time or the human
question turned upside down in poetic theatre. Thus the initiation is multilevel
and multivocal with Deezo learning about himself as a moral, political, and
creative being. And since the inhabitants of the four scenes repeat with seemingly endless variations the images accumulating as the action unfolds, I will
concentrate on only a few.

In the first scene, a woman who claims to have been an Italian immigrant
in the "old days / in Ybor" (224) contemptuously repeats the anarchist slogan
of not betraying the cause because the cause did not serve the anarchists; they
did not benefit from it. Actually a mambo, a Haitian voodoo priestess, she
tells Deezo that she once knew another Deezo who fought with Charlie Wall
over a girl and suffered at her hands as he is suffering, unable to find the answer for which he quests because he is under the influence of a ball of hairs
"willed by Evil Forces" (225). With Fnu Lnu, the only one who would know
the answer, "gone," she sends him to the reptile gods in the "hidden regions
of the / underworld" (226), the only time in the play the word is spoken.

The second scene is the descent's nadir. Although the middle one of the
three alligators connects Deezo and Fnu Lnu by comparing the former's
glowing to that of the latter as the latter "used to . . . / do" (230), this alliga-
tor does not know what a Ybor or a Y is. The other two define Y for their fellow reptile in language that impedes meaning because the definitions are dictionary entries, signifiers leading to more signifiers, as in "A Y is an ordinate
in a rectilinear co- / ordinate system" (229). Not comprehending what an an-

archist is, they nevertheless suggest that he find Ybor City's oldest anarchist on an ascent that returns to the surface of the present city's Seventh Avenue though still in the kingdom of the dead. The inhabitant of the next scene knew Mikhail Bakunin, who died in 1876.

That the energy that Wellman calls anarchy disconnects images from earlier meanings and associations in the play as well as outside the play to connect them with new meanings and associations is never more apparent than in the third scene. Though no counterpart to the hero of Aeschylus' trilogy, Orestes diFannelli Flannagan's name arrests the spectator's attention. Testifying to the decline and death of anarchism as a positive force, he had doubts about Castro even before the exiled revolutionary returned to Cuba. That was in 1955 when Castro visited Ybor City; at the time of the play—the present— he has no doubts that "it's as if ideals mean nothing at / all" (231). Regardless of his name, the oldest anarchist is ineffectual as a positive force. Not knowing how to answer Deezo's question about the Y and dismissing Fnu Lnu "as cold / as a cup of coffee at the North Pole" (233), all that he can do is reminisce about the good old days of Ybor City and Bakunin and advise the quester to talk to the Flim-Flam Man, the shade of Charlie Wall.

Approaching *Fnu Lnu* as a reimagining of Aeschylus' *Eumenides*, I expected gambling kingpin Charlie Wall, mentioned throughout the play, to be Agamemnon's counterpart, but the only correspondence is that Wall was killed in his home in Ybor City a few years after an extended absence and Agamemnon was killed in his palace upon returning home from the Trojan War. The shade of Wall appears as the Flim-Flam Man in the fourth scene unlike the Argive warrior, who does not make a ghostly appearance in *Eumenides* as does Clytemnestra. Wall is closer to Dante's Dis in canto 34 of the *Inferno*, though he does not rule in hell as does the poet's Satan. His force rules on earth, for it is in Deezo's chair that he sits awaiting the quester in a movement that is circular. In the 1997 revival that opened the Wellman festival, one actor played Deezo, the demented person, Orestes, and the Flim-Flam Man. In scenes involving these characters, the hero is listening to voices within himself. He keeps returning to himself, each circle to a greater degree of penetration until he confronts his unacknowledged self, the force from which he split off at the Y's fork.

The Flim-Flam Man links images with Ybor City's historical personalities in a tale that is so finely spun and richly textured that it is a narrative within the play's narrative, thereby fulfilling Deezo's opening-scene premonition that the action would unfold like "something nested in an image of itself" (211). The ball of hairs is Castro's beard, which abandoned the dictator as his plane flew over Tampa on its way to a North Pole tea party thrown by the Devil. The list of attendees is bizarre—in addition to Castro, Wall, and Kim

Il Sung of North Korea are Ronald Reagan, Ross Perot, and Frank Sinatra—but both the location and the rationale for being invited are not. The North Pole, "where / the Devil lives, like a great, creaking heron" (235), is the earthly counterpart to Dante's Cocytus, where Satan lives, so furiously beating his wings and thereby freezing the water that flows into the pit that he creates the ice in which he is encased. The tea-party guests are not the March Hare, the Hatter, and the Dormouse but if Castro and Kim Il Sung are the norm, betrayers of anarchism's ideals, the counterparts to the three guests in the *Inferno*: the betrayers Judas, Brutus, and Cassius, clamped on Satan's teeth. The mambo is the first inhabitant of the initiation phase to intimate a correspondence between Wall and Satan when she tells Deezo that "what is irrational" has him "in its mouth, like food. Like Charlie Wall. / Like Charlie Wall and the devil" (226).

The shade repeats the Zobop sorceresses' connecting of the Y's "fork" and "choice" (222): "'Y' is / split right down the middle. 'Y' implies choice" (234). In "split" he also repeats the sorceresses' image of Deezo's being "split off from someone else" (223). He therefore answers Deezo's question of why the Y in Ybor. Energy originating in the chaos or anarchy flows through a single stem until it bifurcates into positive and negative forces. The anarchists who worked in the cigar factories actualized their principles and ideals positively, as Wellman comments in the play's prefatory note, by building "schools, hospitals, and mutual aid societies" (207). Without being coerced by externally imposed rules, they chose to act on their freedom as individuals for the group's good. The mambo, however, contemptuously rejects the anarchists' slogan, and the ineffectual Orestes can only deplore the death of anarchism's principles and ideals in the present Ybor City.

He who in life was Charlie Wall identifies the two forces in the bifurcation. The sorceress' tale of the two demons responsible for Florida's existence connects the two forces, but the shade links them so as to explain why Deezo has split off and why only one of the two channels in the fork is functioning. Deezo is the first to raise the possibility of a connection when in the opening scene the demented street person claims that he, Deezo, owes his soul to the numbers boss, Charlie Wall, causing him to speculate about being in love with a demon in a former life. The mambo does more than speculate. She says she knew a Deezo who fought with Wall over a girl. The shade identifies the three in the triangle. The mambo was his girl "till Fnu Lnu showed up" (236). In his linkage Deezo and Fnu Lnu are the same person actualizing one of the two forces: the positive one. But since Deezo does not know who he is when he sets out on the quest and since Fnu Lnu is "gone" (226), the positive force is dead, leaving the field to the shade of Charlie Wall, who is the negative force: the Devil, the spirit of the univocal meaning of which he is sole possessor.

In an echo of Dylan Thomas' "The Force That Through the Green Fuse Drives the Flower," he who is the Devil declares his rule:

> I am the letter Y.
> I am the question Y.
> I am the answer Y.
> I am the force that drives the winds (237).

Just as below ground the alligators defeat meaning by impeding the energy's flow, above ground he defeats choice by channeling the energy's flow into a single prong. And by defeating freedom of choice, he defeats freedom of co-operation, anarchism's driving force and the basis of the polis. As he says about the North Pole tea party where nothing flows, "Each speaks to the other in his / own language . . . / so no one has much of a grasp on the / gist of the conversation" (235).

The Devil's negative force in the drinking, guns, and vandalism of the present city rules because Deezo's positive force ceased flowing as evidenced in the play's opening scene, where he does not know himself, fails to understand the significance of the museum's contents, and bolts from the demented voice. When he does seek an answer to the question, he undergoes an adventure that is a descent into the life and death within himself, for the play's characters are his "gaggle of familiars" (208). By the ultimate scene, he discovers what Wall's shade, the negative force within himself, told him in the penultimate scene: Deezo-Fnu Lnu is dead. He therefore cannot complete the hero's quest. He cannot return to the quotidian world with the boon gained from the adventure: showing others how to choose between life and death by descending into themselves to discover the potential to be creative in their personal, political, and artistic lives.

Fnu Lnu, however, shows the audience how to discover the potential. It defeats the negative univocal, dictionary meaning by dramatizing multivocal possibilities. One example will suffice. The Figures' appearance in red as Zobop sorceresses, which coincides with Deezo's recognition that he has left the bus and is "someplace else" (218), may signal their becoming Eumenides who are assisting Deezo on his journey. Yet later the bus driver and another man named Beano report to the Flim-Flam Man that they followed his instructions by taking Deezo off the bus and putting on the "Zobop regalia" (234). In the ultimate scene, morgue attendants put the time of death as a "day / or two" (239) and go on to explain that Beano claimed the suitcase with the ball of hairs in it. The implication of this sequence is that Beano and the bus driver took Deezo off the bus and either killed him or had him killed, ensuring that he would approach Wall's shade as a dead man. In the same scene, one of the sorceresses reappears. Speaking as Castro's beard—according to the shade, the real identity of the ball of hairs—she puts the time of death at "forty- / two years" (241) and identifies the killer as the mambo, retaliating when she realized that Deezo, who had been hired to kill Wall, was using her to get to the vice lord. Finally, she says that the slain man will "be back / before too long" (241), presumably because he is a hero and heroes journey through the quest's initiation. Knowing he forfeited his identity by not choosing to act is the impetus to choose to return to life with the boon gained from the adventure.

How a spectator responds to the possibilities depends on the spectator. In the political dimension, possibilities offer choice, which promotes political consciousness and generates the birth of democracy and civilization. A diverse audience stimulated by Deezo's quest to pursue their quests for meaning within the collective theatre experience in which one's ideas and insights interact with others' ideas and insights reflects a more desirable society than a society in which one author(ity) imposes his or her univocal meaning. It reflects the last paragraph of the longest section of "A Chrestomathy," which opens with these two sentences: "That the terminology of Marxism seems stale, morally nil—if not reprehensible—does not mean socialism itself is dead. Surely, the age-old vision of a secular *paradiso*, with room for all peoples, of all races, ethnicities, and cultural propensities and affiliations is still an overwhelming one" (14).

Eliminating choice not only solidifies the flowing subsurface to shut off one of the two bifurcating prongs so that the present political-social-economic realities are fixed on the surface—the situation at the play's opening—it does so in the linguistic and theatrical dimensions or realities. Eliminating choice in multivocal meanings, as univocal language does, eliminates the tension between possible meanings, the tension that comes with making a choice, and the tension of maintaining in equilibrium multiple meanings to enrich the experience. Poetic theatre appeals because it violates geezer or naturalistic theatre's sanctions, but it does not abolish them. Witness the tour guide's description, Deezo's linear journey, and the Flim-Flam Man's narrative. Theatre that experiments with narratives other than linear excites the imagination weaned on linear narrative, yet an all non-linear theatre would eventually dull the imagination. It would be as monolithic as naturalistic theatre. For creativity to flourish, the subsurface energy has to flow into two surface prongs that interact, stimulating choice, for it is choice in double-pronged poetic or experimental theatre that engages the spectator. That is why a Wellman play is daunting for an audience accustomed to single-pronged theatre that makes the choice or resolves the conflict for the audience. The poetic theatre, however, so structures the experience that the spectator has to make an effort to participate in the creating of the play or be frustrated. Of course, even making an effort, one can be frustrated, yet not to be responsible—not to exercise political and poetic freedom—is to be a Fnu Lnu: first and last names unknown, an ignominy the playwright does not suffer.

Richard Maxwell has made a name for himself by turning naturalism's strength against itself. Although praising Maxwell's "exceptional ear for the ragged nature of everyday speech," Charles Isherwood sees him as a "gifted naturalist who is at war with naturalism, which in the theater he sees as deeply artificial."[13] The artificiality is in naturalistic theatre's glib capacity to articulate. Overmyer summarizes the way actors naturalize a non-naturalistic text. "This usually consists of *relaxing* the language, adding *ums* and *ahs* and halts and pauses and stutters; restoring articles and conjunctions that the writer has deliberately pruned, running sentences together, ignoring carefully constructed rhythms, and generally rewriting so that the language feels more 'natural' to the actor."[14] Wellman has his own list of reasons why a naturalistic play's language is unrealistic. In real life "people don't always know what they mean when they say something, people tell lies, kid themselves, are mistaken, self-deceived, ill-spoken, at a loss for words at the critical moment (the Billy Budd syndrome). Sometimes people don't even know—literally—what they are saying" (9).

Maxwell's strategy for countering the artificiality whose hypertrophied surface masks a shallow depth is to so flatten the language that it is stuck on the surface. In an interview the playwright called his style "'anti-style. It's about coming as close to neutrality as you can.'"[15] *Showy Lady Slipper* opens with three young women entering a performance space, minimal against a painted backdrop, in which a telephone is ringing. Lori picks up the phone and says, "Hello?" The word "*Pause*"[16] appears on the text's printed page, but the text's "*Pause*" cannot convey the pause in the performance space, where the women stand for minutes with deadpan faces and without speech or movement until Lori hangs up and announces to Erin and Jennifer that John is "driving over" (145). The three speak in monotone on subjects such as cars and travel, their mothers and guys they know, uttering sounds that form words, but the delivery is affectless. In addition, the sounds alternate with periods of silence, gaps that create a disconnection, to which this examination of *Showy Lady Slipper* will return. When the speaking resumes, the speaker does not necessarily resume the train of thought so that she can be disjointed within what she is saying or coherent, but if the latter she might go to the other extreme and speak repetitively on the same subject. Sometimes the three do not reply to one another because they seem not to understand, thereby defeating conversation. Other times they reply with, "Yeah" (148), even though the train of thought to which they reply was convoluted. And still other times they reply with understanding because they pick up on what was said. No matter what direction the speaking takes, though, it is invariably monotonic, even when the text has utterances implying excitement such as "Oh my God," sometimes with an exclamation point and sometimes without it (148 and 149).

That from time to time the three women utter "Oh my God" with or without an exclamation point makes it a stock utterance devoid of any significance. And even were it spoken so selectively as to have emotional significance, the delivery from deadpan faces and stiff, awkward bodies would stifle the emotion's expression. For example, at one point Jennifer mentions someone they know, Tracy, who "made a lot of money" (153). Lori criticizes the way in which she made it by wasting her talent and college education making designs for t-shirts. She concludes her criticism by saying that unlike Tracy, she can manage her situation. Following Lori's and Erin's comments on being an "organizer-type person" and a period of silence, Jennifer resumes by suggesting that Tracy "may have skills" (154), a suggestion that Lori interprets as criticism of her so that despite Jennifer's protest that she was talking only about Tracy, Lori feels insulted. After more gaps in the speaking, Jennifer, in an attempt at reconciliation, gives Lori a necklace she made with the words, "It looks nice on you" (156). What makes the scene different from a comparable scene in real life is the affectless delivery. The play's physical activity delivers the same difference. Lori hugs John when he arrives and later "*throws*" (171) Jennifer to the floor for "messing around with" him (169), but the activity is performed robotically.

Discrepancies, contradictions, and ambiguities are rife. Reviewing the Performance Space (P.S.) 122 premiere, Marc Robinson called attention to the two chairs on the set's painted backdrop and the two real chairs in the space, "made more tangible by the contrast."[17] For Shawn-Marie Garrett, the women are "barely out of teenybopperdom."[18] She is right in language and behavior. "Come on, you guys" (161), Lori leads the exit to their rooms where they change into clothes they bought to show John. Returning, she and Erin join Jennifer, who preceded them, to stand motionless and expressionless awaiting his approval as if they were children obeying a parent's directive. "Good" (163) is his affectless judgment.

For Peter Marks, the three are "young women on the cusp of adulthood."[19] He is right in age and experience, for they must be at least college age. They share an apartment to which they have returned after shopping at the mall. Before John arrives, Erin proposes that they see a movie that night. After John leaves, Lori and Erin, not realizing he has told Jennifer he will come back for her, retire for the night, but Jennifer declines, saying she will "stay up a little longer" (167). The lone woman about whom they talk, Tracy, has been out of college for some years working as a designer of t-shirts. Lori, who thinks

Tracy is wasting her talent, draws a contrast with herself. She, Lori, is "into trying to make all" (154) of her projects work to her own benefit; the implication is as an entrepreneur. For experience, they date and party. Lori not only spends time with John in his apartment, she has gone away with him at least one weekend. She and Erin reminisce about vacations they have taken to sunny islands, and although Erin was probably with her family, as Lori describes one vacation, she was by herself or not with her family. Lori is also privileged. When she was nine, her father gave her a horse for a present.

Even within the sisterhood the three form, discrepancies, contradictions, and ambiguities are rife. Lori does not speak into the phone in the opening scene, other than "Hello?" To the other two, however, she says that John is "driving over . . . to see what we bought" (145). Yet when he arrives, she has to introduce her two friends. Since he knows how to find his way to the apartment and since he knows she shares the apartment with others, comprising the "we," the audience has to assume that they have always been out when he arrived. Furthermore, although Jennifer knows that Lori spent Mardi Gras weekend with John, Erin did not know; apparently the matter never came up for discussion. Finally, they have a terrible time remembering names of guys they know, but one would think each knows the names of the other two. Yet Lori introduces Jennifer as "Lisa" (161) before getting the name correct.

These incongruities do not minimize the fun in a performance. John's arrival provokes two of the play's funniest exchanges, and I am not including the arrival itself, although he enters not with a fire chief's helmet but with a racer's helmet, which he apparently wears when driving at race tracks and through the streets. After the three women retire to their rooms to change back into the clothes they were wearing when he arrived, Jennifer is the first to reappear so that she is alone with John. As they talk facing each other, the corners of their lips twitching, he asks, "Are you smiling?" his hope that a smile will signal a reciprocal interest. "I'm not," she answers; "That's my face!" (164) Undeterred because the answer would be a squelch only if expressed with emotion, he proceeds to propose an evening drive. The second exchange, which follows moments later, recalls the scene in *The Flu Season* in which the lovers convert what should be a tender overture that leads to snuggling into crazy dialogue about what they are thinking. Those two have an excuse; they are mental patients. What excuse Maxwell's would-be lovers have, if any, remains to be seen. When Jennifer declines John's proposal for a drive to an observatory because she does not believe they have enough time, he counters with, "But it's fast":

Jennifer: Okay.

John: Okay, you'll go?

Jennifer: No. Okay I get it.

John: But what about go?

Jennifer: To the observatory?

John: Let's do that (165).

Showy Lady Slipper is not simply satirizing a particular generation. Every reviewer familiar with Maxwell's theatre detects the existence of a depth, stifled though it is. Here is Ben Brantley reviewing *Boxing 2000*: "By slowing down rhythms of speech and inflating pauses, he [Maxwell] parses the banalities of everyday talk and finds the whispering fear and confusion beneath. . . . Platitudinous these people may be, but there is a genuine yearning that emerges, despite itself, from their numbness."[20] Maxwell's characters can talk, even volubly, on mundane matters. They experience emotion, as Lori does when she orders Erin out of the room so that she can deal with Jennifer's betrayal and then throws the latter to the floor. What the plays are doing therefore is dramatizing the inadequacy of naturalistic language to express the depth. There are moments when the characters recognize the problem. In the dialogue just quoted, rather than mouthing the perfunctory "Yeah" or "Okay," John wants Jennifer to clarify her "Okay." In a more insightful instance, Lori expresses her disappointment with her boyfriend's laconic judgment on the new outfits they bought: "'Good.' That's all he can say" (163).

In the interview from which this study quotes, Maxwell called his plays musicals. The remark is tongue-in-cheek, as the interview clarifies, but it is illuminating nonetheless. In musical comedies, operettas, and operas, characters express their deepest feelings in soaring songs, arias, and duets. Maxwell's linguistically deprived characters resort to songs to express the depth of their feelings, yet the lyrics are banal. The gaps that every reviewer comments on are pauses during which characters turn inward to summon the depth. It is not the emotion that is wanting, however; it is geezer language that cannot express the depth. As Jennifer pauses to decide whether or not to go on the evening drive with John, he delivers a song for which the first stanza is the following:

> Give me an answer
> What will it be
> I won't wait forever
> Will you comfort me.

If the play's language is to be heightened, it should be in the song. Instead, he sings, "Higher and higher / I'm reaching higher" (165), while standing flat-footed and vocalizing flat-voiced.

In the play's closing scene, the young women learn of John's death in a car accident, at which time they sing, "I'll never be the same again" (173). The absence of inflection in their voices and animation in their bodies belies a change in them, but perhaps the change should be taking place elsewhere. About a song delivered in deadpan style that closes another of his plays, Maxwell commented on the limitations he imposes on his theatre. "'If you're saying these words and not trying to attach some personal psychology to them, what else is there? You compress something so much, it's inevitable you're going to create some kind of combustion.'" By themselves, these statements imply that the combustion will eventually occur in the characters, yielding emotion in expressive language. Yet he also stated that he was "'not interested in the autobiographical, the personal, or the emotionally invested.'"

Granting that the interview can contain the same discrepancies, contradictions, and ambiguities found in the plays, one can nevertheless locate the combustion's site offstage. In addition to exposing the characters' disconnection from their depth, the alternating of flattened language and yawning gaps draws the spectator into the play, as Maxwell himself likes to be imaginatively engaged as a spectator. "'I'm interested,'" he said in the same interview, "'as an audience member, in being able to project whatever I want onto a piece of theater.'"[21] The longer the spectator has to wait for the onstage combustion, the greater the tension he/she feels and the greater the emotional response he/she will have when the moment arrives when the combustion should occur but does not. A later play supports the strategy of building tension offstage to effect its release in the audience, though I have not seen the play, and it is not in the collected edition. Reviewing *Good Samaritans*, Isherwood quotes a character named Rosemary saying toward play's end, "'I don't feel anything,'" as "her triumphant emergence" from emotional turmoil, an admission he hears as "heartbreaking."[22]

It is difficult imagining how Melissa James Gibson could sustain the three parts or acts of her play *[sic]* with the following dialogue, even though it is spoken with affect. One of the three onstage characters, tenants of an apartment building, knocks on the door of one of the other two.

Babette: I'm going to the store downstairs Do you need anything from The Store Downstairs

Theo: No Uh Yes I need candy bars Could you pick me up some Candy Bars

Babette: How many candy bars

Theo: Six or seven Candy Bars

Babette: Six
Or Seven candy bars

Theo: Seven Candy Bars

Babette: Do you have Uh money.[23]

The repetition is typical of act-1's dialogue. Another example is in the third character's, Frank's, questioning of the other two about their ownership of a cassette player that he can borrow. Although they tell him that neither has one, Frank keeps asking. In this instance he withholds the direct address until midway through the repetition: "I need a Cassette Babette Tape Player" (15). Repetition is not the dialogue's sole characteristic. In the midst of a three-way conversation following Babette's return from the store, Theo says, "Let Her Love The Kitchen" (22), a non sequitur worthy of theatre of the absurd. The utterance does have a referent, but it comes earlier in the act when Frank, receiving notice from the building's management about his situation as sublessee of the apartment he occupies, asks Theo, "What rhymes with / Letter of Eviction" (21).

The spectator does not have to imagine the play sustaining uninterruptedly such dialogue for two more acts because Gibson does many things with and to the language to create non-naturalistic modes of presentation and genres that interact with the dialogue. Structurally *[sic]* is balanced halves. The first-half's naturalistic language reveals disconnections in three senses. The characters are disconnected from the world outside themselves. The play opens with the offstage voice of an old woman, a fourth tenant named Mrs. Jorgenson, singing *"with gusto"* (9) sexually suggestive lyrics. But the three do not react to the singing, and Frank ignores what the others tell him about not having a cassette player because the information frustrates his need. They are disconnected from one another except when they need something. As Babette asks Frank whether he wants anything from the store, they shift the conversation to the preceding evening unaware that Theo, who did not close his door all the way, is listening. Confronting them, he claims to have seen them from his window together outside the building. They deny having been together. In fact, Frank protests, he stopped by to see Mrs. Jorgenson. At this point Theo catches them in the lie. Not only did the old woman inadvertently reveal that they went to a movie together but she added that they asked her not to mention their going out to him. Yet they go to him to borrow money and a cassette player. They are disconnected from their deepest selves as sexual, social beings. A shop owner, Larry, to whom Babette gave some items of her furniture to sell for her, was Frank's lover before he rejected the tenant. Theo makes an effort at connecting with a partner to replace his wife, who left him, except that he insists that Babette be the partner, a relationship she steadfastly resists. She is unable to admit that she has any desire. She concedes that she had a sexual encounter of some sort with Theo but dismisses it as of no consequence because she was drunk.

Frank's refusal to accept Larry's rejection of him and Theo's refusal to accept Babette's rejection of him are but two instances of the three characters not listening to the voices that speak to their deepest selves. One reason is that they are absorbed in their surface selves as yuppies "well past the point," as Gibson characterizes them in the author's note, "when being a wunderkind is a viable option" (5). This self-absorption disconnects them from their deepest selves as creative beings. As Theo explains to Frank in act 3, he is a "classically trained composer who attended a genuine School / of Music / or or Conservatory" (85–86), but he has taken a commission to compose a theme song for an amusement-park ride. Act 1 finds him "*in compositional hell*" (23) either staring at the synthesizer keyboard or playing the same bars over and over. In the same scene, the audience hears Larry's "*barely concealed laughter*" (27) when Babette, phoning to check whether he sold any of her furniture, refers to the book she says she is writing, a situation that prevents her from taking a more lucrative position than the sometime editorship she holds and that forces her to sell her furniture to tide her over. Frank needs a cassette player so that he can practice the tongue twisters in the auctioneering training program he is taking.

Though they resist the voices speaking to them, the chinks in their defense mechanisms are apparent. Their resistance stiffens the self-absorption from which they suffer in that they cling more tenaciously to their career choices, for the alternative is admitting that they made a mistake and are wasting their talent. The resistance exacerbates the paranoia from which they suffer in that each suspects that others perceive the mistake. After Babette returns from the store, Theo ends the hallway conversation by announcing that he must get back to "work" on the theme song. When Babette says that the "first two bars Still sound really good," he asks, "Did she just Hit that adverb with something akin to / Mockery or was that Merely my iMagination" (23). Intelligent and verbal, they parry with barbs—in this case what may be Babette's damning the composition with faint praise by Theo's referring to her in front of her as an unidentified third party: "she" (23). Dispersed, they return to their apartments—into themselves—for the apartments function as images of the solitary self whereas the "shared hallway" (5), as Gibson describes the play's setting, is an image of the possibility of communal life.

The drama at the play's core is the three tenants' struggle to discover themselves and their place in the contemporary world. Gibson's treatment of the drama, however, is both naturalistic in language and non-naturalistic in modes of presentation and genres that interact with the naturalistic language. The contrast between the solitary apartments and the shared hallway is symbolic, and the dispensing with the stage's invisible fourth wall, as the three are about to do by speaking directly to the audience, is experimental as is the

altering of the narrative mode that occurs later in the action. As this examination of Gibson's play will develop, *[sic]* is the new type of play first encountered in the study in Groff's *What Then*.

As disconnected as they are, they would like to connect, on the simplest
level as neighbors in the apartment house and as friends, as they explain in
act-1's second scene in which they relate to the audience their overcoming
initial dislike of one another when first meeting at Larry's shop to discover
they would be neighbors and could be friends. The tension between not listening to the voices that speak to their deepest selves and the psychological
need to escape from their doubts and insecurities and the spiritual need to
commune with other selves creates the rapid succession of mini-scenes within
the divisions designated as scenes: two scenes for each of the play's three
parts or acts. In the author's note, Gibson calls these mini-scenes within the
scenes "moments" (6). Act 1 ends with one such moment: Theo playing his
composition and then looking "*expectantly . . . toward his friends*" for approval of nonexistent progress, for the "*development . . . is virtually indis-
cernible.*" They do not speak. Instead, the audience hears an offstage voice
having a "*good laugh*" followed by the repeated interjection, "Alas Alas"
(35).

By closing act 1 with a verbal image, Gibson reinforces language's role in
the characters' disconnections and anticipates its role in their connections: the
focus of the play's second half. In a "work that is, at least partly, concerned
with the sound and power of language,"[24] it not only reveals disconnections,
it disconnects. The first moment in which one of the three is alone occurs after Babette and Frank, caught in a lie, exit the stage, the former to shop downstairs and the latter to disappear behind his closed apartment door. The audience sees Theo playing a few bars on his synthesizer before he stops, rises,
and opens his apartment window. His stopping reflects his doubt about his
ability to compose a theme song; his standing motionless at the window reflects his self-absorption because he does not react to an exchange by the couple whose apartment is beneath those of the three and the clipped sounds of
whose voices carry through the building's airshaft and his open window. The
man's question, "Did you throw that," to the woman about the "*sound of a
bowl falling to the floor*" (19) is even more provocative than Mrs. Jorgenson's
lyrics that open the scene. Yet Theo has no reaction to the ensuing exchange
despite a parallel between them that Gibson draws in the cast listing. Of the
play's eight voices, five are those of characters in their thirties: the three onstage characters and the downstairs couple, designated the Airshaft Couple.
He does not mention the exchange to Frank, who knocks at the door, and his
shutting the window shuts out sounds from the world outside the enclave the
three inhabit.

A comparable moment occurs at the scene's end. It follows Babette's yelling in frustration in Larry's direction because he keeps putting her on hold when she tries to learn whether he sold any of her items and Theo's cursing his synthesizer for failing to deliver a song. Frank stops practicing tongue twisters and opens his window, allowing the Airshaft Couple's voices to enter his apartment. Their situation deteriorating, their sounds are increasingly clipped, disjunct, estranged, and even hostile. He throws keys from his room into hers, they argue about whether or not they have to arrive together probably at a lawyer's office, and she throws toast from her room into his. Their language is disconnecting them from each other, but like Theo earlier in the scene, Frank shows no reaction.

All of the three characters' disconnections come together in their disconnection from their subsurfaces. Like Maxwell's characters, they are stuck on the surface, but unlike Maxwell's characters, they are so absorbed in their pursuits of careers and partners that they do not pause, other than a few times, which pauses would create gaps. The few times that they do pause, they are so self-absorbed they do not listen to voices other than those on the surface, and to those not intently, and when not pausing, they talk incessantly because talk is their defense mechanism against voices from the subsurface rising to the surface and penetrating their self-absorption.

The verbal images make a stronger impression if the production follows Gibson's stage design. As she conceived of her play, three actors, two men and one woman, appear onstage. Yet when New York's Soho Repertory Theatre produced *[sic]* in 2001, another man and woman—the Airshaft Couple, present only in their voices in the original conception—were brought onstage although in an apartment with a ceiling so low that the audience had only an obstructed view of them. Finding the production aesthetically pleasing, Gibson nonetheless states in the author's note to the script that "in future productions, whether the Airshaft Couple is partially visible or remains a pair of offstage voices, it is vital that the concept of an obstructed view be explored in some tangible sense within the production as a whole." After giving instances of how a director can obstruct the view, she writes, "In this way, the visual perspective of the audience is at times as limited as the outlook of the main characters, whose self-absorption makes them prone to misinterpretation and paranoia at every turn" (5). The implication is that the bringing of the Airshaft Couple onto the stage as characters can not only divert attention away from the three but also away from the Couple's voices.

Since their voices are more important than their persons, in a production that follows Gibson's conception, the disembodied voices are non-naturalistic, resonating in a cramped apartment that becomes symbolic of the cramped self. Channeling offstage voices through portals when opened is but one of the things Gibson does with naturalistic language to produce a non-naturalistic effect. The characters' rapid opening and slamming of apartment doors not only signal changes in the mini-scenes or moments, they invoke the disorienting nature of Feydeauvian farce especially when these sounds compete with those of clipped dialogue, torturous tongue twisters, and abortive bars of music.

Yet it is the altering of the mode of narration that marks the division in the play's balanced halves. Disconnection is the first half. The second half has voices that effect a change in the three tenants' self-absorption connecting them to the world outside themselves, one another, and themselves. The second half, however, does not begin until midway in act 2. When the act opens, the three are still disconnected, in the hallway, their attention directed toward the fourth apartment door in Gibson's stage design. Though the door does not open in act 1, the audience knows who the occupant is. The offstage voice of the sung lyrics and the repeated interjection, the owner of a cassette player whom Babette recommended to Frank in his search to borrow one, and the confidante who inadvertently revealed to Theo Frank and Babette's dinner out, she is Mrs. Jorgenson. Her door does not open in act 2 either because she dies at the act's opening, but her death does not prevent her from playing a greater role than those of act 1. As the act opens, the three occupants of the doors that open and shut are discussing Frank's revelation that he discovered the old woman's body early that morning, a discussion that lasts many minutes. Frank has not notified anyone of the dead body. "What's the rush," he asks; Theo concurs, "I guess you're right" (37). Instead of notifying the building's superintendent or the police, they express their admiration for the two-word note she left—"See ya" (39)—and look at photos of her presumably in the altogether.

The audience cannot be offended by their lack of respect because the combination of other genres and modes undercuts the force of the naturalistic drama at the play's core and the social issues it typically addresses. Exaggerating a visual image while tossing off verbal images adds comic opera to the symbolic theatre, experimental theatre, and Feydeauvian farce. Reacting to the realization that the death makes Mrs. Jorgenson's apartment available to anyone looking for an apartment—evicted Frank, for example—Theo and Babette "*put their fingers on their chins for a moment and shift their eyes in unison.*" When they speak, the stage directions grant each any two of three stock responses: "Oh that's right / Of course / Yes you do" (39–40). Yet in language and characterization, [sic] is naturalistic. Mrs. Jorgenson's dominant characteristic in the first act and a half is her sexual nature. Described as a "*very old woman,*" she nevertheless sang the opening sexually suggestive lyrics "*with gusto*" (9). She confided in Babette, who tells Frank, that she "was in love with" him, a possibility he would have rejected had he known because she "wasn't" his "gender," although he concedes she had "great ankles and wrists" (48). Undeterred, she found another young partner. Early in part 2, Babette retrieves from a photo developing service what she thinks are photos of a trip she took but upon opening the packet discovers that she was given by mistake photos belonging to Mrs. Jorgenson. From the two men's offer to take possession of the photos and Babette's refusal to part with them, calling the two "perverts," they capture her flagrante delicto with a "guy" who "looks young" in "terms of what" they "can see" of him (41–42).

It is not, however, Mrs. Jorgenson's sexual nature that figures in the play's pivotal mini-scene. It is her voice, for even though she is dead, her voice lives on in Babette's voice. Midway through the middle act 2 of a three-act play, Babette is speaking on the phone with someone. To this point she was on the phone once, calling Larry to check on the sale of items she left with him. While on hold she received a call from someone trying to collect money lent, but she pretended to be the tenant who moved into the apartment vacated by Babette's death. The act-2 mini-scene or moment is a radical departure from the act-1 counterpart. It is not a stifling of communication by being put on hold but a "*torrent of words*" (52). It is not spurts of clipped exchanges but a sustained monologue, the longest narrative in the play. The act-2 moment is also a radical departure from act-1's truncated interactions. It is not a withholding of information such as Babette and Frank did when Theo asked whether they had gone out together the preceding evening but a recreating of the first meeting with Mrs. Jorgenson on the subway. It is not a withholding of the self by pretending to be someone else but Babette's placing herself in the experience: "It was on a subway train I was / headed uptown and I / sat down next to a Strange Old Lady. . ." (52).

The experience is a shared one. To the unnamed party on the phone, Babette relates how having forgotten to bring reading material she started reading over the Strange Old Lady's shoulder a book she, Mrs. Jorgenson, was reading page after page "at exactly the same speed" (52) until she realized that Mrs. Jorgenson had fallen asleep. She then began turning the pages until the book's owner awoke and resumed reading until she realized the page was wrong and while turning back to the page she was reading when she fell asleep asked Babette what she had missed. The first meeting ended with Mrs. Jorgenson making a date for the return subway that afternoon at which time they continued reading together.

The mini-scene is pivotal for a few reasons. It connects with act-1's final scene that ends with Mrs. Jorgenson's "Alas Alas." As Babette narrates the subway experience, the two read until one of the characters "uttered his Last Words / which were / Alas Alas." But she immediately corrects herself, remembering that the character said, "Alack Alack," and explaining the difference between the interjections: "Alas implies pity whereas Alack says regret" (57). The repeated interjection that ended act 1 therefore points up the contradiction that is Mrs. Jorgenson, who implied pity by saying, "Alas Alas," while having a "*good laugh*" (35). An old lady, she sang lyrics with sexual innuendoes and had herself photographed flagrante delicto with a young partner. Not depressed by her declining years with their diminishing capacity to delight, she can be an inspiration to anyone who does not fit into a groove, particularly those whose career aspirations marginalize them. Neither should they feel they are alone. As she wrote in her farewell note: "See ya."

The mini-scene leads into the future. By recreating a scene that took place outside the apartment and the building, Babette opens herself to other voices outside her solitary apartment, voices that speak to her within the apartment that is an image of her self-absorption. As Gibson writes in the author's note, "The Airshaft Couple was originally imagined as a pair of voices that, in every sense, speak to the main characters from an offstage source, presumably another part of the building" (5). The phrase "in every sense" is the passage's key segment. In act 1 both Theo and Frank opened their apartment windows, acts that allowed the Airshaft Couple's voices to enter their apartments. The Airshaft Couple are breaking up, headed for a divorce, an estrangement increasingly reflected in their voices. But although Theo and Frank suffer estrangement by having their wife and lover desert them — divorce them, so to speak — they did not react. The voices did not speak to them, perhaps because they have had no experiences outside their self-absorptions since the desertions. The voices speak to Babette. Interrupting the monologue relating her subway experience with Mrs. Jorgenson to open her apartment window, she "*becomes distracted*" (53) by the voices of the Airshaft Couple as they claim their possessions. She becomes so distracted that she forgets that she in effect put the other party on hold until she remembers and resumes her narrative. That the Couple are sorting books is a bit obvious given the experience she is relating of Mrs. Jorgenson's sharing a book with her but effective nonetheless, for Gibson suggests that the monologue be scored by the repetition of the two words coming up from below: "'*Yours,*' '*Mine,*' but mostly '*Mine's*'" (55).

By so summoning Mrs. Jorgenson from the dead for the recreated subway experience that she confuses the old woman's last words — her voice — with a character's last words in the romance novel they were reading — his voice — before correcting the error, she becomes conscious of voices that she has not wanted to entertain heretofore, for the Airshaft Couple's voices are those of self-absorption taken to its inevitable conclusion. That the voices penetrated her consciousness a moment that follows substantiates. The books sorted, the Couple decide what each wants for dinner they will have delivered to their apartment. She agrees to have the Chinese food he will order "but / nothing too eggy" (58). When Babette proposes that Frank have food delivered for them, it will be Chinese with her individual order "Moo Shoo Easy on the egg tell them" (60).

Mrs. Jorgenson is the voice of sharing, and sharing implies connecting. Her sharing her book with Babette connects her to the younger woman, just as Babette's narrative, empowered by the subway experience, connects her to the older woman, the outside world, and her deeper, moral, self. At the first mention of Mrs. Jorgenson's name in conversation with the other two tenants following the pivotal mini-scene, it is Babette who thinks that the three "should call someone" (67) about the dead body. She is ahead of the other two in connecting, but they catch up. The three have experiences outside their apartments. Theo has a session with his therapist, and Frank tells Theo that the tunes he offered him as possibilities for the amusement-park theme popped into his head while he was in a supermarket's "checkout line" (84). Babette has a phone conversation with someone unnamed, the subject of which is her attitude toward an unnamed woman whom she would like to like but cannot. Piling up hyperboles, Babette and Theo fill in for Frank, who was not invited, details of Larry's party, the "most supportive and fun party ever No question" (101) in the history of partying.

Although the examination will return to this next connection—with one another—it comes up now because it is the second in the order that the first half's disconnections were examined. The three enter and exit their apartments in the first half, but no mini-scene involves two or three of them in one apartment, which is its occupant's sanctuary from engagement outside the self. When in a mini-scene just before the pivotal monologue Theo tries to jam his foot in the doorway to Babette's apartment so that he can talk to her, she *"slams her door"* (51). Mini-scenes after the subway monologue take place inside apartments involving two and even all three characters. In act-3's opening moment, Theo knocks on Babette's door while she is on the phone. When she opens it, Theo either follows her into the apartment as she tells the party on the phone that she will call back or talks to her from the doorway. In moments that follow, Frank enters Theo's apartment to offer tunes for the amusement-park theme and then Babette's apartment while she is on the phone talking about the woman she would like to like, mimics some of the conversation, and with Babette's approval vacuums her apartment. Act-3's first scene ends with Theo's arrival at Babette's apartment while Frank is still there. Act-3's second scene begins with the three in Frank's apartment talking about Larry's party.

The three also share in one another's career choices, at least to a greater degree than in act 1. Not only does Frank offer to Theo the catchy tunes that popped into his head while checking out of the supermarket, he plays two of them on the synthesizer before Theo declines the offer. An offer Theo and Babette accept is playing Frank's bidding game in which the winner learns a fact relevant to him or her while Frank gets to practice being an auctioneer. The two bidders do not give their undivided attention—each continues with his and her self-absorption—but they play, and by winning Theo learns that his ex-wife, who has been seen with Larry, is coming to the apartment house to claim her personal belongings.

The three connect with themselves. In the moment that ends act 2 in which the three lying in their respective beds reveal their wish to "wind up with someone . . . glad to see" them (72–73), each discloses something from the past: an incident at a party, a part-time job as a teenager, a question about why he does what he does. In a moment toward the beginning of act 3, the three in their respective bathrooms continue the introspection. Babette reminisces about the time she worked in an office, Theo broods on his marriage's dissolution, and Frank excludes words inappropriate for auctioneering. Much later in the act, they delve more deeply into the past: to childhood, coincidences in one's life, and courtship.

They connect with the voices speaking to them "in every sense" (5). For the first time since a distracted Babette interrupted her subway monologue to listen at her window, the Airshaft Couple speak. Now for the first time the three at their respective windows listen, and what they hear are the voices of a couple no longer able to share who are breaking up. Connected, the three can and do share. Not only does Theo accept the finality of his divorce, he confides the acceptance to Babette, who admits, perhaps as a dawning recognition of her sexual preference, that she would like to be friends with an unnamed woman. The two play Frank's bidding game, and for the play's closing moment, the three are together on the apartment-house roof hearing the Airshaft Couple part. Here Soho Rep director Daniel Aukin and designer Louisa Thompson's set supported Gibson's conception. Instead of the four apartments, the fourth being Mrs. Jorgenson's, on the same floor with the Airshaft Couple offstage, they had three apartments on one floor, the older woman's apartment on the floor above the three and the Couple's apartment on the floor below them. That staging suggested a cosmic design with Mrs. Jorgenson, becoming symbolic at the second half's opening in that the three characters cannot stop talking about her, the voice from above of sharing and the Airshaft Couple the voices from below of self-absorption so severe that they cannot live together. The staging prompted reviewer Bruce Weber to write that Mrs. Jorgenson is an inspiration to the three "with her open-mindedness, friendliness and curiosity. After her death halfway through the play, she becomes a kind of angelic presence overseeing the goings-on in the apartment house."[25]

She haunts the minds of the three, for hearing the Airshaft Couple part, they "*share a simultaneous recollection*": "MRS. JORGENSON" (128). Since the three recollections are also identical, their voices are the second half's closing counterpart to the first half's voices that disconnect. The second half opens with Babette and Mrs. Jorgenson connecting. The play closes with the three voices connecting the tenants with one another and with Mrs. Jorgenson and then, after one of the parting Airshaft Couple sneezes, with the Couple because the play's final words are the three tenants' simultaneous, identical "Bless you" (128).

Fnu Lnu dramatizes the descent into the subsurface chaos that generates heightened—that is, imagistically charged poetic—language. *Showy Lady Slipper* dramatizes the flatness of language—language that neither rises nor falls—that is stuck on the surface because the characters are. *[sic]* dramatizes the complementariness of the depths and the heights in creating language that falls and rises. Midway through act 2, Babette's recreating her underground experience with Mrs. Jorgenson leads her to hear the subsurface voices of the Airshaft Couple. In act 3 the three friends' listening to the Couple's voices leads them to the closing scene in which they not only share a recollection of the woman who lived above them, and still lives above them in their minds-memories, but can respond with generosity to the Couple below them.

Were the second half a naturalistic drama and nothing more, the closing scene would be a resolution not only of the three characters' efforts to discover themselves but also of the first half's absurdity. Overcoming their self-absorption, connected with the world outside them, one another, and their deeper selves, the three would be ready to pursue more realistic careers than the ones on which they were wasting their talent. Naturalistic drama, however, is only the play's core in either half. With naturalistic language Gibson has been creating other genres and modes to interact with the drama. Even though Babette's sustained narrative in the pivotal scene appeared to end the other genres and modes and the absurdity their interaction created so that the action could move toward a resolution, Gibson has not stopped experimenting with interaction. It increases in the second half.

The language becomes more naturalistic in the sense that it incorporates street language, the four-letter kind. Threatening Frank in act 3, Theo tells him that if he ever again approaches the synthesizer keyboard to play tunes, "I will be / forced to Kick Your Ass No No I won't / kick your ass I'll Break Your Fingers" (86). In act 2 Babette tells Theo, "I want you / to leave me the four letters sound like duck alone" (61). In act 3 she drops the duck rhyme when she says to him, "*You are so pre*-dictable just so utterly fu-*cking*-pre-*dictable*" (121). By act 3 Frank's tongue twisters have devolved: "Cut the cake cut the crap the cardinal can't come over" (114).

The tongue twisters also increase in frequency. Before the pivotal mini-scene, Frank practiced three of them. After the mini-scene, he practices nine, eight of them in the third act, and four of the eight one after another. But the most annoying of all is an extended one, the story of a Betty Botter who bought bitter butter, and not simply because it is extended. His objective in this session is to practice his delivery while listening to an instructor's tape recording of Betty's story, but since he is able only occasionally to speak in sync with the tape, much of the story is garbled, and in one sequence the synchronized word is "seventy-five" repeated ten times before he breaks the monotony by synchronizing the word *"butter"* (75–76). Yet Gibson is not finished testing the audience's patience. In a mini-scene toward the end of act 3, Frank appears in a window-washing harness outside of Babette's window; inside the apartment are the other two characters. Since Theo wants to talk privately to Babette about returning his ex-wife's clothing that he said she could have and she does not want to engage in a private conversation but wants Frank to hear what is being said, the two keep opening and closing the window with the result that some words are heard and some are not. The fracturing of the language produces gibberish with such perversity that the mini-scene becomes a Dada performance staged to provoke a cretinous audience's reaction.

Language in *[sic]* communicates and obfuscates. And when it communicates, it can be absurd. Tongue twisters are one example. The best example, however, of Gibson's interacting other genres and modes with naturalistic drama to create absurdity is Babette's book because not only do the three persist in their career choices, they do so with intensity, the *"anguish and frustration"* (123) of not making progress notwithstanding. Babette's thesis is that emotional outbursts provoked incidences that changed the course of history. The second of two episodes she relates is that a dispute in 1914 over who had a right to the last cold beverage in a Sarajevo shop led to a Bosnian nationalist shooting the archduke and thirsty duchess and the outbreak of World War I.

Simultaneous with the increase in naturalistic language and absurdity is an increase in the stylization of the mini-scenes. Act 2 closes with the three awakening from sleep to make animal and other shadows with their hands while articulating in overlapping sequence the wish to be connected with someone "glad to see" them (73). In an act-3 introspective moment set in the respective bathrooms with Babette shaving her legs and Frank and Theo their faces, the three are positioned so that the audience sees them *"through the reflections of their mirrors"* (80). A late act-3 moment repeats act-2's closing moment with the three in *"their respective beds"* waking in sequence and making *"elaborate shadows on the ceiling"* (113) while delving into the past.

After an intervening moment, the three *"sit in their apartments next to the phone,"* only to discover the numbers they phoned are busy. *"All three hang up the phone in frustration"* (117–18).

The interaction of naturalized language and stylized mini-scenes can be thought of as surrealistic in the sense of a yoking of incongruous images to startle an audience into awareness. The play has a justification for the yoking and the continual interaction. As Babette narrates the subway experience, when Mrs. Jorgenson awoke and discovered that she, Babette, had read beyond the point at which she, Mrs. Jorgenson, fell asleep, she asked what she had missed in the story. When Babette said that the heroine escaped her confinement on an island by making a raft from wood, the older woman dismissed that explanation because of the absence of wood on the island. She must have hitched a ride on a native's raft. When the younger woman counters that that explanation is impossible because there are no natives or neighboring islands in the story, Mrs. Jorgenson rebukes her: "Oh spare me your Knee-jerk Literal-minded Bourgeois World- / view would ya It's a Gee Dee romance novel for Crying Out / Loud." A stung Babette, protesting that she is not bourgeois, retaliates by accusing Mrs. Jorgenson of being "literal minded about the trees." The old woman does not yield. "That's different," she says; "That's internal logic" (56).

We can appreciate the disagreement by substituting naturalistic for bourgeois and applying the substitution to *[sic]*. If the play is nothing more than a naturalistic drama, Mrs. Jorgenson's death is a matter for a police report, her dead body a matter for the health department, and her attitude toward life and sharing a matter for an obituary. If, on the other hand, other genres and modes, styles and tones interact with the naturalistic drama, the interaction is not governed by principles external to the play but proceeds according to the internal logic it generates. *[sic]* therefore demonstrates that a playwright can retain a naturalistic drama and naturalistic language yet wage war against the naturalistic play by interacting and interpenetrating the non-naturalistic elements with the retained naturalistic elements to create the new type of play first encountered in this study in Groff's *What Then*. While creating tension between the incongruous elements, *[sic]* also tightens and relaxes tension in the audience. The door and window slamming while characters are speaking is particularly exasperating, but the alternating of the slamming and tongue twisters, for example, with reflective mini-scenes keeps the audience engaged. And although the closing "Bless you" (128) lessens the tension, it does not eliminate it because of the yoking of naturalistic language to startlingly incongruous images, verbal and visual. The result is multiple possibilities much closer to real life than the single-tracked naturalistic drama. The action is absurd and reasonable, for the interaction and interpenetration disconnect and connect, subvert and create. In a naturalistic play, Mrs. Jorgenson is a woman of contradictions, not the least of which is sharing with Babette while being estranged from her own children. In a symbolist play, she is an angelic presence. In *[sic]* she is both.

Given the multiple possibilities, the closing "Bless you" bestowed on the sneeze is a perfunctory reaction to an involuntary action; an ironic comment on two persons who cannot even be civil to each other; a benediction on a couple who, finding that they cannot live together, are parting to go their separate ways into the world that lies before them; and a reminder to the audience that though they failed to sustain a relationship, they deserve the audience's good wishes. The play's title also reminds the audience that what it is hearing is not a mistake. Given the multiple genres and modes with multiple levels of reality, each individual spectator has to decide how to interpret the remark and the play.

Having met the second defining objection to the naturalistic play, encountered in Eno's *The Flu Season*—that it cannot actualize more than one level of reality—the study turns to the first defining objection, encountered in Ludlam's *The Artificial Jungle*—that it eliminates mystery. The study turns by way of a transition. The descent into the subsurface to release its contents and thereby change surface reality is still present but with less significance through the final chapters than in the preceding works. Secondly, the two works in the transition, which dramatize the interaction and interpenetration of naturalistic and non-naturalistic behavior, prepare for the next chapter in which works dramatize the encounter with something or someone mysterious whose appearance changes the protagonist's behavior or is supposed to.

As Richard Foreman describes his theatre, it is not naturalistic, for it is anti-representation and characterization, social interaction and linear narrative, empathy and resolution: identifying elements of naturalistic theatre and traditional theatre in general. His plays take place in the ground of the subsurface: the generating energy of consciousness, choice, and creativity. Except for occasional moments, the plays do not depict the descent into the subsurface; rather, the subsurface activity of "mentation, mental-acts," takes place "on an outside surface . . . not hidden away inside."[26] The element examined in this subsurface brought to the surface is behavior by comparing a Foreman play, *Paradise Hotel*, with a few of Georges Feydeau's boulevard plays or farces. About his own early plays, Foreman said, "The situations depicted were normal, bourgeois theatrical clichés, domestic triangles, things like that. That's why I called my theater 'Ontological-Hysteric,' because the basic syndrome controlling the structure was that of classic, middle-class, boulevard theater, which I took to be hysteric in it [sic] psychological topology."[27] The syndrome holds for the later *Paradise Hotel*.

In one of the prefatory essays, "On the Plays," to the volume in which *Paradise Hotel* is included, Foreman declares what his theatre is and is not: "In the plays I write, there is no 'story' in the normal sense. But there is definitely a SITUATION. There is no story, because IMPULSE is set free to deflect normal linear development. Linear, narrative development in the theater always ends with a denouement that delivers a 'meaning'—i.e., a moral." Because a theatre of linear, narrative development reinforces the "spectators' behavioral conditioning" and his plays attempt to change the spectators' perception to see possibilities for living other than those that "society" or the "superego" sanctions, his theatre is one "of SITUATION and IMPULSE."[28]

Foreman's theatre therefore would seem to be the antithesis of the theatre of Georges Feydeau, master of the "conventions of the well-made play," the reigning dramatic form in late 19th-century France:

> In this, the plot (usually in three acts) begins with an exposition which tells us the background history of the characters and also that there is a secret whose discovery will change all their lives. It starts at normal pace, but gathers momentum irresistibly until the first-act curtain comes down on confusion (often caused by revelation of the secret in question). There follows a series of *quid-proquos*: mistakes, ironies, deceptions, misunderstandings, which always lead to a reversal of the hero's situation, from heights to depths or vice versa. The third act then explores the way this reversal affects every other character, and tidies up loose ends.[29]

But since Feydeau also "brought to his choice of situations the same relentless discrimination that Paul Valéry used in selecting each word of his poems,"[30] the Frenchman's theatre affords a basis with which to compare the American's theatre, for in setting and language, characterization and resolution, the former's theatre is naturalistic. By his own admission, Foreman is one of a "group of so-called difficult, or transgressive, artists" (8). Comparing a play of his with a few of the Frenchman's naturalistic plays that are similar in situation should illuminate the Ontological-Hysteric Theater that he founded in 1968, making it less difficult.

As soon as the cast of *Paradise Hotel* assemble and begin dancing, a voice announces that the title really is "'Hotel Fuck,'"[31] the title that in an addendum to the text the playwright notes was the title when the play was performed in Europe. The impulse signified is the one that drives many of Feydeau's characters to the act-2 assignation, usually in a hotel. Act 1 of *L'Hôtel du libre échange—Hotel Paradiso* in a 1966 film adaptation starring Alec Guinness, Gina Lollobrigida, and Robert Morley—is exposition with a story line easy to summarize. Pinglet, an engineer whose wife, Angélique, is a shrew, is attracted to the wife, Marcelle, of an architect colleague, Paillardin, who is unhappy because her husband is such a workaholic that he has little time for her. When Paillardin's announcement that he must spend the night investigating strange noises in a hotel provokes a quarrel with Marcelle, Pinglet seizes the moment to propose to her that they spend the night together to take revenge on him, especially since Angélique will be away for the night visiting her aunt. Their decision is the farce's equivalent to the secret in the well-made play that can change lives; its power to involve others is felt at once. Mathieu, a friend with whom the Pinglets stayed the previous summer, comes calling with his four daughters, expecting to stay until the girls return to school. Because the couple cannot accommodate them, they must find a place that can. Mistaking Pinglet's giving of the love-nest address to Marcelle as the address to which he should turn, Mathieu leaves for the hotel, which just happens to be the hotel where the court-appointed investigator will be spending the night.

Act 1 of *L'Hôtel* also develops characterological qualities. Pinglet and Paillardin have professions and professional disagreements—over structural materials for buildings, for instance. They are married to women who, like them, have attitudes toward the marriages. The couples have extended relationships and hierarchical relationships. Angélique has an aunt; Paillardin's nephew, Maxime, is a student; Pinglet's housemaid, Victoire, is attracted to Maxime. Mathieu is a friend from the south of France whose luggage porters carry into the Pinglet house. All of these relationships are a microcosm of the larger relationships that constitute a society the conventions of which act 1 establishes. When Marcelle arrives, she teases Pinglet for receiving her in a dressing gown, the implication being that were they not friends, decorum would dictate a more proper attire. Mathieu took the Pinglets' invitation to reciprocate his hospitality by arriving with four daughters and multiple trunks. As she is leaving to visit her aunt, Angélique locks Pinglet in his room to prevent him from dining out. "Because you're a husband," she reminds him. "And husbands don't dine in restaurants without their wives."[32]

Foreman's theatre does not represent an absent larger society. Neither are the performers characters in a naturalistic sense, though they can be referred to as characters because the term is standard in dramatic criticism. "All of my plays," he writes in another of his many volumes, "are about my attempt to stage my particular rhythm of perception, which is to say, admittedly, the plays are about *me*."[33] The stage that he designs for his productions is not a naturalistic image of the man as a socially conditioned self, although to the newcomer to the annual Foreman play in his New York theater, the performance space appears to be naturalistic until the newcomer adjusts his/her perception. A hallmark of the naturalistic stage is excessive details creating a representation of the drama's milieu. Foreman's space is cluttered too, but the clutter is awry. If books are present, they will be scattered about. Papers will be attached to the walls. Clocks will be multiple, at odd angles, and display-ing different times. The stage is an isomorphic image of the playwright as a creating artist; the stage images his mind. The actors and actresses who per-form impersonate his impulses. They fall into two classes. In *Paradise Hotel* are five who, dressed alike and made up to negate individuation, form a cho-rus of *"potential hotel guests"* (252). As in any Foreman play, they pulsate back and forth across the stage, serve as markers by pointing or stretching taut string, and engage in the action by dancing, dispersing, falling, and so on. By the time the play opens, five *"principals"* (252) have emerged from the name-less chorus. Each is dressed—or undressed, since a Foreman play usually has some nudity—in his/her unique style, and they have names such as Julia Ja-cobson and Ken Pussy Puss.

The two groupings simply appear. They are present without a past or his-tory or relationships or anything that constitutes a society. The lights come up on the performance space, and they dance a *"frantic Charleston"* (252): what Foreman in another essay calls the "dance of manic theatricality,"[34] for they are the impulses that, impinging on the artist's mind, create consciousness and with which he generates theatre. There is no exposition, yet they too are going to the hotel for the same reason Pinglet and Marcelle are going though without the emotional ambience that envelopes the French couple.

Perhaps the principal convention in act 1 of *L'Hôtel* is the romanticizing of the carnal impulse. Feydeau both incorporates it into the action and satirizes it. After Paillardin, tired of Marcelle's complaint that he ignores her for his work, challenges her to find someone who will appreciate her, Pinglet pres-ents himself, courtly lover to his idealized lady. At the completion of his ten-dering of devotion, Marcelle, accepting his offering, gives him permission to speak. Were it not for the approaching sound of Angélique's voice, he would have to repeat the ritual; instead, in hurried whispers they commit themselves to a nocturnal tryst.

As Foreman explains in "On the Plays," his performers do not reflect the "spectators' behavioral conditioning—conditioning provided by the world which exists as we have been conditioned to perceive it by physical reality, society, inherited psychological patterns, et cetera" (7). Feydeau's characters are so conditioned. Foreman's embodied impulses are not, as their language indicates. Their motivation, or perhaps raison d'etre is better, is to fulfill their potential and damn social niceties. To Julia's question about what the five principals will do when they reach their destination, Ken blurts out, "Fuck our brains out, possibly!" (255)

Foreman's principals nevertheless share some traits with Feydeau's ec-centrics. Paillardin's nephew, Maxime, persists in reading philosophy despite

Victoire's caressing him. So long as the sun is shining, visitor Mathieu speaks normally, yet when rain falls, he stutters, and thunder and lightning render him speechless. Camille in *La Puce à l'oreille* must wear an artificial palate to pronounce consonants. With it he speaks normally, but as one can imagine, he loses it in the act-2 confusion. Because Foreman's principals are individual impulses that have emerged from the indiscriminate energy, they have individuating quirks. Tony Turbo, for example, dons a dress and a bonnet. The impulses also have their conventions and standards. When Julia invites Ken and Tommy Tuttle to fuck her simultaneously, they decline. Individually they would welcome the opportunity, but together they risk losing their "individual body orientation" (264).

While there is no division of exposition in a Foreman play, performed without intermission in the theater, the above discussion can serve that function in an analysis. The body of the analysis follows. We will begin with the Frenchman's act 2 and divide the discussion into two parts, each part followed by an examination of the corresponding part in the American's *Paradise Hotel*.

Feydeau's characters go to the hotel to act on impulses suppressed by society and the superego. The question therefore is What prevents the experience from being fulfilled? The answer on the level of surface action is that one character's desire to fulfill a suppressed impulse activates a counterimpulse in another character. *Le Dindon* is the second of the three farces this study takes as models. Annoyed that her husband, Crépin Vatelin, excuses the philandering of a friend, Pontagnac, his wife, Lucienne Vatelin, vows that should he stray, she will take a lover. When Pontagnac, hoping to be her choice, alerts her that Vatelin plans to meet a woman that evening in a hotel, she follows with the informer to retaliate. And so do others—the woman's husband and Pontagnac's wife among them—descend on the hotel, which is the perfect place for confusion. As guests come and go, other guests dissatisfied with their rooms vacate them for different rooms, leaving luggage to be redistributed by harried porters, who deposit the pieces in the wrong rooms, usually occupied by philanderers pushing their companions into concealment in bathrooms and closets until order prevails. It never does, however, because still others are filling the building. The Pinchards, an elderly army doctor and his deaf wife, are mistakenly given the room Vatelin booked. They leave for the opera before he arrives. They return to the room while he is downstairs with the woman's husband; at the sound of their arrival, she hides in the bathroom.

The commotion caused by many people moving about the building accelerates the action with characters dodging one another and bumping into one another and with doors slamming and bells ringing. The result is that the impulses are frustrated, for just as it appears that a character will satisfy the impulse that brought him or her to the hotel, someone or something intervenes, separating the character from the object of the impulse. The frustration increases the acceleration to a frantic pace and compounds the impulses. As the play unfolds, characters decide to act on individual impulses, but as the frustration and acceleration increase, they experience multiple, conflicting impulses. They want to catch their partners flagrante delicto while hoping the partners have remained faithful; they want to escape detection by getting out of the building as quickly as possible while wanting to stay and satisfy the original impulse. The frustration and pace come to a head in *Le Dindon* when the various characters including the police burst into the room where moments earlier Pinchard discovered a sleeping Vatelin next to a sleeping Madame Pinchard and where moments before the discovery Lucienne and Pontagnac wrestled in the dark with Pinchard, whom they mistook for Vatelin.

Since Foreman's characters are not conditioned by the same forces that condition Feydeau's characters, the question is Why do not his impulses immediately fulfill their potential? The answer on the level of surface action is twofold. In the second of the prefatory essays, "Rules," to the volume *Paradise Hotel and Other Plays*, the playwright advises the would-be writer to look "deep inside yourself. Look deep—that's the true fact of being human, the fact that every impulse gives rise at the same moment to its counterimpulse" (12). As soon as the cast of *Paradise Hotel* assemble and begin dancing, a voice speaks. The cast bolt at the sound because it is evidence of still another voice within the being's energy. The founder of the Ontological-Hysteric Theater would say that we do not embody a monolithic impulse, but that many impulses, many voices contest within us. Just as Ludlam creates conflict in his theatre by colliding plots—*Thérèse Raquin* and *The Postman Always Rings Twice* in *The Artificial Jungle*—so Foreman creates conflict in his theatre by colliding impulses. In *Paradise Hotel* the principals disagree on whether they feel emotional and whether they can control sexual emotions. They disagree on how to dress and whether simultaneous or individual intercourse is better. With dialogue "*continually underscored and punctuated by a series of high-pitched pings, cymbal crashes, drum thuds, and deep resonating gongs*" (251), the cast dance, run, and collide with walls and one another. The principals shoot themselves, fall to the floor, and rise again. They appear nude, seminude, and fully clothed, sometimes with elongated phalluses strapped onto them.

The second of the twofold reasons Foreman discusses at length in an essay contained in another volume. "In my plays," he writes, "I try to separate the impulse from the object that seems to evoke it, and in doing so, clarify the quality of the impulse itself."[35] He describes two of the several strategies he uses to separate them. The first is interrupting the activity. The example he gives is having two characters stop interacting and start dancing. *Paradise Hotel*, like all his plays, abounds in such interruptions. When the cast assemble and start dancing, they bolt from the performance space. When they dash to get to the bus to Hotel Fuck, they *"smash into the walls and fall back with a crash to the floor"* (256). The second strategy is the "'double bind'"[36] in which the characters contradict themselves. In the play after Tommy rises from a self-inflicted gunshot to the head, the others hug before running to the bus stop. Tommy does not hug with them because as he asks, "Why do I feel like I'm already inside the Hotel Fuck?" (260)

The purpose of these frustrating strategies is to draw the spectator's habitually oriented attention away from the object and to focus instead on the impulse—to enable the spectator to perceive the impulse from a new or changed perspective. And just as the contesting among the principals interferes with their satisfying the impulses, so too does the separating. The result is similar to that of Feydeau's theatre. The frustration increases the acceleration to a frenetic pace heightened by moments of intervening silence that dissolve into renewed frustration and acceleration. Unable to locate the bus, the impulses *"stop in confusion."* After Ken gets stuck in his "one hundred percent sex memories," Tommy hits a light bulb with a stick to produce a flash of light signaling a resurgence of his sex memories. The female cast members *"tumble into the room"* (260–61) with badminton rackets at the swishing of which Ken covers his crotch, presumably to protect his memories. One of the women with a dildo strapped onto her dances across the stage whipping the *"dildo as if she were urging on a racehorse"* (265).

Foreman wages war against the naturalistic play by exaggerating its four-letter language and its bedroom behavior. Since nudity and an erection are prerequisites for sexual activity, his characters are sometimes nude and sometimes wear dildos that they whip as they prance about the stage. Other behavioral hallmarks of a Foreman production are characters assuming awkward, unnatural positions; interrupting the action to perform an activity at odds with the one interrupted; and stopping the action altogether to gaze motionless at the audience. Like the disconnection between the representational set the audience expects to see in a theatre production and the disequilibrium it actually sees, these strategies build tension onstage and offstage, preventing the spectators from settling into passive observers. The effect, however, is not a "cacophony of images or crazy characters,"[37] publisher Gould's description of contemporary theatre that strives to be different just for the sake of being different. The Ontological-Hysteric play has an internal logic driving it and a destination. Yet one quarter into the play, the impulses do not know "how to get inside the fucking front door of the fucking Hotel Fuck!" (269)

So far we have been looking at the surface action in both theatres. We now have to look beneath the surface in Feydeau's theatre. Translator McLeish cites *Le Dindon* and *L'Hôtel du libre échange* as two plays that "make use of the hotel setting in order to create a space situated half-way between the private and the public, a space where desires which cannot be spoken of in a polite bourgeois salon emerge and press for satisfaction. . . . *Heart's Desire Hotel* is justly one of the most famous comedies of assumed identity in the repertoire."[38]

We will take McLeish's second point first. A quarrel between Marcelle Paillardin and her husband provokes Pinglet into declaring his feelings for her and their decision to go to a hotel that evening, unaware it is the hotel where Paillardin will be investigating noises said to be caused by ghosts. Complicating matters, a visitor to Paris, Mathieu, overhears the address and assumes it is meant for him. When Pinglet and Marcelle encounter Mathieu and his daughters in the hotel, they have to pretend they are not together and that each is there for a reason other than the errant impulse. About to escape, they rush back into the room when Paillardin sees their figures in the dark and assumes they are ghosts. Pursued, she pulls a hat over her face, and he, his face covered with soot, comes out of the fireplace into which he fell and punches the court-appointed investigator. Arriving police prevent physical harm but subject the couple to a greater harm: scandal. Their sole hope of not being held with the other detainees is convincing the police they are husband and wife. Interrogated separately, she identifies herself as Madame Pinglet and he as Monsieur Paillardin.

For McLeish's first point, the hotel serves as a symbol of a realm beneath society and the superego. Meeting the object of one's impulse there is exhilarating because the assignation subverts the controls that prohibit such liaisons. And the assignation not only satisfies sexually, it fulfills spiritually. The experience liberates adventurous souls from the otherwise confining restraints of everyday existence; it frees them to be their existential selves. The experience also terrifies and for the same reason. Freeing them to encounter their existential selves, the experience interrogates their identity. As they are caught up in the whirlwind confusion, they have their socially conditioned selves stripped from them, and in Feydeau's imaginative world, characters are socially conditioned. The farceur satirizes the social conditioning by exposing cultural pretensions, for example, in the lawyer's bogus art collection in *Le Dindon*. It is one thing, however, to have one's identity satirized and another thing to have it taken away. "What is at stake for the characters in Feydeau's farces is not their lives but their reputations. Feydeau's men are solid, bourgeois and middle-aged. His women, as he said, 'breathe virtue and are forthwith out of breath'. . . . It is the terror of losing their precious reputations which makes Feydeau's characters hide, lie and pretend to be each other."[39] In the three farces this study uses for comparative purposes, the four principal men are an architect, an engineer, a lawyer, and a branch director of a life-insurance company.

These are their identities upon entering the hotel. What happens to the identities is exhilarating and terrifying. Architect Paillardin perceives the soot-covered figure coming at him from the fireplace to be a ghostly chimney sweep. Back home after posting bail, engineer Pinglet is visited by Marcelle, who has him look in a mirror to see the soot on his face. Although he wipes his face clean, the other characters continue the search for the chimney sweep's identity. Paillardin arrives to explain that the figure that blackened his eye was Pinglet's size. The police arrive for documentary evidence of the characters' identity. If Paillardin is not the figure who claimed to be the architect the preceding night, then who was in the hotel? Pinglet is saved from exposure only because Paillardin's nephew, who was there with Pinglet's maid, attempts to flee the room, covering his face with the towel the engineer used to clean his face.

An even better example occurs in *La Puce*. Convinced that her husband, the branch director of an insurance company, is having an affair, Raymonde Chandebise appeals to a friend to write as a secret admirer a letter inviting him to a hotel assignation, but he assumes a mistaken identity: the letter is really meant for their friend, Tournel, who, unknown to him, is Raymonde's would-be lover. By the end of act 1, the following characters are destined to appear in act-2's hotel: Chandebise; his wife Raymonde and her letter-writing friend; the friend's husband who, upon reading the letter, recognizes his wife's handwriting and concludes that she has a lover; Tournel; Chandebise's nephew with his mistress, the family cook; her husband, the uncle's manservant; and the insurance company's doctor. At the hotel are other characters, one of whom is Chandebise's double, the drunken porter, and as Harry Levin observes in his study of the nature of comedy, mistaking doubles for a single is fundamental to farce.[40] His presence converts farce's ordinary confusion to extraordinary heights, or depths from Chandebise's perspective, for the branch manager has to suffer the ignominy of the hotel manager kicking and berating him for not performing his duties while forcing him to don the porter's uniform and the bewilderment of his wife and friends judging him mad for behavior they perceive as irrational. It is not until act 3, with all the characters reassembled at his home, that he regains his identity but only after he comes upon the porter, a man named Poche, asleep on his bed. "And I saw . . . myself,"[41] he tells the others. When the hotel manager invites him to the hotel to meet Poche, Chandebise declines the invitation.

Going beneath the surface action for the corresponding analysis of the On-tological-Hysteric Theater does not require a new orientation. We have been in the realm of pure impulse from the opening moment of *Paradise Hotel* be-cause the stage is an isomorphic image of the artist's creating mind. We have also answered the question why the impulses do not immediately fulfill their potential: because Foreman interrupts the action and frustrates the lust so that the spectator focuses on the impulse separated from its object. A second an-swer is that the birth of an impulse produces its counterimpulse with the re-sult that, as impulse Giza von Goldenheim says, "There is never immediate resolution to a complex web of superimposed appetites" (264). (Interestingly, love is the example the playwright uses in one of his theoretical writings of an experience with contradictory impulses.[42]) There is a third answer to the question, but it must be deferred until we examine the complex web and the changes it effects.

The voice that speaks in the opening moment and that disperses the cast in panic makes two statements in American productions but only one in Eu-ropean productions. The first statement is that the play is really "'Hotel Fuck.'" The second statement in America, which is the only one in Europe, is that another play, "'Hotel Beautiful Roses,'" threatens "to replace . . . 'Ho-tel Fuck'" (253). Since Foreman does not write allegories in which stage re-alities bear a one-to-one relationship to absent realities, Hotel Beautiful Roses cannot be reduced to a single meaning. What it does invoke, however, is the idealizing of the carnal appetite but without the satirizing that Feydeau applies to the idealizing in act 1 of *L'Hotel* when Pinglet petitions Marcelle for her favors. The impulses do not want to go to the second hotel because a play with that destination is to them an "insipid" and "boring" play (258–59). They are giving their point of view. The audience sees the action from the perspective of impulses for whom love dilutes their power, and they want to be lustful. Hearing of the possible supersession by a play about beau-tiful roses, the impulses accuse one another of being "selfish" (258): of clinging to their lustful selves. Yet so long as fulfillment is delayed, they be-come vulnerable to the forces that condition Feydeau's characters—indeed, all people in and out of the theatre.

The artist does not live in a vacuum. In the preface to *What Did He See?*, the playwright raises issues attendant upon leading the reclusive life of the artist, one of which is questioning whether he is "making enough of a social contribution."[43] The artist must interact with the world outside the mind, and the interaction can lead to love, imaged as beautiful roses. As soon as the voice introduces the image, the principals begin asking whether they feel emotional. Giza's concession that all are "victims of sexual emotion" (254) prompts Ken's proposal that they go directly to the hotel. Since they do not, to remain unconditioned impulses, they have to cling to their lustful selves, even if that means displays of bravado such as yelling, "Well, fuck you" (254), at one another. Yet they are fighting a losing struggle, for they are divided between going to the hotel and holding back, between reveling in lust and succumbing to love.

The situation actualizes not the experience's unitary meaning that traditional theatre dramatizes but the "multitude of meanings and realities . . . available."[44] As the pace becomes frenetic, more of the women in the cast wear dildos and prance across the floor, they cheer as a cart approaches with luggage topped by a miniature hotel, and Tommy appears wearing a rabbit hat and munching a carrot. As if their tongues were reproducing—and Giza contemplates "licking and fucking and sucking" (272)—he and Julia ecstatically repeat the verb "fucking" (278–80). Yet with these images, they repeat images of mommies, daddies, bonding, and family life: the development of society. The experience gives rise to ambivalent feelings because the play is not depicting a physical reality but is presenting a state of mind that is not unitary and fixed. A key to the confusing, multivalent stage action is the principals' referring to mental adjustment, reading another's mind, and imagining another possibility. Another one does appear but not without warning, for it has been implicit from the play's beginning.

The best way that I can indicate how the play prepares for the opposing possibility is to refer to another Foreman play, *Bad Boy Nietzsche!*, which presents the philosopher's descent into madness, an experience both terrifying because madness is a loss of control and exhilarating because irrationality is the ground of the unconscious and therefore of creativity. At one point a cast member contemptuously says to Nietzsche, "Are you crazy?" He answers, "No, but I'm getting there."[45] *Paradise Hotel* has been getting where it is going from the time the voice warned that the play might be superseded by another play. The impulses interweave images of manic intercourse and burgeoning family life. Giza's suddenly handing Julia a bouquet of roses should come as no surprise, but it does because he is in the persona of a dirty old man lusting after schoolgirls. The Hotel of Beautiful Roses is an "alternative reality" (282) to Hotel Fuck, yet the play contains the two so that the experience in the inseparable hotels is both consistent and contradictory, both a "voluntary self-transformation" (257) and an "unwelcome idea" (284). The encounter between the two realities may create drama, but that is not the reason they collide. The impulses contesting for recognition have to encounter each other because the one being generates them. They are constituents of the being whose energy the stage images, unlike Feydeau's characters, who are constituents of the society that the stage represents. The Frenchman's opposing realities encounter each other because their collision creates drama. The critic Marcel Achard quotes the farceur's "first and most important commandment: 'When two of my characters should under no circumstances encounter one another, I throw them together as quickly as possible.'"[46] Differences aside, in the two theatres the encounters cause pandemonium.

Midway through the French theatre's second act, most of the other characters who are society's constituents are involved: hotel guests and staff, for instance. Other constituents are involved in the American theatre's turmoil too, one of which the prefatory essay, "Rules," anticipates in its discussion of language, for just as an impulse generates a counterimpulse, so should verbal images generate counter images, providing the would-be writer looks deep inside himself/herself. In the play the frenzied vulgarity of language releases not only idealized language that accompanies the proliferation of roses but its opposition: images of anal discharge. As Tommy complains about excreting a "million dried-up words and words and words—," Ken *"whirls into the room covered with roses, including a crown of roses on his head"* (285–86). Images beget images, verbal and visual. Images of genital penetration beget images of anal penetration, which in turn beget mythological images. With Tony in position to be sodomized, Julia puts a target on his bottom for one of the chorus to take *"aim, Cupidlike,"* at it (288), and Giza enters wearing Greek cothorni, a Louis XIV wig and embroidered coat, and an elongated phallus.

"You know what I think?" Julia interrupts the action. "It's too bad there aren't enough cute little roses in the Hotel Fuck so it could simultaneously be the Hotel Beautiful Roses" (292). If the two "rival hotels" (292) were to cohere into one, the play would be over because Foreman's theatre presents a multitude of possibilities. If the hotels were to remain as two but be balanced in a harmonious relationship, the play would be over because the Ontological-Hysteric Theater actualizes the tension between the possibilities. *Unbalancing Acts* is the title of the volume of plays that opens with the essay, "Foundations for a Theater." Balancing creates a stasis, a condition the playwright addresses in the essay, "On the Plays," that opens the volume containing *Paradise Hotel*. He proposes that the "most desirable human condition is that where one is able to avoid stasis—spiritual and emotional—by continually subjecting oneself to the nonstatic unbalanced state, where impulse is continually permitted to introduce a creative wobble to the straight and narrow of well-disciplined mental life" (7–8). The image is prophetic. The principals wobble as they examine their shoes for the muck they discover on Giza's cothorni. A typical Foreman image, it eludes a precise meaning while suggesting the excrement of words and images in which they have been running amuck.

Given the principle that an impulse generates a counterimpulse, the compounding of impulses generates simplicity and the wobbling generates stability so much so that Giza urges them to step in the direction of their "choice" (295). An essay in *Reverberation Machines* distinguishes between traditional theatre, which shows "what choice to make," and his theatre, which shows "that which . . . stands under what is chosen, so that choice is alive and energized."[47] The play shows the consequence of making a choice that excludes all other choices. Each cast member carries two suitcases. That is, by so choosing, each assumes the conditions such as inherited psychological patterns that the Ontological-Hysteric Theater subverts. And not only do they carry their baggage through life, they begin talking about their "personality," about themselves as "ME" (298). The antithesis of the socially and psychologically conditioned "ME" is the ground of being. As the philosopher does in *Bad Boy Nietzsche!*, the impulses reach the ground of irrationality beneath the two hotels, which reveals itself as a voice. When it first speaks in the opening moments, the cast run in panic. They do not panic now because they have been changing since the opening moments and because the voice calls them by name. In imagery recalling the god of Job and the god of the Delphic oracle, the core of life is described as a "whirlwind" (302): the source of energy which makes choices possible and from which, in a voice that in productions is Foreman's, emanate cryptic, contradictory messages.

Symphony of Rats is a Foreman play that depicts the descent into the subsurface. Since this innermost reality is a mystery, it can only be imaged metaphorically. In Wellman's theatre the energy is imaged as chaos that flows into a single stem that bifurcates. In Foreman's theatre the energy is imaged as a whirlwind: "Tornadoville, where nothing stands still" and where "something gives birth, a holy spirit ignited, unlocatable, burning." Contact with this "invisible center" does not eliminate suffering; on the contrary, contact makes humans "comfortable with suffering,"[48] for the descent renews them for the surface, where they will experience the tension between competing impulses.

From here to the end is a welter of impulses-messages. We will look at three that the play subverts. The first, verbal, is a traditional message of society, psychology, and theatre. Tommy relates a story—and the fact that he tells a linear narrative makes it traditional—about a time when, "not getting fucked," he renounced sex and found bliss in freedom from "turmoil" in that he was burned "empty of all anxiety and suffering." The second, aural, underscores the first. As Tommy begins his narrative, the cacophonous music *"softens to a soprano voice sustaining one clear note."* Traditional religion supplies the third, visual, in a figure masked *"as if a white-bearded and ancient God were approaching"* (310–11). With Tommy's admission that he never again found that bliss, the figure disappears, the music changes to a jazzy dance tune, and Tony charges about the room whipping the dildo strapped to his body. The Ontological-Hysteric Theater subverts these traditional messages in order to change the spectators' perception so that they can see other possibilities for living. The change involves the perception of identity.

As we saw earlier, the second act of a Feydeau farce is an exhilarating experience because it releases the would-be adulterer from the restraints of society and the superego and a terrifying experience because the hotel guest loses the identity that society and the superego confer on one who honors the restraints. Putting aside the satirizing of bourgeois values, we can say for comparative purposes that the goal of a Feydeau farce is getting through the second act's turmoil, which divests one of identity, to the third act's normalcy, where one's place in society determines identity. That is not the goal of a Foreman play. When the voice announces in the opening scene of *Paradise Hotel* that Hotel Beautiful Roses may supersede Hotel Fuck, the latter hotel-play tries "desperately to hold on to its proper and genuine self" (253). The cast want to remain pure impulses.

That goal is impossible, however, because they generate counterimpulses, interaction with whom generates change. They develop "personality" (298) imaged as the baggage they carry as they become socially and psychologically conditioned. But they lose the conditioning too because nothing is permanent in this welter of contradictory forces. The exhilaration is the transformation of imperial monarch to naked bellhop, orgies of Rabelaisian appetites to ceremonies of Blakean innocence and the turmoil of anxiety and suffering, horseplay and creativity. There is a terror and it is the loss of identity, but the loss is the surrender of the turmoil and the multiplicity of possibilities and meanings for a self conditioned into a fixed, unitary identity. Thus one way of summing up an essential difference between Foreman's theatre and Feydeau's theatre is that the entire play in the American's theatre is equivalent to the play's second act in the Frenchman's theatre. By getting through the turmoil to the third act, Feydeau's theatre restores the naturalistic play's conventions and proprieties. By staying in the turmoil, the Ontological-Hysteric Theater rejects the naturalistic play's conventions and proprieties.

If Foreman could only stay in the void from which flows the turmoil experienced as tension, he might experience the bliss that Tommy once experienced but lost. As he writes in the preface to *Lava*, "I carry within me the dream that I should be able to remain suspended in the live thing, in the gap of the non-representable, rather than falling back into the production of dead, representable, and materialized action." But he cannot remain suspended. He knows he cannot, and his plays present the flow toward fulfillment. Deferred earlier, the third answer to the question why the impulses do not immediately fulfill their potential is that Foreman delays the inevitable as long as he can because once the process of creating starts, it will eventually assume a form as a surface reality, terminating the flow from the inner reality. Hence the prefatory passage concludes: "That's why in *Lava* I suggest that the ideal theater would be a theater of nonacts, because the minute that anything is concretized, and is given a form, it becomes part of the fallen world."[49]

What to do, then, if one cannot resist the flow to resolution because in life one must make choices? Feydeau's plays end with the characters' act-3 resolutions. They have strayed but, chastened, they choose to remain in their socially and psychologically conditioned identities. Vatelin in *Le Dindon* sobs because he believes his wife Lucienne has taken a lover in retaliation for his indiscretion. Learning she has not, he confesses his one lapse, a confession that elicits her forgiveness, and the two pledge their love to each other. *L'Hô-tel* ends with Pinglet, who just managed to escape detection as the mysterious figure with the soot-covered face, vowing not to return to the hotel. Chandebise in *La Puce* declines the invitation to come to the hotel to meet his double, Poche. Having been mistaken for the drunken porter, having been kicked and insulted in the hotel, he chooses to remain where he is, the branch director of an insurance company.

Foreman's plays do not have acts or resolutions. *Paradise Hotel* closes with the cast repeating the opening image: "*dancing a frantic Charleston*" (318), their faces apprehensive about returning to the turmoil. The choice is not between having impulses, born in Tornadoville, or not having impulses. The choice is in what to do with the impulses because once the process is completed, the product is concretized. The choice therefore is whether to retire or begin anew. To renew themselves, the impulses must fall back into the void, the burning center, the "flux-fluxity-flux-flux"[50] and begin anew the journey to the hotels. Not all of the cast are apprehensive, however. They have undergone change in the process; they are unbalanced. Apart from the others, Tommy, the one who experienced the bliss of stasis, is excited, bouncing up and down and "*shouting, 'Hotel Fuck! Hotel Fuck!'*" (318) Knowing that life is in the turmoil and the tension and not in the resolution, the creative self returns to the turmoil and the tension. If the tension is eliminated, if the war between the surface reality and the inner reality is over, creativity shuts down as do consciousness and choice, and freedom of choice, in Feydeau's theatre too, defeats philosophical naturalism.

Paradise Hotel actualizes the energy that changes behavior as well as language. The next play actualizes the energy channeled into the prevailing surface behavior and the energy that effects the change. The threat to civilization in Groff's *What Then* is ecological. To combat it, Diane releases a subsurface energy that changes the other characters, empowering them to change their behavior, joining forces to combat the threat. According to the program for the 2006 Clubbed Thumb production, *What Then* was originally commissioned by Clubbed Thumb and developed, with a different title, beginning in 2003. The threat to civilization in Groff's *Inky* is moral and ethical. According to the program for the 2005 Women's Project production, Clubbed Thumb workshopped an earlier version and co-produced the work with Salt Theater. The program gives no date, but an interview with Groff gives 1999 as the year of the co-production. The information is relevant because although *What Then* has greater characterization and takes place now whereas *Inky* is set in 1986, in terms of waging war *Inky* should be the later of the two plays, and it may be if the 2005 Women's Project version is very different from the 1999 version and if *What Then* has not undergone major changes in conception and revision from its 2003 development. The energy Diane releases empowers the other characters to perform a scene, the cabaret scene, for a new type of play. *Inky* is the new type in that it dramatizes the interaction and interpenetration of two clashing styles throughout the play.

From the outset of *Inky*, the couple in whose apartment the action takes place embody the corrupt values that threaten civilization. The husband, Greg, steals from corporate America through crooked accounting practices. The wife, Barbara, greets him upon his daily homecoming by turning his pockets inside out while they assume sexually provocative positions, for money is her aphrodisiac, and it is a consuming one. They have two children, one a baby and one grammar-school age, but they do not command Barbara's attention. She spends much of the play goading Greg to get more money so that they can move into a more luxurious New York City apartment, vacating the modish but limited representational set. In behavior and language, lifestyle and aspirations, the couple are presented naturalistically as pursuing the American Dream of upward mobility in contemporary America bereft of traditional values.

The character for whom the play is named is the couple's au pair. From bandanna to sneakers and speaking an undefined European accent, Inky is an indentured servant, for an au pair exchanges services such as caring for a child or domestic work or both for the opportunity to learn the host family's language and culture. Her goal is the couple's goal, achieving the American Dream, but they are not her model. In behavior and language, she chose Muhammed Ali, a non-naturalistic choice and the antithesis of the host couple's behavior and language. She adopts a prizefighting stance to bob and weave, jab and spar around the apartment while spouting Ali quotations such as proclaiming the ability to float like a butterfly and sting like a bee. Her language is not as original as Wellman's metaphoric language in *Fnu Lnu*, but it is figurative nonetheless and therefore poetic: the antithesis of geezer language.

Since the couple and the au pair share close quarters, inevitably they interact. One scene opens with Inky turning Greg's pockets inside out though with disdain because she is retaliating for his sexual advances on her. A quick learner of the culture, she has begun to pursue the Dream aggressively, creating tension. That is, her prizefighting stance is not symbolic; it has become her modus operandi. Since the three pursue a common goal and since they interact, inevitably the colliding styles interpenetrate, heightening the tension. Barbara does not bob and weave, but having come under Inky's influence, she challenges Gerg to hit her. Responding, in the interview referred to above, to the interviewer's admiration for the mounting tension in her plays, Groff said, "'When it's really working, it should be as if the audience is saying, "I don't know what's going to happen next . . . but it's going to be something really *bad*!"'"[51] The interviewer then quotes as an instance of mounting tension Barbara's challenge declined by her husband, who exits the room.

Greg's not hitting his wife contributes to his gaining sympathy as a character driven to corporate wrongdoing to satisfy her. Conversely Inky, who is initially a sympathetic character because she is a servant in a culture in which the acquisition of money is the supreme achievement, loses some sympathy because her method for getting the money, which she substitutes for the couple's methods, is tainted. When her charge, the grammar-school girl, is mugged by teenage boys, she teaches the girl the prizefighting maneuvers so as to be able to defend herself. That method is commendable, but she goes one step further. Make it two steps. She supplements her income by mugging teenage boys, and she coaches the daughter in skimming money from the sale of Girl Scout cookies. By play's end, however, her style prevails. In what can be considered a coda, Inky brings the daughter onstage for her sole appearance. She too adopts the prizefighting stance. With her parents' approbation, she will aggressively claim her due rather than badger someone or wile someone—a partner, for example—to get it for her.

Though the final scene can be considered a coda, it is no traditional resolution. One of the play's challenges is determining what to make of Inky's modus operandi for success. In his review Isherwood states the challenge: "It is hard to tell whether Inky's obsession with Ali is meant to be a symptom of the era's warped ethical values or a healthy route to feminine empowerment. It cannot logically be both."[52] Encouraging the girl to be assertive is commendable; the tainted values are not. With Letts' *Bug* I want to say that the play satirizes the characters' behavior. It was good theatre but a put-on even before the opening scene. Upon entering the Julia Miles Theater, where the Women's Project was producing Groff's play in the spring of 2005, the ticket holder was given a souvenir three-inch, red and white boxing glove and a program. The latter's centerfold has an advertisement for a hidden video surveillance to check on the nanny's behavior with her charge and a variety of photos—one of Ali, for example—and quotations, each with authorship. One states that not only is greed "'all right,'" it is "'healthy.'" Another reads, "'When there are no values, money counts.'" Yet I cannot be certain that *Inky* is a put-on.

However one interprets Groff's play, the objection to naturalism implicit in Eno's *The Flu Season*, that a naturalistic play cannot simultaneously accommodate more than one level of reality, has been met. Playwrights no longer have to dramatize the descent into the inner reality to release its force or energy. Some do and the descent can be spellbinding theatre, but it is not a prerequisite for battle because the unruly subsurface has been released into the ruled naturalistic surface where the war is being waged. Answering the question whether the released reality is a mystery or a mechanism that can be explained, as Zola set out to do in *Thérèse Raquin*, will meet the objection implicit in Ludlam's *The Artificial Jungle*, that a naturalistic play eliminates mystery. The way to answer the question and restore the mystery is to examine a few plays in the next chapter that dramatize the surface encounter with something or someone embodying the unruly inner reality and/or the encounter's consequences.

NOTES

1. Christopher Gould, "A Note from the Publisher," in *Anti-Naturalism* (New York: Broadway Play Publishing, 1989), v-vi. Hereafter to be cited parenthetically.

2. Overmyer, "The Hole in the Ozone," 451.

3. Eric Overmyer, *On the Verge* (New York: Broadway Play Publishing, 1988), 75. Hereafter to be cited parenthetically. I quote from the single edition because it contains production notes omitted in the collected edition.

4. Ludlam, *Ridiculous Theatre*, 104, 63.

5. Mac Wellman, *Fnu Lnu*, in *Cellophane*, PAJ Books (Baltimore: Johns Hopkins UP, 2001), 207. Hereafter to be cited parenthetically.

6. Porter Anderson, "Fidel Castro Slept Here," *American Theatre* 12, no. 1 (1995): 8.

7. Mac Wellman, *Sincerity Forever*, in *Grove New American Theater*, ed. Michael Feingold (New York: Grove, 1993), 99.

8. Mac Wellman, "Figure of Speech: An Interview with Mac Wellman," by Marc Robinson, *Performing Arts Journal* 40, 14, no. 1 (1992): 46.

9. Joseph Campbell, *The Hero with a Thousand Faces* (Cleveland: Meridian-World, 1956), 51–53.

10. Campbell, 77.

11. Campbell, 97.

12. Anderson, 8–9.

13. Charles Isherwood, "When Naturalism Isn't Natural, Subvert the Realism," *New York Times*, 12 Oct. 2004, E5. For Alexis Soloski, "Cowboys and Indians," *Village Voice*, 30 Mar. 1999, 145, he is "defiantly non-naturalistic."

14. Overmyer, "The Hole in the Ozone," 449.

15. Margot Ebling, "Flat Land," *Village Voice*, 24 Nov. 1998, 140.

16. Richard Maxwell, *Showy Lady Slipper*, in *Plays: 1996–2000* (New York: Theatre Communications Group, 2004), 145. Hereafter to be cited parenthetically.

17. Marc Robinson, "On with the Shoe," *Village Voice*, 2 Nov. 1999, 71.

18. Shawn-Marie Garrett, "The Awkward Age: New York's New Experimental Theater," *Theater* 31, no. 2 (2001): 46.

19. Peter Marks, "Taking the Mall Mentality to Its Ultimate Vapidity," *New York Times*, 29 Oct. 1999, E3.

20. Ben Brantley, "Burned Out but Not Down for the Count," *New York Times*, 21 Sept. 2000, E5.

21. Ebling, 140.

22. Isherwood, "When Naturalism Isn't Natural, Subvert the Realism," E5.

23. Melissa James Gibson, *[sic]* (New York: Dramatists Play Service, 2004), 14–15. Hereafter to be cited parenthetically. Since the text has no punctuation marks, I put a period to indicate the end of a quotation even if the quotation is a question.

24. Bruce Weber, "3 People at an Uncertain Stage Making Their Uncertain Way," *New York Times*, 20 Nov. 2001, E3.

25. Bruce Weber, "*[sic]*," in *The Best Plays of 2001–2002*, ed. Jeffrey Eric Jenkins (New York: Limelight, 2003), 133.

26. Richard Foreman, *Reverberation Machines: The Later Plays and Essays* (Barrytown, NY: Station Hill, 1985), 189.

27. Richard Foreman, *Unbalancing Acts: Foundations for a. Theater*, ed. Ken Jordan (New York: Pantheon, 1992), 75.

28. Richard Foreman, "On the Plays," in *Paradise Hotel and Other Plays* (Woodstock, NY: Overlook, 2001), 7. Hereafter to be cited parenthetically. For analyses of Foreman's theatre, see *Richard Foreman*, ed. Gerald Rabkin, PAJ Books (Baltimore: Johns Hopkins UP, 1999); Marc Robinson, *The Other American Drama*, PAJ Books (Baltimore: Johns Hopkins UP, 1997), 150–77; and Andreach, *Creating the Self in the Contemporary American Theatre*, 142–51 and *Drawing Upon the Past*, 83–103.

29. Kenneth McLeish, introduction, *Georges Feydeau, Plays: One*, trans. McLeish (London: Methuen, 2001), xii-xiii.

30. Marcel Achard, "Georges Feydeau," the introduction to *Feydeau's Théâtre Complet* (1948), trans. Mary Douglas Dirks, in *Let's Get a Divorce! and Other Plays*, ed. Eric Bentley (New York: Hill and Wang, 1958), 358.

31. Richard Foreman, *Paradise Hotel*, in *Paradise Hotel and Other Plays*, 253. Hereafter to be cited parenthetically.

32. Georges Feydeau, *L'Hôtel du libre échange*, in *Georges Feydeau, Plays: One*, 37.

33. Foreman, preface, *Symphony of Rats*, in *Unbalancing Acts*, 207.

34. Foreman, preface, *Reverberation Machines*, viii.

35. Foreman, *Unbalancing Acts*, 7.

36. Foreman, *Unbalancing Acts*, 8.

37. Gould, v.

38. McLeish, xvi. *Heart's Desire Hotel* is McLeish's title for his translation of *L'Hôtel du libre échange*.

39. John Mortimer, introduction, *Georges Feydeau: Three Boulevard Farces*, trans. Mortimer (Harmondsworth: Penguin, 1985), 9.

40. Harry Levin, *Playboys and Killjoys: An Essay on the Theory and Practice of Comedy* (New York: Oxford UP, 1987), 76–78.

41. Georges Feydeau, *La Puce à l'oreille*, in *Georges Feydeau, Plays: Two*, trans. McLeish (London: Methuen, 2002), 472.

42. Foreman, *Unbalancing Acts*, 20–21.

43. Foreman, preface, *What Did He See?*, in *Unbalancing Acts*, 263.

44. Foreman, *Unbalancing Acts*, 53.

45. Since the play has not yet been published, I am quoting from my memory of the 2000 premiere.

46. Achard, 359.

47. Foreman, "Things I Tell Myself When I Fall into the Trap of Making the Writing Imitate 'Experience,'" in *Reverberation Machines*, 205.

48. Foreman, *Symphony of Rats*, 238–39.

49. Foreman, preface, *Lava*, in *Unbalancing Acts*, 316.

50. Foreman, *The Universe*, in *Paradise Hotel and Other Plays*, 67.

51. Rinne Groff, "Framing Rinne Groff," interview by Deron Bos, *The Brooklyn Rail* Apr. 2005, 45.

52. Charles Isherwood, "Who's Minding the Baby? It Sounds Like Ali," *New York Times*, 15 Mar. 2005, E5.

Chapter Three

The War in Character Behavior: Albee, Greenberg, and Donaghy

Edward Albee has been challenging the naturalistic play's conventions from the beginning of his career. In the stage directions for "The Sandbox," which premiered in 1960, one of the five players "is doing calisthenics; he does calisthenics until quite at the very end of the play. These calisthenics, employing the arms only, should suggest the beating and fluttering of wings. The YOUNG MAN is, after all, the Angel of Death."[1] He is present for the death of Grandma, who speaks from the sandbox in which her daughter and son-in-law "*dump her*" (11) to the audience and the Young Man about the play they are performing. At one point she even calls to the offstage technical crew that the lights should be dimmed to indicate time's passage. Another of the five performers is a musician, who does not speak but plays when directed to by any one of the other four. In *The Goat or, Who Is Sylvia?*, however, an Albee character crosses a boundary with the revelation of the crossing coming after the play establishes the naturalism—the boundaries.

John Arnone's set for the 2002 New York premiere of *The Goat* was an impeccably appointed living room. Mercedes Ruehl and Bill Pullman were actors playing two of its occupants: happily married characters Stevie and Martin preparing for the arrival of their friend Ross, a television journalist coming to tape an interview with Martin on his fiftieth birthday, for not only is he the recipient of a distinguished architect's award, he has been chosen to design the dream city of the future. With the architect so distracted that the journalist decides to reschedule the taping at the studio and with Stevie shopping, the two friends talk, the latter picking up on the former's admission that "something's the matter"[2] until the "something" becomes the admission that he is in love with his wife but also outside of the marriage. The first of the play's three scenes ends with the revelation. Martin produces a photograph of his secret beloved. "YOU'RE FUCKING A GOAT!" Ross yells at him, to which he replies after a "*long pause*": "Yes" (23).

Since Martin's reply is "*factual*" (23) and he is carrying in his wallet a photograph, which records surface features, he would seem to accept his experience as naturalistic. Yet he does not, and the tension between his perception of the experience and Ross' perception of it generates the scene's movement. For Martin, if a word has to describe the experience, it is love; for Ross, "'in love'" means "Ficky-fack! Humpty-doodle!" or, dropping the euphemisms, fucking. Martin's observation, "You say fuck a lot," has the journalist naturalism's representative. Ross' rejoinder, "You say fine a lot" (17), though it draws a laugh from each, would have the architect the representative of another perception in language but not in fact because for Ross, an extramarital love yields only one interpretation. The separation between them continues when Martin, explaining that he never cheated on Stevie even before they were married, reminds his friend of the college reunion when they had two bimbos brought to their hotel room but he could not perform while Ross, already married, did perform. The entire scene is a widening of the gap between the two men, but one excerpt will suffice. It occurs after the architect relates how on an excursion to locate a "real country place" (20) that he and Stevie had been talking about buying, he came upon a sylvan scene where he "saw her" looking at him "with those eyes." The journalist assumes he means someone like the cartoon Daisy Mae with "big tits in the calico blouse."

Martin: You don't understand.

Ross: No? It *wasn't* love?

Martin: No. Yes; yes, it was love, but I didn't know it right then. (*To himself.*) How could I?

Ross: Right then it was good old lust, eh? Dick starting to get big in your pants . . .

Martin: (*Sad.*) You *don't* understand. (*Pause.*) I didn't know *what* it was—what I was feeling. It was . . . it wasn't like anything I'd felt before . . . (21).

Since Ross can only understand Martin's experience naturalistically, following the revelation he writes a letter telling Stevie that her husband is having an affair with a goat.

Having failed to get his friend to understand his experience in the country, Martin knows that his wife, who has read the letter by the time scene 2 opens, "won't understand" (28), a conviction repeated more than once until it is not only she who cannot but "nobody understands" (39). Nevertheless he has to repeat the account because Stevie insists that they "talk about this" (30). For her, the marriage is at stake. The extended talk, twice as long as that with Ross, gives the husband the opportunity to attempt to clarify the essence of the experience. Martin's language is that of divine possession: "It was as if an alien came out of whatever it was, and it . . . took me with it, and it was . . . an ecstasy and a purity and a . . . love of a. . . ." The experience was not naturalistic because it relates "to nothing *whatever*, to nothing that can be *related* to!" What in scene-1's description was a union in which he and the goat Sylvia were attracted to each other becomes in scene-2's description a communion. The experience is religious: "And there was a connection there—a communication—that, well . . . an epiphany, I guess comes closest" (39–40).

For Stevie, like Ross, the experience is naturalistic. Not only is her husband an "*animal* fucker" (42), a "goat-fucker" (44), the experience falls under the purview of a "psychiatrist" (40); it is psychological and not religious. Her emotion, however, is rage because the relationship with the goat involves her as it does not Ross, for she is married to the architect with whom she shares her life, values, and bed. The emotion builds to rage as the scene with their son out of the room and just the two of them talking builds. To Martin's protest that he loves her, she begins to cry: "How can you love me when you love so much less?" (25) Sylvia, the ruminant mammal, is less than human; it is a "*thing*" (31). When Martin refers to Sylvia as "her," Stevie's temper flares: "Stop calling it *her!*" It is not a person, a "*whom*," but a "*what*" (32). Neither is it a subject, which presumes cognitive development, but an object: not "those eyes" but "THEM eyes!" (39) By the time he invokes the religious imagery, the emotion is unwavering. The goat is neither elevated above the human nor equal with the human. So far beneath the human that it is not even a whole thing, it is a piece of an animal: a "cunt" (42). The scene ends with Stevie reversing the scene's opening. Now, she screams at her husband, it is he who cannot "understand" that by professing to love her and a goat equally, he has brought her down to its level, and since he cannot understand, she leaves vowing to "bring" him "down" (44).

Though both Ross and Stevie condemn Martin's act, they do not present a united front. Ross' hypocrisy exposed in scene 1 in that he endorses extra-marital affairs so long as they fall within acceptable boundaries, scene 2 exposes his real reason for writing the letter to Stevie. The fear that exposure will ruin "'Martin's public image'" (24 and 27) is his fear that his own public image will be ruined by his friendship with the architect, his college roommate and the subject of more than one of his television interviews. His own image is at stake. So too is Stevie's image, though for a different reason. Her self-image was largely formed by her marriage. As she says to her husband, "I rose into love with you and have—what—*cherished*? you, all these years"

(37). Since her experience of divinity was in the marriage, his desecration of the marriage desecrated her self-image.

Ross' hypocrisy is contemptible, but his shock at learning the details is understandable. Even more so is Stevie's rage at the insult to her understandable. Their shock and rage hearing the details that they demand Martin twice relate keep the three characters' perceptions of the country experience forefronted for the audience and thereby enable Albee to shift from one to another. Responding to interviewer Stephen Bottoms' comment about the play running the "*gamut back and forth between total hilarity and quite gut-churning dramatic moments*," Albee said, "I like catching people in the middle of a laugh, and them realizing that it's not funny—or catching them in the middle of something awful, and realizing that you can laugh at it."[3] The shift becomes hilarious as Martin's description of the therapy session for people whose problem is interspecies congress, punctuated by his wife's incredulity, progresses from a pig to a dog to a goose. The question for the imaginatively engaged spectator is How does one do it with a goose? No wonder the audience laughs and Stevie crashes a vase on the floor!

The shift also works for the dramatic moments. Martin's description of the experience as supernatural jolts because it climaxes his relating naturalistic details and because Stevie's rage reduces the supernatural revelation to a perverted naturalistic act. For example, when he says that he realized he and Sylvia "were going to go to bed together," she counters with, "To stall together! To hay! *Not* to bed!" (41) But he does not perceive the act as a trampling of a boundary; he does not think he violated the animal. Humans "fall in love with *many* other creatures . . . dogs and cats," he reminds her, only to have her interrupt him: "We don't *fuck* them!" (42) The problem for the audience midway through the play, however, is not with the hilarity or the dramatic moments. It is perceiving a tragedy that, in response to another of Bottoms' comments, Albee qualified as "not part of the title—it's a parenthetical comment" and "a definition. Not *the* definition, or a redefinition. 'Notes Toward a Definition of Tragedy.'"[4]

In Greek mythology divinities assume theriomorphic form for congress with mortals, but in no extant Greek tragedy does a protagonist relate such an experience that happened to him or her. In the Aeschylean *Prometheus Bound*, Io tells the tale of her transformation into a heifer, but she is given a theriomorphic form, and she is not the protagonist. That Martin alludes to the Eumenides in scene 1 suggests an allusion to the third play in Aeschylus' *Oresteia*—the play Wellman reimagines in *Fnu Lnu*—invoking Greek tragedy, but the allusion does not take on significance until scene 3, where it will be examined. For John Kuhn, "Ross functions as the funny watchmen do in Aeschylus' *Oresteia* and Sophocles' *Antigone*, or the Corinthian messenger in Oedipus [sic]."[5] The *Oresteia* has comic relief. Told by Clytemnestra in *The Libation Bearers* to summon Aegisthus back to the palace to hear what she believes is news of Orestes' death, the nurse pauses to comment on her experience attending to the unpredictability of a baby's excretions. *The Goat*, though, does not draw smiles or chuckles. It elicits prolonged laughter so much so that one critic calls it "vaudeville–cum–tragedy."[6]

J. Ellen Gainor suggests that, rather than Aristotle's *Poetics*, "Nietzsche's speculations from *The Birth of Tragedy* seem more apt as a gloss on the significance of the tragic form for Albee."[7] She is referring to the preface to the 1886 edition. I want to extend her suggestion to *The Birth* itself. For Nietzsche, tragedy originated in the chorus as witness to the suffering of the god Dionysus: "In its vision this chorus beholds its lord and master Dionysus and is therefore eternally the *serving* chorus: it sees how the god suffers and glorifies himself and therefore does not itself *act*." Nietzsche goes on to write that since the god was imagined as present in the oldest period of tragedy, "originally tragedy was only 'chorus' and not yet 'drama.' Later the attempt was made to show the god as real."[8] If the Nietzschean model is Albee's model, by the end of scene 2, the audience, the contemporary theatre's counterpart to the ancient chorus, is witness to only one character's suffering. The tragedy is Stevie's.

In tragedy the hero or heroine typically has a recognition of complicity or transgression or simply having been chosen for an experience that challenges normal boundaries. Yet the perception's religious imagery notwithstanding, Martin is untouched by his experience. The sole difference in his behavior as witnessed by Stevie and Ross is his distraction. In the opening scene, he cannot remember where he put the new razor head or the name of Ross' son, yet as he details the country experience, his wife questions his previous day's behavior: "There are some things you *can* remember, eh?" (40) Not only was he the lone person at the therapy session who was not unhappy in his love for an animal, he could not understand why the others were unhappy, "ashamed, or—what is the word?—conflicted" (34). He is so insouciant that he is impervious to Stevie's suffering. Before son Billy leaves the room, he revises a sentence to clarify his meaning, archly adds "Of comfort and joy?" to Stevie's reading of the word "'tidings'" in Ross' letter and "Poor Dad?" to Billy's "Oh, Dad!" thereby forming part of the title of Arthur Kopit's absurdist play (25), breaks down the word "haberdasher" (30) into its two components, and picking up on his wife's disgust, asks whether he should scar her before or after vomiting on her. His "Sorry; sorry" (38) is an attempt at appeasement. For another critic, the play's theme is "pretentiously tragic."[9]

When scene 3 opens, Martin is still insouciant. To Billy's remark upon arriving home and surveying the damage his mother wrought that "You guys really had it out, hunh," he is *"almost laughing"* as he agrees (44). He also corrects his son for mixing metaphors. Only when Billy breaks down telling his father how much he loves him and how painful it will be for him at school when the story about the goat becomes known does Martin show a depth of sensitivity. Billy's suffering, however, qualifies him as the play's tragic hero on two counts. In one of the summary passages in *The Birth of Tragedy*, Nietzsche identifies the hero of Greek tragedy in its earliest form as the "suffering Dionysus of the Mysteries, the god experiencing in himself the agonies of individuation, of whom wonderful myths tell that as a boy he was torn to pieces by the Titans and now is worshiped in this state as Zagreus."[10]

The Nietzschean model is not the sole explanation, or theory, for tragedy's origin. For the second count, Gerald F. Else begins his explanation for the origin and early form of Greek tragedy, in the chapter "Dionysus, Goat-Men, and *Tragôidia*," with a critique of the Nietzschean explanation and other explanations, or theories, all of which he rejects. A later chapter refers back to the etymology of *tragôidia*:

> We saw in the first chapter that both the etymology tragôidia="song of goats" and the historical development to which it commits us are impossible. *Tragôidia*, as we said there, is not a simple compound of *tragos*, "goat," and *ôidia*, "song," but a secondary compound formed from the primary compound *tragôidos*, "goat-singer." Thus the beginning of the development must be sought in *tragôidos* rather than in *tragôidia*. And there is good reason to believe that "goat-singer" referred originally to the poet-actor, the reciter of spoken verses, rather than to the chorus.[11]

Since *tragos* is the he-goat or billy goat, son Billy is the goat singer, and the song he sings is that of the pain of individuation: the separation from the group he will suffer once the story of his father's perversion becomes known.

Whether it is the Nietzschean model or another model, tragedy implies isolation from the group. In the third scene, a sobbing Billy, holding his father, kisses him on the mouth. Martin shoves him away, but then responding to his son's pain, holds him, the interaction watched by Ross, who, unknown to them, has entered the apartment. Once aware of him, Martin defends not only his behavior with his son but in an exchange with the television journalist his behavior from the time he first encountered Sylvia. Their exchange serves as a recapitulation with Ross condemning the behavior because inevitably the goat lover will be exposed and Martin assailing Ross' hypocrisy: that behavior, no matter what form it takes, is acceptable so long as one can get away with it. The architect finally recognizes that no one understands his experience. "Why can't anyone understand this," he wails, "that I am all *alone* . . .

all . . . *alone!*" (54) His recognition puts him with his son and wife as tragic hero/ine.

There remains one more candidate in the play, however. In a short article, Jean-Pierre Vernant takes the position that Else takes in his book-length study: that Greek tragedy did not originate in the religious world of the Dionysiac cult. He then addresses the theory that the *tragôidos* sang to win a goat as prize or sang at the ritual sacrifice of a goat. "Unfortunately though, this goat, the *tragos*, is nowhere to be found. No goat—male or female—was sacrificed either in the theater or during the Great Dionysia. Furthermore, when, in other contexts, Dionysus is given a religious epithet suggesting some kind of goat, it is the term *aix* (she-goat) that is used, never *tragos*."[12] For anyone who has seen the play, the last line leaps from the page because in the closing scene Stevie enters dragging a goat's carcass. Is scapegoat Sylvia really the theriomorphic form, the she-goat form, of Dionysus or any divinity? Before we address this issue, we have to finish with Greek tragedy.

John Simon's review of *The Goat* is very critical. "One problem with the play," he writes, "is that it makes no sense"[13] that a happily married, professionally successful man enjoying a good sexual relationship with his wife and tolerant of his son's homosexuality would fall in love with a goat while looking at farm properties in upstate New York. Although I agree with Simon that the play is seriously flawed, sense can be made of it, but the sense begins in scene 1 with Ross hearing the sound of "wings" that Martin opines may be caused by the "Eumenides" (12). Had he said the Furies, or Erinyes, who become the Eumenides, or the Kindly Ones, in the *Oresteia* by accepting Orestes' acquittal in return for reverence in Athens, the audience might in the opening scene have made a specific connection with Greek tragedy. In the first play in Aeschylus' trilogy, conquering Agamemnon returns to Argos with Cassandra as part of the spoils of war. After he enters the palace, she directs the elders' attention to the roofs where the Furies are dancing or chanting. As proof of her divinatory power, she knows the House of Atreus is cursed.[14]

Ross is no Cassandra and Martin misidentifies the sound, but the momentary calling attention to the Greek chthonic deities indicates a curse on Martin's house. Without information about the family in which he originated, we cannot speculate about a curse in the past. In the present we do not have to speculate. The architect committed bestiality. But with whom or what? Exploring the possibility that Sylvia is a deification of Nature, Kuhn asks, "If Sylvia is divine, a nature goddess or god to Martin, how can his act (or any loving act) with her be low and unnatural?"[15] The exploration takes him into a discussion of scene 3: homosexuality as a natural or unnatural act. Relating Albee's Sylvia to Shakespeare's Sylvia in *The Two Gentlemen of Verona*, Gainor writes that the goat "mirrors her both as a real object of love and desire and as part of a contemporary rural and agricultural idyll, a locale equally remote, fertile, and mythic." She too moves to a discussion of scene-3's implication for sexual desire among other implications. Albee "confronts the dominant, hetero-normative culture with its designation of gay sexuality as aberrant, and challenges it to rethink not only these categories, but also the impossibility of making clear-cut distinctions among the manifold, polymorphously perverse expressions of sexual desire."[16] The two discussions of the play's implications for sexual desire make sense. So does Gainor's citing of Billy's closing words as indicative of a renegotiation of roles in the family. A critic might see in the play's constellation of father, mother, and son a parallel with the constellation in *Who's Afraid of Virginia Woolf?* I do not because for me the earlier play is a comedy.[17] What is interesting, however, in Billy's closing words and his proposal to his father earlier in the scene to set the room right is a parallel with the general outline of the tripartite *Oresteia*: the toppling of the triumphant masculine power, the toppling of the reigning feminine power, and the son's assumption of the role of redeemer.

Whether or not the parallel makes sense, the problem remains. The play's title is *The Goat*; its subtitle is *Who Is Sylvia?* If she is a naturalistic ruminant mammal and nothing more, Martin is deluded to believe he had a religious experience with her, and his hypocrisy notwithstanding, Ross is right in telling his friend that he needs professional help. The problem, however, is not Sylvia. She should be ambiguous, leaving open the possibility that she is other than or more than a naturalistic ruminant mammal. The problem is Martin, who in scene 3 insists that he continues to love the goat as well as Stevie. He also bemoans the fact that no one understands his experience, yet how can anyone be expected to understand it when he shows no effect beyond having a lingering caprine odor on him? A theatre audience wants to suspend disbelief, yet there must be something in the theatre experience that encourages the suspension. The scene-1 distraction that Martin exhibits is not serious enough to qualify as a radical change that an encounter with the Holy, whether a deity in theriomorphic form or the deification of Nature, would effect. He and Stevie joke about his distraction, and Ross' reminders, "Put on your public face. . . . And don't switch in the middle" (12), indicate that the journalist is accustomed to the architect's fluctuations.

Simon's criticism—that regardless of what happened in the country or what is happening in the apartment, the characters are detached enough to "continually and gratuitously correct one another's grammar and metaphors"[18]—cannot be ignored. Martin's insouciance and lack of sensitivity to Stevie's rage and Billy's pain detract from his claim to an encounter that drew him across a naturalistic boundary, a crossing that has continued to the present. The play does not open with Stevie trying to understand the change in her husband's behavior because there is no change. The combination of title, subtitle, and parenthetical comment imply a mystery, and Martin claims he experienced the mystery. The play, however, does not make it convincing.

Richard Greenberg's *The Violet Hour* premiered in 2002, the same year that *The Goat* premiered. Reviewing the Chicago production, Ben Brantley saw in it the author's "willingness to break through the boundaries of naturalism to explore the inexplicable."[19] But *The Violet Hour* comes after two decades of writing plays whose mode of production is primarily realistic-naturalistic though mixed with other modes and styles. A guide to the experimenting with the mixture is in Greenberg's experimenting with the dramatic use of the literary allusion, which yields a major theme in his work and takes us to the boundaries breakthrough in *The Violet Hour*. The one-act play, "The Author's Voice," opens in the apartment of Todd, author of a first novel, to which he has brought, at her request, his editor because she cannot work with a writer unless she feels she knows him and the environment in which he creates. Portia's reaction is "House of Usher."[20] The reaction is understandable given the apartment's gloom, but the Poe allusion is the insertion of a blind alley, a stratagem Greenberg is not averse to using. In an interview he gave for the magazine publication of *Three Days of Rain*, he explained that one character's name is symbolic. A son, Walker, was so named by his father because the latter "would like to have been a *flaneur*—a walker." Another character's name, however, is not symbolic despite invoking *Great Expectations*. To the interviewer's question about the name Pip, Greenberg replied, "I kept it for fun—yes, the play deals with inheritance and there's a Pip, but there's no connection. It's a blind alley. I think the character is a pip, that's all—Dickens be damned."[21] The allusion as device for invoking a shaping influence on the play does not appear until the closing scene, but the audience can follow the action without it.

Todd's apartment is described as *"strangely shadowed"* with a *"door in the back wall."* Despite Portia's interest in him, and like him, she is described as *"young and beautiful"* (173), he is not only unresponsive, he is anxious to have her leave, which she does but not before remarking in jest as a way of accounting for the discrepancy between his bland personality and passionate, tormented writing that "Behind that door, there's some horribly twisted gnome who does all your writing for you—." After she leaves, the door opens and a *"horribly twisted gnome emerges, carrying a sheaf of papers"* (176–77). "The Author's Voice" actualizes a basic Jungian concept. In Jungian psychology the shadow is that part of the personality that the ego relegates to the unconscious because it contains qualities deemed unacceptable. Of course, the process of individuation requires that the person come to recognize and accept the shadow.

With the contrast of ego and shadow, Greenberg constructs a drama of creativity. A gnome is an ageless creature who lives in the earth and guards treasure. Symbolically named Gene, Todd's gnome guards the treasure of the unconscious, the images released into consciousness that the artist seizes and forms into art. The play's protagonist is a divided self. Todd is a physically and socially attractive aspiring writer who first met Portia at one of the clubs he frequents, but his verbal images, when he is not speaking the images Gene supplies him for the novel, are as bland as his personality. Gene is a misshapen gnome, but his verbal images are the contents of art. His desire to come out of the shadows in which he feels he is kept prisoner and be acknowledged by both Todd and Portia as guardian of the treasure causes the conflict that generates the drama's action.

Profound in theme, the play nevertheless has funny scenes. Once the audience realizes that Gene is the author's voice, they assume the voice is oracular. Hence when the gnome coaches his conscious self in how to speak seductively to Portia so as to maneuver her into bed, the assumption is that his approach, as opposed to Todd's, will be successful. Claiming a libido dulled by a surfeit of sexual encounters, Todd is not interested, but since he has to respond to the editor's overtures if he wants to be published, he agrees to be coached so long as he does not have to speak the lines, "'Darling, I want you'" and "'Be mine,'" preferring instead the line, "Do you want to sleep with me?" (191–92) Gene prevails, however, and the seduction is underway in the next scene. Laughing at the coached lines, an eager Portia, positioning herself on the bed, uses her line on the reluctant lover, "Look, do you want to sleep with me?" (196) The scene ends when a frustrated Gene, protesting that intimacy should be beautiful, bursts into the room. Believing that when Portia sees his inner beauty she will love him, he kisses the editor, who faints.

The informing allusion appears in the closing scene, the second scene after the abortive seduction with the intervening scene one in which Todd forcibly remands Gene to the shadows on the other side of the door. Reviews praise the first novel as the "'best first novel of the season, perhaps the decade'" with the "most memorable opening since, 'Call me Ishmael'" (201–02). *Moby-Dick* is a blind alley, but another Melville tale is not. "Bartleby, The Scrivener" can be read as the interaction between the conscious ego or personality and the Jungian shadow. The conscious self is the tale's narrator, who describes himself as "one of those unambitious lawyers who never addresses a jury, or in any way draws down public applause; but in the cool tranquillity of a snug retreat, do a snug business among rich men's bonds and mortgages and title-deeds."[22] His business increasing at the time of the tale, he had to hire an additional scrivener, placing him behind a folding screen in the corner of his office, isolating him from the other scriveners and himself.

Bartleby's only view therefore, through a small window that once had looked out upon backyards and bricks, was of a wall a few feet away that formed a shaft through which some light filtered down—a situation echoed in the opening paragraph of Todd's novel as quoted in the reviews: "'I live alone. There are no neighbors. There is no neighborhood. Brick has vanished. Tree and sky, too. When I peer through the narrow, grimy shaft that is my window, I see horizon and murk'" (202).

Bartleby was the narrator's shadow, magnifying his traits of lack of ambition and retreat from life. Unacknowledged, the scrivener further retreated, first by reiterating his abstention, "'I would prefer not to'" (11), from the proofreading of copied documents; then by not venturing from behind the screen, which had become his "hermitage" (13), or the chambers, which had become his home, until he became a fixture in them, for he no longer copied. A ghostly figure standing at the window, he was "absolutely alone in the universe" (22). Since he would not quit the premises, the narrator moved to new chambers, though he could not remove Bartleby from his memory or conscience, visiting him in the prison where the building's landlord had him taken and where he died.

Greenberg's Gene is no scrivener by profession, and his play is not a Melville tale. With Bartleby ensconced behind the screen, the focus is on the effect on the narrator of his refusal to participate in the office's routine. Gene does not refuse to participate in Todd's routine; he rebels against the routine by becoming a scrivener. "The Author's Voice" ends with his revelation to Todd that the novel which he supplied from behind his screen, his door, and which is garnering accolades is actually an out-of-print novel by a Canadian author who, having been apprised of the plagiarism, is approaching the apartment.

The differences notwithstanding, "The Author's Voice" does allude to "Bartleby, The Scrivener." Its introduction by way of the reviewer's contrasting Todd's face on the book jacket with that of Herman Melville is awkward and quoting the opening line of *Moby-Dick* is a blind alley, yet by recalling the 19th-century tale that on one level is a writer's withdrawal from life, the 20th-century play also offers a contemporary perspective on the consequences of denying one's voice, nature, inner self: the wellspring of one's creative power. As Greenberg's theatre develops the allusion's function, his dramas develop the relationship between the conscious ego, which is better called the disengaged ego, and the unacknowledged self.

Thus the theme that the one-act play yields and that becomes a major theme in Greenberg's theatre is the need to acknowledge the unacknowledged self. In this study's terms, the playwright is developing the relationship between the outer and inner realities of ruled surface and unruly subsurface. The relationship is also connecting with the allusion as he experiments with different modes and styles. The largely symbolic mode of "The Author's Voice" gives way to the thoroughly naturalistic mode of *Eastern Standard*. With its sets of restaurant interior and summer-home sundeck, language, and cast of instantaneously recognizable yuppies, waitress, and bag lady, the play was Greenberg's most successful play prior to the 1990s, premiering in 1988 and after runs in Seattle Repertory Theatre and Manhattan Theatre Club productions, moving to a commercial Broadway theater in 1989. Prior to 2003 it was his sole play to be produced in a commercial Broadway theater. A *New York Times* article of the late 1990s on the scarcity of new American plays produced in the commercial sector cited Greenberg as a playwright enjoying considerable success in New York and around the country but, with the exception of *Eastern Standard*, not produced in the big Broadway theaters. The article raised the possibility that his being gay writing about gays might have some bearing on the issue. He disagreed. "'It may have made me a little more concerned with the position of the outsider, which is often one of my themes,' Mr. Greenberg said. 'But so has being Jewish or being a playwright in a culture that provides more rewards for other kinds of endeavor.'"[23] *The American Plan* has more than one outsider and more than one gay character, one of whom is the unacknowledged self.

A detailed examination of *The American Plan* would take too much space, but a summary is in order. The play is a reimagining of Henry James' *Washington Square* with Lili the counterpart to James' Catherine Sloper, Lili's mother Eva the counterpart to Catherine's father Doctor Sloper, Lili's fiancé Nick the counterpart to Morris Townsend, and a fourth character for whom there is no Jamesian counterpart. In *Washington Square* Morris betrays Catherine when he realizes that Dr. Sloper will disinherit her should they marry. In *The American Plan*, Nick betrays Lili, her inheritance notwithstanding, when Gil, his ex-lover, reappears. Gil is the unacknowledged self in that Nick does not acknowledge him when he attempts a reunion with Lili years later despite her knowledge of their relationship, since Eva, suspicious of Nick's motive for courting her daughter, saw them kissing. *The American Plan* also allows Greenberg to experiment with James' great theme of the boon conferred by and the price exacted for the gaining of consciousness. To escape the humiliation she suffered, Lili has disengaged herself from her consciousness of herself as the fragile daughter to become her impervious mother: a reclusive self in which she is imprisoned at play's end.

The Violet Hour, the final Greenberg play to be examined, opens in 1919 in the Manhattan office of John Pace Seavering, who with old money, for he is a Princeton alumnus, is starting a publishing firm, although the office is in disarray because he has just moved in and the firm has yet to publish a book.

With him is his factotum, Gidger. The few minutes they are together before a third cast member appears establish their relationship and the playwright's theme. Gidger gave his employer something he wrote to read. When John is evasive in replying to Gidger's query about his reaction, the factotum asks whether he prefers the free verse or the sonnet, only to spring the trap: "IT WAS PROSE!"[24] To Gidger's question about their professional relationship, the would-be publisher identifies him as a nondescript "employee." To the former's question whether he thinks Gidger is a first or last name, the latter admits it never occurred to him that "it was your *name* at all"; he thought of it as "sort of . . . in *lieu* of a name" (10–11). John is the disengaged ego, and Gidger is one of the play's three unacknowledged selves.

Since the cast listing describes Gidger as "*ageless*" (5) and since a later reference identifies him as a "'woman'" (114), he is a development of gnome Gene in "The Author's Voice," and as comic actor Mario Cantone played him in the New York production with exaggerated, drag-queen mannerisms in spiking the language when speaking and throwing a "*hissy fit*" (11), he appears to be androgynous. The offstage anteroom in which he works is a development of Gene's shadowy room in the one-act play. Shortly after the second unacknowledged self arrives and the factotum returns to his workstation, a machine is delivered to the anteroom. Gidger informs John of the delivery, but even though it was not ordered, the publisher is too busy with the new arrival to take a look. Gidger subsequently informs his employer that although he did not turn the machine on, it is running and then that it is spewing paper with writing on it, but neither time does John show an interest in it. About the time the third unacknowledged self arrives, the factotum enters the office carrying a stack of pages. Once again John declines to look at the machine, at which point Gidger cries out, "WHY WON'T YOU ACKNOWLEDGE ME?" (37) His cry connects him, the machine, and the anteroom in which it releases the image-laden sheaves of paper.

With two plays, *Take Me Out* and *The Violet Hour*, running simultaneously in commercial Broadway theaters, the year 2003 marks a turning point in Greenberg's career. This study does not include *Take Me Out* because the unacknowledged self is acknowledged early in that play, diluting the major theme and eliminating the mystery. I am not implying any debt or influence, but one avenue for approaching the mystery in *The Violet Hour* is through a metaphor in Richard Foreman's theatre. His plays are reverberating machines. The hum the audience hears from time to time in a Foreman play is the energy generating the images that stimulate the imagination and the impulses that create consciousness and choices. Gidger's machine serves the same function as Foreman's metaphor: to stimulate the imagination by having characters in the play and spectators in the audience seize the released images and convert them into consciousness, choices, and creativity. Since the anteroom, like Gene's room in "The Author's Voice," is a symbol of the unconscious, the images flow from the room to John, the disengaged conscious ego. Christopher Barreca's set for the New York production was naturalistic, and the characters behave naturalistically, yet it is possible to see Greenberg experimenting with a merger of naturalism and symbolism in the stage design. In the clutter, disarray, and mounting contents of the office, one can see a stage image of John's pressured mind, a possibility that will loom larger in act 2 when the publisher, his imagination stimulated, makes a decision.

Although Greenberg materializes the energy source, his treatment of the transmission of the contents is truer to the nature of the unconscious, the inner reality that is the repository of stored images, than the comparable transmission in the earlier one-act play. Gene consciously writes the sheaves of paper he gives to Todd. Although Gidger is the room's custodian or guardian, he is unconscious of the machine's source—that is, who delivered it—or why it spews pages or what the contents are. By the end of act 1, he discovers that it is turning out pages from the future so that as act 2 opens, he and John are reading pages in the office and therefore learning about the past and the future, both of which the writing realizes in verbal images. Yet the images mysteriously flow through Gidger. At one point in act 1, he exclaims, "I'm a little DUTCH boy, I'm STEMming a FLOOD!" and then *"appears in the doorway, dripping pages"* (33–34). While he and John read in act 2, a *"chorus of 'Que Será, Será' hums itself* through *him. He has no idea what it is"* (77). Minutes later he is *"flabbergasted by the festival of alien slang he's unleashed"* (83).

Gidger, however, is only one of three unacknowledged selves. The other two arrive at the office, each from a different time in John's life: Denny McCleary, his best friend from the past, and Jessie Brewster, a colored singer with whom he says he is in love in the present. John tries to keep his relationships with them separate from each other, but the visits overlap as do their expectations, and from his point of view, the expectations are competing pressures because each submitted a manuscript to be published. Since each wants to be published, each is an unacknowledged self and being published is the equivalent to being acknowledged. Yet although he expresses admiration privately for each one's manuscript, John argues that his restricted financial resources allow for only one of the two to be published but the one not accepted is no less an aspect of his life. As he says to Jessie, "Part of me screams out no, I don't want to publish it—I want to *private* it. I want to secret it beneath my pillow and have it for my dreams" (42).

There may be another reason for his trying to keep the relationships separate and accepting only one of the two submissions, for once the manuscript is in book form in the public world, it acknowledges a relationship between the author and the publisher. When Denny thinks he hears an acceptance from his college friend, he *"kisses him passionately on the mouth"* (31). With the image recalling a similar image of Gil with Nick in *The American Plan*, the drama of John, Denny, and Jessie becomes a development of the drama of Nick, Gil, and Lili. Denny also figures in the development of another drama in *The American Plan*. Both authors have compelling reasons for wanting to be published. Jessie wants to win an audience—the year is 1919—larger than that of her devoted but limited number of black fans. Denny has to prove to his fiancée, Rosamund, that he holds the promise of success for her to win the approval and wealth of her family; should she marry him without the promise, her parent, perceiving him a fortune hunter, will disinherit her.

Since Denny figures in the two dramas, he plays a more important role in the play than does Jessie and for other reasons too. The machine's arrival in the anteroom coincides with his arrival in the office, and the title of his novel is the title of the play. Greenberg said he found the image "in one of [Alfred] Kazin's books of memoirs."[25] It is not in *A Walker in the City* or *Starting Out in the Thirties*. Furthermore, if the image is in one of his many books, I am sure that Kazin attributes it to its author. In *A Walker in the City*, the literary critic recounts his boyhood in the Brownsville section of Brooklyn until the time he graduated from high school. During the high school years, a boy in the neighborhood who aspired to be a poet was always reading Eliot's *The Waste Land* and writing commentaries on it so that whenever Kazin and a few other boys went to the tenement house in which his family lived, they would be present at another reading of the poem. *Starting Out in the Thirties* opens with Kazin unemployed in the summer of 1934, between his junior and senior years in college, but with an interest in the works of Eliot and other poets. A decade later in wartime London, he got to meet Eliot when he interviewed him.[26]

Why does Greenberg mistake the attribution? One explanation is confusion. As is his habit, he did some research for the play but admitted, "'I tend to get my facts wrong.'"[27] A second explanation, and the one I accept, is the incorrect attribution is a blind alley. "At the violet hour" are the opening words of the central section of the middle part III of the five-part *The Waste Land*. The violet hour is the time when offices close for the day, releasing the typist "home at teatime" to await the "small house agent's clerk," who arrives for a scene perceived by Tiresias, who having foresuffered the sexual experience as both man and woman "foretold the rest." To compensate for Juno's condemning Tiresias to blindness for siding with her husband in a dispute, Jove gave him the gift of prophecy. In the note for the section, Eliot writes that "what Tiresias *sees*, in fact, is the substance of the poem."[28] What he sees is the sterile ritual of the clerk's lust coupling with the typist's indifference. That Greenberg is familiar with *The Waste Land* Lili establishes in *The American Plan* by quoting the poem's opening and closing lines.

Explaining how he got the idea for the title of his novel, "The Violet Hour," Denny tells John that it came to him at the hour "when clerks and secretaries started to emerge from office buildings and scurry . . ." (29). If the 1920s word for secretaries, typists, is substituted, the hour is that of the opening lines of "the violet hour" section of *The Waste Land*. Ageless, androgynous, characterizing himself as "proficient and gifted and wise beyond" his "years" (7), Gidger is act-1's Tiresias, the custodian of the machine that foretells the future, the "invention" to which he is "talking" (32) when Jessie arrives. As the act makes clear, he sees in John's indifference the sterile ritual of publishing without passion and commitment: without engagement. John has the self-assurance of a conscious ego in that he believes that whatever choice he makes will be "*right*" (45), but he does not know, given his limited financial resources, which is the right choice. "If only I could *know*—" (49), he pleads with Jessie. The two unacknowledged authors give him a deadline for making his choice.

By play's end he chooses to publish the two manuscripts. The two reasons he gives are valid. Both manuscripts are "authentic . . . in their ways" and "it makes no difference what" he does—"it will happen as it happens. The century will take its course" (122–23). The second reason requires a little explanation. Early in act 2, from the window John sees a woman on the street below looking in a shopwindow while unknown to her a photographer is taking her picture. Toward the act's end, Denny and Rosamund burst into the office talking about the woman at the shopwindow being photographed so that John realizes that all the intervening time has taken place in his mind. Since the machine releases verbal images that stimulate the imagination, his imagination has been interpreting the scenes in the sheaves of paper. That is, Greenberg transforms the office into a theatre of the mind for actualizing the scenes. John is also under pressure to make a decision from the threats of Rosamund to commit suicide should he not select Denny's manuscript and from Jessie to break off their relationship should he not select her manuscript. "Is it all right to fuck a nigger but you don't want to be a nigger press?" (49), she taunts him. When he tells her the future the machine revealed for her during the intervening suspension of time, she protests, "No—*no*—that's not me—that's *you*—That's all you can imagine for me—" (113). What he learns from these scenes is that he cannot control events involving other persons' choices and lives.

The unspoken reason for his decision to publish the two manuscripts is the gaining or intensifying of consciousness. In act 1 Denny brings Rosamund in to meet him and then leaves them alone, their hope being that she will so charm the college friend that he will commit the firm to publishing Denny's manuscript. After she sketches in what will happen to her and her fiancé should he not publish the novel, John says, "You have the gift of prophecy," and she counters, "I never said it was a gift. . ." (63). In the course of the conversation, she asks him, "Do you ever have presentiments?" (59) All of this talk about foretelling the future prepares for act 2. Its crucial piece of evidence is the revelation the machine releases in pages from a 1995 book by a Violet Haze that quotes from Jessie's recently discovered diary. The entry, dated 1919, records her coming upon "John sharing a passionate kiss" with Denny: a "*most erotic*" scene for the diarist (116). In this scene from a book the name of whose author invokes Denny's novel, John has his relationship with his college friend both ways. He becomes act-2's Tiresias, perceiving the action in which he is engaged but disengaging himself from it. "But it isn't *me*. . . ," he says to Gidger (118). Just as what Eliot's Tiresias sees is the substance of *The Waste Land*, so what Gidger initially and John finally see is the substance of *The Violet Hour*: the would-be publisher's disengagement. With the machine issuing three tickets to go with the two he already has and with real time resuming, the publisher invites the four, Gidger included, to accompany him to the theater, for what he learns from this scene is that he can control events involving his choices and life, especially when the choices involve persons about whom he cares.

It is not only the publisher that the play integrates. Greenberg integrates modes of production and philosophical positions, a point Brantley made in his review of the Chicago production before the play came to New York when he praised the "fine blend of wit and wistfulness, of philosophical darkness and bright social satire."[29] He achieves the integration by stretching the tension between the opposing forces before reconciling them. The play opens in John's office where he is absorbed in satisfying his need for a career that makes something worthwhile of his life. The setting is the naturalistic surface because he has the resources to rent an office and publish a book and the career is a glamorous one, but he is disengaged from the three unacknowledged selves who constitute publishing's ground: its raison d'etre. Since they have the same need for careers to make something worthwhile of their lives, they pressure him to be acknowledged. Their threats of estrangement and suicide at act-1's end take him to his inner reality in act 2, a change that is reflected in the office becoming symbolic. Given the deadline and the increased pressure that an acknowledgment of relationships with Denny and Jessie in 1919 puts on the risk of public embarrassment and career failure, the tension reaches a breaking point. John, however, takes the risk. His recognition that he cannot control other people's choices—that, in other words, there are forces over which he has no control—is a naturalistic tenet, yet it is followed by his recognition that he can control his own choices—that, in other words, he has free will to direct his life. No longer disengaged, he acknowledges the unacknowledged selves, and the five leave the integrated naturalistic-symbolic office for the theater and participation in the larger community.

John takes the risk because having turned inward, he has to continue. The privileged characters in *Eastern Standard* have the boon that consciousness confers—they know who they are, what they want from life, and how to enjoy their privileges—but except for a stirring in one or two of conscience for their insensitivity to the underprivileged, they do not suffer the ordeal of consciousness: the price the gaining exacts. By not turning inward, they therefore remain superficial characters. Lili in *The American Plan* suffers the price without the boon, and the price is so terrible that she escapes by becoming her mother, the person from whom she so desperately wanted to escape, but by disengaging herself from her consciousness as Lili, she becomes trapped in her consciousness of herself as Eva. Of Greenberg's plays that this chapter examines, *The Violet Hour* is the most mature treatment of his major theme. To grow as an individual, regardless of choice of career, the ego has to accept the unacknowledged selves, whether misshapen or fragile, eccentric or marginal. The acceptance with its risk is the price to be paid, but the acceptance is the gaining of consciousness, and it is consciousness with its price and its boon that can render life fulfilling. By acknowledging the images his unacknowledged selves generate in their manuscripts, John realizes his public power, for creativity in publishing gives him his status in society. By acknowledging the images the machine generates for the act-2 scenes, he realizes his personal power, for consciousness and choice give him his status as a moral being.

Since writing and publishing are allied activities and since I suggested that the metaphor of reverberating machine in Foreman's theatre provides an avenue for approaching Greenberg's theatre, Foreman's advice for the would-be writer is good advice for the would-be publisher too. He should "look deep" inside himself.[30] The instrument for going deep and gaining consciousness in *The Violet Hour* is the machine that foretells the future. About the gap that exists between the self and the ability to create language to express the self, Foreman writes that the "gap is the field of all creativity—it's an ecstatic field rather than a field of despair. It's the field of the unconscious, of God; it's the unfathomable from which everything pours forth."[31] I cannot claim similar words for Greenberg's machine from which everything pours forth, but I like Brantley's term for it: "deus ex machina,"[32] and in this play the source of the unruly subsurface reality whose images impact the ruled naturalistic surface reality is at the other extreme from naturalism. It is a mystery and one that changes behavior, for John's behavior changes, as Martin's does not in *The Goat*. The trouble with the machine, however, is that it is a one-time dramatic device, inexplicable though it is. Characterization is a more permanent site for a mystery as in the theatre of Tom Donaghy.

Michael Feingold began a 1998 review of three plays with observations on the trend in playwrighting of mixing modes:

> Trying to squeeze two modes of work into one script will give you anything but a fully realized vision. And the theater seems in a mood to try this squishy approach: Where it occasionally used to spice up mode A with a hint of Mode B, it now mixes them casually, with results that are usually disconcerting, and at times disastrous. Oldsters who grumble that you can't tell the girls from the boys any longer should try a few weeks of play reviewing, and learn how tough it is to tell the Chekhov from the ghost stories; gender's an easy guess in comparison.

As problematic as the mixture may be, it works in the Donaghy play being reviewed, as Feingold went on to admit: "Trying to marry Chekhov, king of naturalistic exactitude, to the supernatural is at any rate piquant, and Tom Donaghy's *From Above*, in which the improbable nuptials are solemnized, has all the pleasures of the unexpected combination: Till you start to discern the familiar flavors, you're willing to swear you've never tasted anything like it."[33] Although the emphasis of this chapter's final section is Donaghy's *The Beginning of August*, the section opens with a brief examination of the "improbable nuptials" of the naturalistic and the non-naturalistic—of exactitude and mystery—in *From Above* as preparation for a fuller examination of the marriage in The *Beginning of August*.

From Above opens with an image of life so fixed in the past that it is an image of death. The lights come up on Evvy, a woman in her forties, staring into the full-length mirror before which she is seated. Her marriage having given her an identity, she cannot liberate herself from that image to discover a new identity, even though a year has passed since her seventy-two-year-old husband, Jimmy, died. She can only see herself as she is, which is arrested in the past, and not as she can become. With money that Jimmy left her, she has purchased some household items, but they remain in the crates in which they were delivered. She "kept"[34] his charcoal sketches and his sweaters because she cannot throw the sketches away or donate the sweaters to a clothing drive, and in a later scene the audience learns that the answering machine still plays the tape with his voice inviting the caller to leave a name, short message, and phone number. She knows that she should change the decor of her house, but she cannot decide on a new decor. She also knows that by not going out into the world, except to go to work as a hostess and shift manager at the nearby resort hotel, she has become a recluse. Getting back into life is difficult, she tries to explain to Linny, her neighbor and co-worker, who stands behind her braiding her hair.

Linny would like to help. She has brought swatches of material for drapes and a suggestion for a new color for the walls. Picking out a dress for her friend, she tries to persuade her to go out that night to a lounge where the two of them can "flirt with fat men" (11). She also tries to suggest that Evvy cannot resolve the grief over her loss because she has never resolved the reason for marrying a man thirty years her senior. Was she marrying a father figure? Linny asks. "We had a good time in bed" (8) is Evvy's answer. Proposing an alternate explanation that she knows will be rejected, the late husband's dubious artistic talent, Linny returns to the father-figure explanation. But Evvy will not grant that there was anything odd in the age discrepancy.

Evvy is not being frank with herself. Neither is Linny frank with herself, for she too has an unresolved conflict, at odds with the suggestion about flirting with fat men. With the widow agreeing to go out that night, the women *"giggle and kiss; but the kiss lasts too long and Evvy pulls away"* (11). Linny's reaction is to bolt. Suddenly remembering that some of the townspeople are meeting that night to discuss an upcoming hotel-casino referendum, she cancels their going out and leaves despite Evvy's offer to make more coffee if she will stay. Her hasty exit precludes any conversation that might yield a clue to her reaction, but her explanation for canceling their girls' night out reveals an unresolved conflict in the community. The lakeside town has fallen on hard times with the resort, the principal employer, catering to a clientele of old people. A referendum to convert the resort hotel to a hotel-casino will bring money into the town that will increase wages and property values, thereby making the town a more attractive place to live and work. But since gambling may also impact the town's image, attracting undesirable elements, the community is undecided on how to vote. Hence the meeting to address the referendum's ramifications.

The mode of this opening scene is naturalistic exactitude establishing the following facts: Jimmy's age and the length of time he has been dead; during that period three of Evvy's girlfriends died too. He sketched dogs in charcoal, not pastel. Sixteen of his sweaters are in drawers. Linny recommends Autumn Crocus Blue for the new wall color, and the meeting is at eight that night. Though not facts, the following issues, discussed with varying degrees of development, come under the naturalistic mode: the effect of the referendum's passage on the area's land values and the two women's working conditions, whether drapes or shutters should replace the blinds on Evvy's windows, and whether the bubble wrap, when removed from the ottoman, poses a threat to turtles or frogs if improperly discarded.

The opening scene also establishes the basis for the supernatural mode. Like the women, the town would like to change its image from that of host/ hostess for old people yet is apprehensive about changing. Like the women, the town is divided in attitude toward the proposed change. The co-worker, who supports the referendum, has an idea for a poster for a public-relations campaign whereas the widow, who has yet to commit herself, does not even know whether she will attend the meeting. Furthermore, the women are divided within themselves. Linny wants Evvy to start making the bar scene again with her, but when her friend pulls away from a lingering kiss, she bolts. As the third act makes clear, she is not a lesbian, but she does not know herself at the play's opening. Neither does Evvy, whose contradictions compound as the scene unfolds. She purchased household items but cannot unpack them. She says that nothing is wrong with her emotionally but considers the possibility that stopping her drinking caused her to stop feeling. She says that she is trying to get back into life but has to be coaxed into going out. She professes not to be lonely but calls after her friend to come back, offering to make more coffee and promising not to have to talk.

For Linny, the resolution to the divisions, conflicts, and contradictions will come through the referendum, as the play's title implies and imagery develops. Her poster idea is an image of dollar bills floating down from heaven. In act 2 another neighbor, Peaches, gives his poster idea: an image of a casino coming out of the clouds. "It's otherworldly," he defends the idea. "It, uh, shows the promise of—it promises something" (35). For these two and others in the town, a casino represents the intervention of a force that promises to liberate them from the drabness of their lives, and the promise lies outside them. Since Evvy has not committed herself to the referendum yet is not opposed to it, her position is different from that of the other characters, as the imagery develops in the opening scene. She tells her co-worker that the preceding evening she purchased three photos from a college student who "flies around in a plane taking pictures of people's houses from a distant perspective" (11). Since the student did not call on Linny, who consequently does not have aerial photos of her house to "*lean against the wall*" (7), the implication is that although Evvy is absorbed in her mirror image, she is beginning to move back to see herself from a new perspective. The dual perspective suggests that a liberating force or forces will come from outside her and within her. Thus the process of self-discovery has begun for her because the focus of *From Above*, as it is with *The Goat* and *The Violet Hour*, is not the mystery, the alleged supernatural, as such but the effect on the behavior of the character or characters who encounter it.

The encounter is not reported as in *The Goat*; it is not postponed until the revelation about the foretelling of the future as in *The Violet Hour*. As soon as

Linny leaves, Evvy encounters the mystery—the supernatural mode—in the person of a man *"in his twenties . . . soaking wet"* who, in answer to her question about what he wants knocking at the back door, identifies himself as her husband "Jimmy" (12). The effect is immediate too. In the 1998 Playwrights Horizons production, Patricia Kalember's Evvy was frightened, understandably so as a single woman living alone, locking doors and shutting blinds as Neal Huff's Jimmy moved about the house's exterior knocking to enter, even to trying to make a phone call for help but suddenly stopping when he shatters the back door and is inside the house. Though the broken glass in which he lands does not come from the mirror, so that the critic cannot argue that he literally crosses a surrealist plane to confront her, the archetypal image of water dripping from him suggests that the mysterious stranger has risen from beneath the surface to be with her: that he is the liberating force outside her. She does not, however, scream for help or bolt as Linny did. When he rises from the floor, she stands her ground, talking to him while having him look at himself in the mirror to see the contradiction: a man claiming to be old yet in a young body. He reacts to his image with awe.

Whoever or whatever he is, the mixture of naturalism and supernaturalism works in the mysterious stranger. He behaves naturalistically, explaining that he is wet because he rescued a kitten from the lake. When a van's horn honks, he runs into the bedroom to get his sketch pad so that he can "draw the cat" (13). He does not hide from Roz, another neighbor and co-worker, who comes in from the van to pick up Evvy for work, or flee the house now that others have arrived. With Roz checking the damage from the break-in, he calmly enters the room, wearing a blanket in place of the wet clothes and smoking one of Jimmy's pipes. He offers no explanation to her for his presence; on the contrary, he refers to "our bed" (15)—his and Evvy's—and proceeds to staple the blanket over the broken back door. If he is Jimmy, he is supernatural, a reality he accepts because he is amazed that he is in a young body. As he says at act-1's end, "I'm young now" (27).

The mixture works for Evvy. The mysterious stranger's behavior is naturalistic. When he rises from the floor, he does not attack her; he goes back outside to retrieve the bag with the rescued kitten. When she tells him to look at himself in the mirror, he does, rendering himself vulnerable to an attack from her and provoking his comment that he looks "boyish" (13). And he knows the details of their life together. Hence when Roz arrives, Evvy does not tell her co-worker to get help; she does not even reveal his presence. He does by entering the room smoking a pipe. Evvy does not accept him as a supernatural reincarnation of her husband, yet she does not reject the possibility either. As late as act 3, following his disappearance, she asks Linny, "What if he was Jimmy?" (46) What she does is accept him as a mysterious stranger who in the present answers her needs for the security of her old husband in the past and the challenge of a new partner in the future. After the others who converge on the house leave, because Roz alerts others and friend Sean, a social worker, did pick up on her attempted phone call, Evvy and the stranger calling himself Jimmy are alone. Reminiscing about their life together, he reminds her of how they spent the cold winters in a drab town in which nothing happens "tucked in bed, watching" (25) the videos he made at their summer barbecues. "Come into the bedroom," he proposes with a kiss; she can call in "sick" for one day. Act 1 ends with her response: "You can stay here, if you like. For a bit. I wouldn't mind it" (27).

Though the tension remains constant between the opposing naturalistic-supernatural interpretations of the stranger's identity, his effect on Evvy, which began as soon as he crashed through the back door, steamrolls, for he has awakened the liberating force within her: her imagination. At the opening of act 2, wearing the dress he chose for her, she decides to shop because they are hungry and the pantry is empty. She does not shop often and then only for necessities, but this time she will shop as she imagines the people on the upscale side of the lake do. Not only does she see them in her imagination walking down the store's aisles, she sees herself in her new role in the aisles: "Take whatever appeals to me." If they see something they like, they buy it; she therefore will buy cheeses because she likes an "assortment of cheeses" (30). Her imagination stimulated, she becomes aware of the condition into which she has allowed the house to fall. By act 3 she has redone the bedroom, replaced the old furniture with new furniture, hung curtains, and started painting the living room. Since the house is an image of the self, as in the aerial photographs, she is changing. At the close of act 2, she erases Jimmy's voice from the answering machine and substitutes her own voice. At play's end she tells the stranger that Jimmy is dead and explains the noise of the cocktail blender revving up in the bedroom as caused by a "friend" (49), a reference to social worker Sean, to whose overtures she is responding.

The stranger is also a catalyst for change in other characters in that his presence gets them to stop phoning and beeping one another and to start personally interacting by asking questions about him and Evvy's relationship with him. Declining handyman Peaches' overtures throughout the play, Linny becomes interested in a referendum polling-place worker named Michael. Responding to Evvy's attempt to phone him in act 1, Sean comes to her house. As he is about to leave, they embrace, an embrace that awakens his desire. When she tells him that he is moving too quickly, he defers to her feelings, only to return that evening in act 2 with flowers and his plea to Evvy that since each is alone and "needing, we're needing," he says, they "should try." He sums up not only for himself but for the play: "We should try to find a

common—people have been known to find a common ground. Together"
(38). When he returns with the ingredients for a romantic drink in act 3, which
takes place a few months later, having "waited a respectable period of time"
(48), they try again.

When the focus shifts back to the stranger in act 3, the mystery is solved.
He is a mentally disturbed young man under partial supervision whom Jimmy
had befriended and who learned details of his marriage through their friendship. The late husband was not the first identity the young man appropriated.
Every few months he wanders off and becomes someone else, he confesses
to Evvy in the play's penultimate scene when he returns to apologize. Yet he
is a liberating force in that he speaks for the necessity of interaction as a
means of connecting with life. More so than the other characters, he feels the
need for personal contact to retain a place in the human community, and no
amount of therapy can convince him otherwise. Just before he leaves, he
struggles to remember what his supervision team want him to learn. "We're
not supposed to need other people or—wait, shit, it's something they make
me say every morning—(*Remembering.*)—we're supposed to stand on our
own. Be self-sufficient" (51). Though he is the patient, he knows better than
the hospital staff that he needs interaction, and he knows the demand that puts
on him. Since he works at Burger King, he has to end the conversation with
Evvy. "I've got to go now, in the morning I'm at the drive-through window.
There's more personal interaction there so I need my sleep for that" (51).

Though the mystery of the stranger's identity is solved, another mystery is
not: whether he and Evvy were sexually intimate after they retired to the bedroom at the close of act 1. When he returns for the play's penultimate scene
and asks her whether they were, she does not answer, and since she remains
silent on the issue, the audience cannot know what transpired in the bedroom.
That he showed an interest in her was enough to stimulate her, and he ap-
pealed to her both as a husband with whom she could reminisce about watching videos on cold winter nights and a new partner for whom she could dress
and shop and with whom she perhaps was intimate. *From Above* does not end
on a note of mystery, but it is open-ended. Evvy votes for the referendum,
which passes in act 3 by a slim margin. As she and Sean watch the final count
on television, an image of her house flashes on the screen as a helicopter fly-
ing overhead transmits images of the town being reported on the news. Noting that the image is closer than that in the aerial photos she purchased, she
wonders "what now" (52) for herself and Sean and the town.

In *The Beginning of August*, Donaghy does not flirt with the supernatural as
he does in *From Above*, yet he has a character whose motivation is more mysterious than that of the stranger calling himself Jimmy in that the character
cannot explain herself as a patient in therapy. She has no simple explanation

for herself. The two plays have the same pattern, though. A protagonist so arrested in naturalistic exactitude that she/he is emotionally dead requires a force outside the self to stimulate a force inside the self. The naturalistic reality requires an opposing anti-naturalistic or non-naturalistic reality to generate tension, drama, and liberation.

Before entering *The Beginning of August*, however, we should look at the epigraph to the published text. The story line does not require it because its significance is not in suggesting the theme. Rather, it provides a term that establishes the basis for the naturalistic exactitude, and once that term is extracted, two others will follow. The three terms clarify the situation into which the character who is a mystery surfaces. The epigraph is the seventh and final stanza of Wallace Stevens' "The Idea of Order at Key West." Through the first four stanzas, the speaker with his companion sought to identify the spirit of the song a woman sang as she walked by the sea at Key West. Stanza five is the realization that the spirit is the imagination and that by exercising it, she became the "artificer of the world / In which she sang." Then they "knew that there never was a world for her / Except the one she sang and, singing, made." One does not impose an order onto physical, material reality but discovers an order in that reality the apprehension of which, by appealing to the senses and emotions, makes the experience pleasurable. The imagination is the function for the apprehending. Ministering to the human being's "rage for order," it makes meaningful the otherwise "meaningless plungings of water and the wind" in stanza four; "arranging, deepening, enchanting night" in stanza six, it reconciles the self with an otherwise alien reality.[35]

That imagination has the power to transform the interaction between the self and the world external to the self is a central theme in Stevens' poetry. Imagination also has the power to effect perceptual change in Donaghy's plays, as in *From Above*, where the mysterious stranger's appeal so affects Evvy's imagination that she sees herself shopping again and begins to address the disrepair into which the house has fallen. Imagination, though, is not one of the three terms. The term in the epigraph is a *rage for order* without which one's universe is meaningless. The other two terms are in the poet's *Notes Toward a Supreme Fiction*. They are *imposing order* onto the universe to render it meaningful and *discovering an order* in the universe meaningful to the self, an order with which the self can harmonize its needs.[36] It is the imagination that enables one to discover an order. With these three terms and naturalistic exactitude, we can enter *The Beginning of August*.

The play's situation is that a wife and mother, Pam, has left her husband, Jackie, and three-month-old daughter, Margueretta, forcing him to have someone baby-sit while he is at work until he learns where Pam is and what her intentions are. He arranges with the recently widowed second wife of his

father, Joyce, described as a *"middle-aged woman."*[37] Two characters interact
with her for short periods during the first of the play's two acts. Ben is a
handyman painting the house on a piecemeal basis. His age is not given, although from his talk and behavior he is younger than Jackie, who is described
as in *"his early thirties"* (179), and Joyce refers to him as the "boy with the
paint" (184). Ted, *"about forty"* (194), thought he had an arrangement to mow
the lawn every third Thursday in the summer.

Each of the four characters who appear in act-1's opening scenes has a rage
to order his or her individual situation within the play's situation, though the
naturalistic exactitude is best applied to Jackie's rage. When Joyce tells Ted
that he must stop mowing because the noise will disturb the baby, he protests
that he has an arrangement to mow. When Joyce does not pursue the conversation because his name is not on the list that Jackie gave her of persons with
whom she may talk, he persists until she relents and they talk but in typical
Donaghy dialogue, which is to say that they do not necessarily talk to each
other. She misinterprets as an overture his suggestion that she might find the
vacation of his choice, a cruise, enjoyable. He in turn attempts to correct the
misinterpretation by granting that though he likes women and she is attractive, he likes men too. "That's why me and Jackie got along," he confides,
mentioning their brief affair when "Pam was gone" (200). Joyce is shocked
by the revelation, and he, realizing that she did not know, is angry at himself
for his indiscretion. Agreeing that they should keep the revelation a secret, he
leaves. He is the fourth in the rage-for-order ranking because the rationale for
the ranking is the degree to which the character either imposes order onto reality or discovers order and not the character's motivation or complication.
Ted may have come to the house on the pretext of mowing in the hope of seeing Jackie, but once he realizes his mistake, he accepts the situation. At least
in act 1, he does.

The play opens with Jackie suspending Ben's services until he, Jackie, has
greater control over his situation, at which time he, Ben, can resume painting.
When the latter protests, arguing that having started he should finish, the explanation seems to be a need to be employed because he has no other work.
His inquiry about "Pam" (180), however, implies that he does not think of
himself as a hired hand, an implication reinforced by his calling to Ted from
a window in the house and using "We" (195) to refer to himself and Joyce as
if he were in the same relationship to the family as she is. He wants a closer
relationship not with the family but with Pam, about whom he erotically fantasizes in the passage beginning, "I love Pam. I wish she'd come back" (202).
Since she did not discourage him, if his claims that he once put his head in
her lap for a moment and that she once let him kiss her on the forehead are to
be believed, he intends to stay until she returns in the expectation that her

leaving Jackie if only temporarily means that she will be more accessible. He is not only adjusting to the reality he discovers, but he also hopes to impose his conception of order onto the reality he perceives.

Unlike Ben, who fantasizes about satisfying his need and conceals his intention behind the excuse that he cannot leave because his paint brushes are still drying, Joyce is honest about her need. She feels so lonely that she tolerates Jackie's rage for order, which he reviews for her before leaving: "The towels, the numbers, the contacts, the clean diapers, the schedule of times, feeding, naps—feeding, naps—pick her up every now and then, play with the brightly colored keys, make words or don't—I'm back at six. Six or so" (190). She screams, "For Christ's sake!" when he adds last-minute prohibitions against making food or dust, touching the phone with sticky fingers, feeding the baby sticky candy and alphabetizing, but she consents to stay nevertheless because, in her words, "I feel needed" (191). Being with a man constitutes her reality. To her handheld tape recorder, she composes a New Year's letter that ends with her brooding on her husband's death: "Friends say I'll get used to it. This loss. I don't believe them. I don't believe them! (*beat*) What do friends know about being lonely?" (194) She therefore justifies not talking with Ted, because he is not on the list Jackie gave her, by deferring to her stepson: "He's the man now" (198). Yet given her need to feel connected with people, she cannot comply with the prohibition. She not only talks with Ted, she misinterprets his remarks about a cruise as an ideal vacation, and by exaggerating her connection with Jackie—"I know all about him. . . . A special understanding that goes unsaid" (199)—she leads Ted to confide his connection with her stepson. The shocking revelation gets her in trouble; her reaction to the trouble gets her the second ranking in the rage-for-order hierarchy.

When Jackie returns from work, he is in a good mood. He has had a fax from Pam indicating that she is coming home, and Joyce appears to have observed all the regulations. Offering her a beer, he urges her to stay until Pam arrives. He thanks her for helping out. He even repeats an image she used earlier when she pointed out a similarity in their situations in that each still uses "we" when referring to the absent partner: "I still say 'we' too [about herself and her dead husband]. Now we're 'we.' Us" (192). He did not pick up on the image then, but hours later he does: "I was thinking also what you said before. (*beat*) That now we're 'we'" (206). Yet as he grows impatient and then angry at Pam's failure to return, she lets slip the possibility that his wife might have a reason for staying away. Suspicious, he probes until she admits that she was talking with Ted, at which point he forecloses any consideration of the more permanent baby-sitting arrangement he suggested earlier. "That's it, it's over!" (213)

Joyce, however, will not let the relationship end, for she will not be re-manded to the emptiness of her house where she would be "alone . . . with boxes" containing his "father's things" (214). Since he is unyielding, she threatens to expose his past should he become involved in a child-custody battle with Pam. She is still being honest about her need and her intention ex-cept that now she is imposing her rage for order onto the situation. Not only will she continue to baby-sit, she will live in his house on a temporary basis cooking and cleaning. "You'll see Jackie," she assures him. "We'll be us. We have to be—we're the only ones left" (215).

Jackie qualifies for top ranking in the rage-for-order arrangement. The first scene of *The Beginning of August* corresponds to the first scene of *From Above* in that each presents a character struggling to adjust to the loss or ab-sence of the partner with Jackie the more deserving of sympathy because his wife's absence is recent and unexpected and he has a baby to care for. Evvy and he also are struggling with contradictions in their makeup. The widow says she wants to get back into life, for example, but does not leave the house except to go to work. Her single physical quirk is pulling away from the pro-longed kiss. In the section on *From Above*, I discussed the pulling away on Linny's part as perhaps a fear of latent lesbianiam in her, but the fear could be in Evvy too. The contradiction is so physically manifested in Jackie, how-ever, that fits and starts could describe his behavior. As the play opens, he is setting up the backyard in preparation for Joyce's arrival to baby-sit so that he can leave for work. As played by Garret Dillahunt in the Atlantic Theater Company production of 2000, his movements were almost spasmodic in opening a lawn chair, placing it in the center of the backyard lawn, looking down the driveway to the unseen street, opening a sun umbrella, placing it, looking down the driveway, and so on. The most pronounced quirk was reaching toward the bassinet, which he had brought from the house, but pulling back, unable to hold his sleeping daughter. And the quirks are verbally manifested too. As he is about to leave, Joyce tells him to say "good-bye to the baby," but he declines because "she doesn't need a lot of handling" (192). Neither does he call his daughter by name; the audience learns the name, Marguerretta, from Joyce.

The setting up of the yard is realistic, yet as Jackie fills in lawn furniture and bassinet, he begins the mode's transformation into naturalistic, particularly as verbal images supersede visual ones, duplicating the process in *From Above* though to a greater degree. The earlier play opens with Evvy and Linny sur-rounded by unpacked furniture. As they talk, they establish the naturalistic ex-actitude with Jimmy's age, specific improvements to the house, and the like. Rage for order would be an inaccurate term for them but not for the characters in *The Beginning of August*, each of whom has a rage that contributes to the naturalistic exactitude, though Jackie's is the most exact. Once he begins with his lists and regulations, he reveals not only his rage for order but his imposition of order. He is a classic ruled surface struggling to keep an unruly subsurface under control, and the subsurface cannot simply be his bisexuality because he has already actualized it with Ted. The second act reveals more about the conflict within him prefigured in his prohibitions against personal contact. Donaghy has a nice contemporary touch in his plays about characters phoning one another and recording messages for one another in lieu of interacting. In *From Above* the phoning and beeping are not oppressive; Jackie's prohibitions are exclusions. In addition to the list of persons with whom she is permitted to talk, Joyce is to ignore Ben, discourage conversation with the neighbor, Mrs. Barnes, because they will not be able to get rid of her, and refrain from inviting to the house a friend she has not seen in years who resides in the area because if one friend is allowed to visit, others will follow. The exclusions do not include his daughter. His periodically reaching for her only to pull back does, though he does not mean to exclude her. The conflict between his desire to connect with life and his imposed rules for connecting exerts so intense a pressure that it affects his speech and body.

If his imagination were awakened, his perception of reality—his rage for order—could change. The one time the audience sees him attempting to use his imagination occurs after he returns home and asks Joyce to stay at least until Pam arrives. To create a natural scene for the latter to walk in on, he asks his stepmother to read aloud from the catalogues his wife enjoys collecting. The result is anything but natural because once again he is imposing his order onto reality. This is the scene that backfires on him. When Pam does not appear, he raves about her leaving him, rhetorically asking, "What did I do? (*beat*) The thing I don't get is what did I do?" (210) Joyce makes the mistake of suggesting that his wife might feel that she has a reason for staying away. Threatened with expulsion, she threatens him with exposure of his relationship with Ted. Silenced, Jackie walks down the driveway to the street a beaten man because he does not want to lose the child in a custody battle, yet to keep her, he must surrender to another's rage for order. When his stepmother follows him, the stage is momentarily empty before the lights come down on act 1, but in those moments something happens that changes the play.

More than once in the act, there is movement on the other side of the backyard fence separating the property from that of Mrs. Barnes. At one point, for example, a hand extends a plate of cupcakes over the fence, which Ben accepts. Since Jackie warned Joyce about the neighbor's attempt to get friendly, and since act 1 is naturalistic, the audience assumes the hand belongs to Mrs. Barnes until a door in the fence opens and Pam steps into the empty yard.

How does the audience know it is Pam? The age of the actress and as played by Mary McCann in the Atlantic Theater Company production, the character was lost but not in the sense of location. She knew where she was but not who she was. She knew she was Pam, but she had the look of a confused, even bewildered, woman staring at the bassinet but not moving toward it as the scene ended. And Donaghy makes this scene more charged than its counterpart in *From Above*, where the mysterious stranger calling himself Jimmy splits the focus with Evvy, who is trying to phone her friend Sean as he crashes through the door. Pam is alone. She is both the confused, frightened inhabitant in that the yard is hers and also the stranger. Another difference between the two plays is that Jimmy disappears in act 2, not to return until act 3, which takes place months later. When act 2 of *The Beginning* opens, Pam is gone, leaving the baby in the bassinet, not to return until later in the act, which takes place that night. The audience does not forget her, however, because more than once a flashlight beams from Mrs. Barnes' yard.

Donaghy is slowly yet surely transforming a play naturalistic in act 1 to a mixture of modes, and though Pam is the agent of the change, it involves all of the characters. While she is gone, the play widens the causes of Jackie's conflict until it is collective rather than individual and universal, historical, and existential rather than personal. The change in the yard from act 1 to act 2 is apparent as soon as act 2 opens. With empty beer bottles, a bottle of tequila, and the television set on the grass, the yard is in disarray. Act 1 reflected Jackie's order in Pam's absence. Act-2's opening reflects the three other characters' orders that fill the vacuum left by the absence of his order, which Joyce's threat of exposure forced him to retract. Each of the three imposes his or her order to satisfy his or her need, the result of which is disorder. We can take them in the same ranking as before.

When Ted, responding to Joyce's message on his answering machine, confronts Jackie, he volunteers to baby-sit because Joyce is not doing a good job. His testimony that she caused the baby to be bruised gives the stepson a reason for terminating the arrangement with his stepmother. But Ted's motive is not simply securing employment, although he has experience sitting for his younger sisters that Joyce does not have. He hopes to develop a relationship with Jackie based on their one episode together. That hope is part of a larger need. When Jackie dismisses the episode as "nothing," Ted repeats, "Don't say 'nothing,'" the second time emphasized with an exclamation point and moments later repeats, "You tell me I mean something," the second time also emphasized (222–23).

When Ben is not painting the fence, he is drinking, sleeping off his drunkenness, or vomiting. He is different in act 2 but only in the sense that he no longer masks his intention. Told by Jackie that he should be home, he fires

back, "Why should I go home? . . . I'm a young person with energy who loves
Pam! That should be taken into account when old people say go home!"
(230–31)

Joyce would have Jackie's home be her home. To that end she watches
Margueretta, cooks some food he can heat up, and washes sheets and towels
and not because the activities are pretexts. She is a responsible person but one
whose heart is not in those activities. Hence she contributes to the disorder by
doing what her heart is in: drinking with Ben, phoning Ted, and inviting old
friends to the house. To Jackie's charge that she is incompetent by causing the
baby's bruise, she explodes, "You can't be incompetent in a job you never
wanted! I wanted to be married! I didn't want children!" (225) Having a partner without the burden of children meant being "popular. Invitations every
weekend, someone's house, cocktails" (220). Widowed in a world of couples,
she so feels the loss of her partner and their social life that she speaks for all
the characters when she says that she wants to "belong" (218). She therefore
resists the dismissal, not by drunken belligerence, although she has been
drinking, but by appealing to a sense of family and community. "What happened to homesteads?" she asks, going on to indict the breakup of the family
as the cause of the contemporary malaise. But her late husband's son will
have none of her argument: "We are not related!" (231–32)

Once Jackie learns that the baby is bruised, he has a reason for dismissing
Joyce, and no longer fearful of her blackmail threat, he can revert to his original order, the one that ruled in act 1 before act-2's disorder displaced it, the
one he imposes in his struggle to control the conflict within him. If the conflict's cause were personal and individual, it would stem from his mother's
death when he was a child and his father's remarriage, a union that left him
more or less to fend for himself. Yet the conflict is larger than personal, individual issues. It is between the need for permanence and stability, which is
every human being's rage for order, and the recognition that everything in life
is temporary and unstable. Jackie's conflict is the most extreme one in the
play because he represses under his imposed order the acceptance of life's
mutability, just as he represses that part of himself that is mutable and disorderly: his instinctive, sexual, emotional nature.

At this juncture Pam, who earlier came through the fence and took the
baby, reenters the yard to continue the play's transformation from naturalistic
to a mixture of modes. I see a similarity between Donaghy's character and the
subject of that strange, haunting tale of Nathaniel Hawthorne, "Wakefield,"
named for a man who absented himself one day from his wife, "took lodgings
in the next street to his own house, and there, unheard of by his wife or
friends, and without the shadow of a reason for such self-banishment, dwelt
upwards of twenty years. During that period, he beheld his home every day,

and frequently the forlorn Mrs. Wakefield."[38] A comparison between the tale and the play yields two points of similarity. As soon as the tale's narrator tries to understand Wakefield, he concludes that he lacked imagination; he had to lack the faculty because he could not have planned to stay away for twenty years. He planned a day or two or three, but once he took the initial step, he initiated the difficulty of returning, and each succeeding day increased the difficulty until he inhabited another universe. He could not imagine the "transformation." Could he, he never would have strayed, for the first night he was gone wrought the "great moral change," and not only could he not foresee it, when the change took place, it was a "secret from himself" (135). The Hawthorne scholar Hyatt H. Waggoner sums up this point: "No one knew, no one can know, Hawthorne makes clear, why Wakefield went off by himself, not even Wakefield."[39]

Donaghy's Pam knows that something had to have happened for her to drive from the store where she was shopping to Mrs. Barnes' house, there to seclude herself while beholding her house, but she does not understand what happened. She is aware that a woman can suffer postpartum depression, but she does not advance that diagnosis as an explanation for her condition. She does not advance any explanation, other than feeling overwhelmed by her responsibilities, because she cannot explain her flight. Zola's naturalistic explanations do not apply. "I don't know what I've done," she admits to her husband, repeating the admission moments later (233–35). Like Wakefield, she is a mystery to herself.

For the second point, "Wakefield" illustrates Hawthorne's theme of the consequences of withdrawal from the human community. By dislodging himself from his place next to his wife's bosom, the man who took lodgings in the next street lost his place in her heart. By absenting himself from love and friendship, he forfeited human beings' common fate for an uncommon but terrible one. The tale ends with the narrator's reminder of the risk a man takes by stepping aside from the relationships and interactions that give him his significance. "Like Wakefield, he may become, as it were, the Outcast of the Universe" (140).

Pam is the one in *The Beginning of August* who absents herself from her partner and home, yet she is not the one at risk of becoming the outcast from the human community. That is, Donaghy splits the Hawthorne conception of Wakefield between her and Jackie. She does not understand why what happened happened, but she knows that "something has happened" (235). Conscious of a change in herself, she knows she has needs. She needs help; she needs "to be home"; she misses "affection" (236). She also knows that she is not ready to be a mother. If she has to be, she tells her husband, she will return to Mrs. Barnes' house. Lodged next door, Pam experienced the "transformation," the "great moral change" (Hawthorne 135) that Wake-field does not undergo; she came to empathize with the woman whom Jackie warned Joyce not to engage in conversation. Feeling disconnected from the world, she could see herself in the older woman, alone and dis-connected, haunting the "attic, the yard, under the stairs by her telephone table. Sitting, pointing a flashlight at the phone. That's how mothers end up. Children scattered" (237). She therefore understands the need of Ted, Ben, and Joyce to belong to a family, and she wants them to stay.

When Jackie objects because they are excluded from the categories that for him constitute a family—husband and wife, for example—she suspends the categories. Although she does not engage in poetic discourse, she says in ef-fect that husband and wife are metaphors whose meanings are not fixed. She, for instance, wants to return as the wife, but that metaphor does not mean that she will sleep in the same bed with him. "At first" she will be "in another room. For a time" (241). She wants Ted to be a friend, and since she saw him embrace the man hired to mow the lawn, she expects that he too wants Ted to be a friend. Joyce, whom she sees as a member of the family, can stay in Mrs. Barnes' house while the older woman is in the hospital. The arrangement will be good for Joyce, who will not have to return to her empty house; for Mrs. Barnes, who will not have to worry about her house being vandalized in her absence; and for herself, who will have as a neighbor a friend and relative on whom to rely for support.

The man who would ignore Ben and discourage Mrs. Barnes because they do not fit into his scheme of reality thinks in categories; for him husband and wife are designations whose meanings are fixed. A wife, no matter what her psychological or physical need is, sleeps next to her husband. Before they go into the house therefore, he has to know in what designations they will enter. "We should—we should—what? Chart it out—in our heads, at least. Is Ben between me and Ted and you? Is that what this is all about? Will you tell me?" (242) Pam cannot. Not only does she not think in categories, it is the catego-rizing of shopping lists and household duties from which she fled the store and the house ruled by rational constructs when the something that happened to her happened in her "head, from thinking all this" (234). Since she cannot impose an order because she is trying to recover from her own disorder, he summons his order, even though the summoning exacerbates his conflict. De-spite envying the furnishings and keepsakes that give Ted's place a "homey" atmosphere (227), he orders everyone off his property, an expulsion that would leave him with only the baby and necessities. "I'M TELLING YOU WHAT'S WHAT! It won't be all—this MESS!" (243) is his ultimatum, re-ferring to the physical mess that the others have made of his property and the moral disorder that they have brought into his life.

Unlike Pam, Jackie does not know that he is sick and needs help, for he and not she is the contemporary counterpart of Hawthorne's Wakefield, who, unable to imagine the psychological and moral consequences of his act, would not only isolate himself from the human community but also his daughter. Knowing in her head that she is sick, Pam, like the stranger in *From Above*, knows in her heart that belonging—being needed and helping others in need—will cure her. Returning from withdrawal, she actualizes an alternative to the others' rage for order, for she is the contemporary counterpart of the speaker of a Stevens poem who discovers the imagination. She discovered hers by empathizing with Mrs. Barnes and by observing reality as she could not when she was overwhelmed by it. That is, by stepping back from her situation, she gained a new perspective on it. She has not yet perceived an order in the reality, but her perception has altered. From her perspective overlooking the house and yard, she saw the potential for a community in the persons who gather there with her husband and child, and she sees the potential in such a community for helping one another to feel that they belong. Yet she can only resist her husband's exclusionary measures. She cannot force him to alter his perception. That change must come from within himself.

It does when for the first time, Jackie holds Margueretta. He has the sensuous experience that in a Stevens poem empowers the imagination. Feeling the life in the baby's body, her reality, pressed against his body, he responds with his heart as characters in Hawthorne's fiction must if they are to be released from solitary confinement. He does not reverse himself because such a resolution would be false. He still insists upon order, and he still imposes his order by assigning each a role in the community they will form. Yet when he says, "Until we decide differently," he acknowledges that they are all empowered to discover new orders, and when he asks, "Is everything, for now, in order?" (246), adding a prepositional phrase to the question he asked Joyce that morning, "Is everything in order?" (184), he acknowledges that his order is temporary. He even calls Margueretta by name. His imagination awakened, he is beginning to change.

Jackie's imagination is awakened by the encounter with his wife's reality as well as his daughter's reality, for the Pam who reenters the yard in act 2 is not the woman he knew or thought he knew before her disappearance. She embodies the unruly subsurface: the inner reality that resists categorization, that rebels against the ruled surface's domination, and that is necessary to have a multivocal drama, for should she disappear permanently, *The Beginning of August* would revert to what it was in act 1—a play of naturalistic exactitude—or what it was in act-2's opening—a play disintegrating into autonomous disorders. A mystery incarnated in characterization without being supernatural while being anti-naturalistic or non-naturalistic, Pam is instrumental in saving her husband and the play. His encounter with her takes the tension to a new level of intensity, but it is an intensity that leads to a new union of the characters and the play's modes. Mystery is restored, meeting the objection to naturalism implicit in Ludlam's *The Artificial Jungle*.

As Jackie steps toward the house at play's end, the *"sprinklers go on, shooting up around the perimeter of the yard"* (247), an image to remind the characters and the audience that life is unpredictable and therefore filled with tension. So too is theatre that is more faithful to life than a mere reproduction of its surface unpredictable and therefore filled with tension because life is the interaction of the ruled naturalistic surface and the unruly non-naturalistic subsurface, the explicable and the inexplicable. Demastes' argument that the interaction of disorder and order is creative can be applied to the plays in this study, most obviously perhaps those by Ludlam and Wellman, Foreman and Donaghy. "Chaos is increasingly being seen—again—as a dynamic blending of disorder *and* order, not as the entropic, final result of *degenera*tion but as embodying the loop and cycle of constant generation, degeneration, and regeneration. To the static 'being' of order and the eruptive 'nonbeing' of randomness has been included a vast middle realm, the 'becoming' of chaos."[40]

NOTES

1. Edward Albee, "The Sandbox," in *The Sandbox and The Death of Bessie Smith* (New York: Signet-NAL, 1960), 9. Hereafter to be cited parenthetically.

2. Edward Albee, *The Goat or, Who Is Sylvia?* (New York: Dramatists Play Service, 2003), 14. Hereafter to be cited parenthetically.

3. Edward Albee, "Borrowed Time: An Interview with Edward Albee," by Stephen Bottoms, in *The Cambridge Companion to Edward Albee*, ed. Bottoms (Cambridge: Cambridge UP, 2005), 239.

4. Albee, 239.

5. John Kuhn, "Getting Albee's Goat: 'Notes toward a Definition of Tragedy,'" *American Drama* 13, no. 2 (2004): 5.

6. Linda Ben-Zvi, "'Playing the cloud circuit': Albee's Vaudeville Show," in *The Cambridge Companion to Edward Albee*, 197, note 33.

7. J. Ellen Gainor, "Albee's *The Goat*: Rethinking Tragedy for the 21st Century," in *The Cambridge Companion to Edward Albee*, 205.

8. Friedrich Nietzsche, *The Birth of Tragedy*, in *The Birth of Tragedy and The Case of Wagner*, trans. Walter Kaufmann (New York: Vintage, 1967), 65–66.

9. Ruby Cohn, "'Words; words . . . They're such a Pleasure': (An Afterword)," in *The Cambridge Companion to Edward Albee*, 229.

10. Nietzsche, 73.

11. Gerald F. Else, *The Origin and Early Form of Greek Tragedy*, Martin Classical Lectures 20 (Cambridge, MA: Harvard UP, 1967), 55–56.

12. Jean-Pierre Vernant, "The God of Tragic Fiction," in *Myth and Tragedy in Ancient Greece*, trans. Janet Lloyd, ed. Vernant and Pierre Vidal-Naquet (New York: Zone, 1990), 185.

13. John Simon, "Baa, Humbug," *New York* 25 Mar. 2002, 134.

14. Aeschylus, *Agamemnon*, in *The Oresteia*, trans. Robert Fagles (New York: Penguin, 1977), lines 1189–1202. For the Furies as winged goddesses, see Lillian Feder, *Crowell's Handbook of Classical Literature* (New York: Crowell, 1964), 148.

15. Kuhn, 15.

16. Gainor, 208, 213.

17. Andreach, *Drawing Upon the Past*, 35–46.

18. Simon, 134.

19. Ben Brantley, "Future As Prologue in Two New Dramas," *New York Times*, 20 May 2003, E1.

20. Richard Greenberg, "The Author's Voice," in *Three Days of Rain and Other Plays* (New York: Grove, 1999), 174. Hereafter to be cited parenthetically.

21. Richard Greenberg, "Life Flows Through It: An Interview with the Playwright," by Steven Drukman, *American Theatre* 15, no. 3 (1998): 20.

22. Herman Melville, "Bartleby, The Scrivener," in *Melville's Short Novels*, ed. Dan McCall, Norton Critical ed. (New York: Norton, 2002), 4. Hereafter to be cited parenthetically.

23. Brendan Lemon, "Unlocking Broadway: Outsiders Seek the Key," *New York Times*, 30 May 1999, sec. 2, 10.

24. Richard Greenberg, *The Violet Hour* (New York: Faber, 2004), 9. Hereafter to be cited parenthetically.

25. Richard Greenberg, "The Busy, Bookish Man of Broadway," interview by Brendan Lemon, *The Financial Times*, 3 Nov. 2003, 12.

26. Alfred Kazin, *A Walker in the City* (New York: Harcourt, 1951), 146–48. *Starting Out in the Thirties* (Boston: Little, 1962), 3. For the interview, see *New York Jew* (New York: Knopf, 1978), 138–40.

27. Jesse McKinley, "Broadway Has a New Heavy Hitter," *New York Times*, 7 Sept. 2003, sec. 2, 6.

28. T.S. Eliot, *The Waste Land*, in *Collected Poems: 1909–1962* (New York: Harcourt, 1963), 61–62, 72.

29. Brantley, "Future As Prologue in Two New Dramas," E5.

30. Foreman, "Rules," in *Paradise Hotel and Other Plays*, 12.

31. Foreman, preface, *Lava*, 315.

32. Ben Brantley, "Jazz Generation Sees the Future: It's Not Cool," *New York Times*, 7 Nov. 2003, E4. McKinley, 6 calls it a "supernatural conceit."

33. Michael Feingold, "Modes of Play," *Village Voice*, 5 May 1998, 151.

34. Tom Donaghy, *From Above* (New York: Dramatists Play Service, 1999), 8. Hereafter to be cited parenthetically.

35. Wallace Stevens, "The Idea of Order at Key West," in *The Collected Poems of Wallace Stevens* (New York: Knopf, 1957), 128–30.

36. For the distinction between imposing order onto reality and discovering it in reality, see Wallace Stevens, *Notes Toward a Supreme Fiction*, in *The Collected Poems*, 403–4.

37. Tom Donaghy, *The Beginning of August*, in *The Beginning of August and Other Plays* (New York: Grove, 2000), 182. Hereafter to be cited parenthetically.

38. Nathaniel Hawthorne, "Wakefield," in *Twice-Told Tales* (Columbus: Ohio State UP, 1974), 130. Vol. 9 of *The Centenary Edition of the Works of Nathaniel Hawthorne*. Hereafter to be cited parenthetically.

39. Hyatt H. Waggoner, introduction, *Nathaniel Hawthorne: Selected Tales and Sketches* (New York: Rinehart, 1950), xx.

40. William W. Demastes, *Theatre of Chaos: Beyond Absurdism, into Orderly Disorder* (Cambridge: Cambridge UP, 1998), xii.

Chapter Four

Naturalism Defended and Three Extraordinary Plays: The Working Theatre, Corthron, Glover, and Foote; Overmyer, Jenkin, and Long

Before concluding this study of the contemporary war against the naturalistic play with three extraordinary plays, the enemy, naturalism, should be permitted to speak for itself, as its opponents have been speaking against it, but through a few kinds of theatre it creates, theatre that without which the contemporary American theatre would be irreparably diminished. The first was a production of The Working Theatre: *City Water Tunnel #3*, written and performed by Marty Pottenger, who identified herself in the 1998 program as a carpenter and trades activist as well as an artist and performer. In the introduction I excluded performance art, and this is performance art, but it was so imaginatively performed that I am including it as an actualization of naturalistic theatre's original mission of creating a set that realizes onstage an everyday work environment. In *Naturalism in the Theatre*, Zola gives as an example teeming with possibilities the main marketplace of les Halles in Paris while listing among other examples "inside a factory, the interior of a mine, the gingerbread market." The criteria would be "detailed reproduction" and "costumes supplied by tradespeople."[1] To quote the 1998 program: "The Working Theatre is dedicated to producing new plays of cultural diversity that explore the lives of working people and the issues they confront in a world of changing values." The Working Theatre is still going strong; to celebrate its twentieth anniversary in 2005, it produced *Disconnect*, which with a cast of four is a play.

Billed as the largest public works project in America, the building of New York's third water tunnel was begun in 1970. The first section, running from Yonkers to Manhattan's Central Park and under the East River into Queens, was opened in 1998. At the time of the performance, a second section was under construction with two more sections planned. On a set constructed by Brendan Atkinson representing a workstation in the tunnel, Pottenger, wearing work clothes, had various props. Most prominent of those she handled were a hard hat and a ladder that she incorporated into her choreography. She also played a video of the chief engineer, Tunnel #3, Department of Environmental Protection, who supplied relevant information. But the best part was her enactments of some of the accidents that killed twenty-four workers as of 1998 and stories that according to the program tunnel workers told her or she wrote from a "brief conversation overheard on an elevator, a shouted greeting yelled out across a construction site, the memory of sunflowers along the wall of a DEP trailer or a tiny photograph in a frame amidst a desk piled with manuals." In different voices with different accents, the stories tell not only of life underground but of the workers meeting, as they go on or come off shifts, in the aboveground trailers where they put on or take off protective gear, play cards, and drink coffee. Each union or function in the project has its own trailer. Membership in a union is frequently family generated with a father bringing in a son or an uncle a nephew, and men outnumber women by a wide margin. The unions tend to be ethnically oriented too with strong Irish and Caribbean representation. As Pottenger impersonates workers relating these oral histories while relating her own, they build a collective experience in which sandhogs, engineers, and administrators identify themselves in relation to their work environment.

The opening scene of Kia Corthron's *Breath, Boom* takes place in a workstation very different from that of *City Water Tunnel #3* with dress and activity very different from those of the tunnel workers The location is a street, and the participants are teenage African-American girls with cornrowed scalps under headbands and wearing guerrilla-styled garb: pocketed shirts with the sleeves cut off, for example. They are gang members, and their activity is disciplining one of them for violating a gang code. They lured the violator, named Comet, to the street by phoning her, an injunction she had to obey though unhappily, as she tells them in the play's opening speech: "*What. (She waits for them to answer. They don't.)* Attitude? Don't even gimme that shit I *told*ju this is my birthday I'd appreciate the night off *please*, Toldju tonight my eighteenth big party *Ring*! Shit! Get the phone. I gotta leave my guests."[2] Too late she realizes that their silence bodes ill so that unable to escape the trap, she is beaten by two members, Angel and Malika, while the leader, Prix, looks on except for administering some blows and the caution, "Don't kill her" (6).

In violence and language, the scene is naturalistic. This study's introduction showed how attacks that Zola's critics directed against *Thérèse Raquin* could be applied to Letts' *Bug*. The attacks could be applied here also. That is, the play concentrates on humankind's baser nature; its characters are animals with nothing human about them. And in diction and expletive, elision and run-on sentences that pause only for words that stand in for complete thoughts and for explosive bursts, the language captures the rhythms of the street. The violence does not cease, however, and neither does the language become more refined when *Breath, Boom* moves indoors. Scene 2 takes place in Prix's bedroom in the apartment house where she lives and where she is the locus of information on rival gangs. While she is talking with Angel and Malika and then Comet, who has been released from the hospital, outside the apartment can be heard the sounds of a fight between Prix's mother and her common-law husband Jerome. Hiding in Prix's closet, the mother hears Jerome enter and, not knowing she is in the closet, come on to Prix only to have her slam "*him against the closet door*" with the words, "I ain't five no more." Suddenly the mother realizes that he abused her daughter, but the teen has no compassion for her mother: "If you weren't always playin' Helen Keller, bitch, you mighta knowed a long time ago" (12–13).

Among Corthron's many talents as a playwright is ending a scene with a line that fixes the scene's characters. In scene 1 Prix stops pummeling Comet when she becomes aware that fireworks light the sky. Angel and Malika stop when they become aware that their leader is looking skyward. "What day's today?" Prix asks. "I dunno," Angel answers. "Memorial Day?" (6) The day is ironic because it is a national holiday celebrating the war dead, yet the three who are looking skyward are standing next to the nearly unconscious body of one of their comrades in arms whom they beat to the ground. The line therefore reveals one of the play's major motifs: the girls' insensitivity—the stunting of their emotional nature.

Scene 2's closing line gives one cause of the insensitivity. Because Prix's mother denied that child abuse was taking place in her home, Prix suffered in silence, shutting down her normal, healthy emotional development until she became the laconic, unfeeling creature she is when the play opens while resorting to violence as a way of striking back at the violence done to her. Child abuse, however, is not the sole cause of the disaffection expressed in violence. Act-1's remaining scenes track Prix's adolescent career in the criminal-justice system. Ordered by her probation officer to visit her mother, in prison for killing Jerome, she sits across from her without speaking while the mother promises upon her release to show her daughter Bronx neighborhoods that are not "just projects and bullets" but "got flowers, butterflies" (14). In a mandatory counseling session, Prix's cellmate, a fifteen-year-old named Cat, talks about growing up in a ghetto overrun by garbage and rats. But the most numbing experience for the audience at the Playwrights Horizons 2001 production was listening to Rosalyn Coleman as Angel identifying the contents of her scrapbook of dead classmates and neighborhood kids who were victims of the omnipresent violence killed, for instance, in drive-by gang shootings while they were playing in the streets. Yet not all the violence is retaliation for the damage done to one's individual soul by others. For many, ghetto life is so stultifying, so destitute of horizons, that violence is their sole experience of self-expression. Relating an emotion told to her by another girl, Cat asks Prix, "The kickin' and smashin' and breakin' bones snap! Somebody lyin' still in a flood a their own blood, somebody dead it gets her all hyped up, thrill thing! And power, them dead you not, *you* made it happen! Them dead, *you* done it! You ever get that high?" (18)

The disclosures of a personal nature such as a scrapbook's contents come from those not totally inured to a life outside the law. Angel has come to the prison to visit her boyfriend and her sister; she and her mother are the only ones who have visited Prix's mother. She also has an independent streak. When Prix asks her about the gang job the next day, she is "takin' the day off" (14), knowing full well since she was involved in Comet's beating that she risks disciplining. To girls more hardened in crime, a counseling session is "talkin' shit" (20). Prix straddles the two groups. She commands so much respect as a gang leader that violence or the threat of it confers self-esteem. To Cat, she is "O.G.": "Original Gangsta" (18). Not given to volubility, she nevertheless has an interior life to go with her rage in killing Jerome in her fantasies, and it is the inner reality that saves her. The girls in the criminal-justice system are expected to internalize the lessons learned in the counseling sessions, specifically that their "errors" are "attributable to social and economic circumstances" of "upbringing as well as to personal choice" (16). In act 1 such lessons are a joke to them, but just as Angel chooses to take a day off, by play's end a thirty-year-old Prix chooses to leave the gang and even reconcile with her mother. The brutality continues in act 2 with some of it very graphic, but with the exercise of free will, *Breath, Boom* ceases to be what it is in act 1: a powerful naturalistic drama in which girls unable to control the social and economic circumstances of their upbringing are driven inevitably to an early death or a life in and out of prison.

This study has been distinguishing between naturalism in the theatre as a mode of production in which sets and costumes, language and behavior exactly duplicate everyday reality and a philosophical position in which the characters cannot understand or control the forces determining their existence; they lack the free will to change their lives. *Breath, Boom* is a naturalistic play in both senses in the first act but only as a mode of production in the second act. Keith Glover's *Dancing on Moonlight* is minimally naturalistic as a mode of production but thoroughly naturalistic philosophically and therefore a good companion piece to Corthron's play as indicated by the following passage. An African-American woman, Neptune, comments to her African-American man, Eclipse, on a scheduled parade to honor an astronaut for his successful flight in outer space. Eclipse disagrees about the flight. It had to be faked because whites—"they"—do not take risks; they use others to test the danger. "Listen baby," he says. "First they'll blast off a dog, then a monkey, then a Nigger, 'fore they even think of sending themselves."[3] Though white culture is invisible in the play, the passage reveals the psychology of blacks in that culture.

Dancing on Moonlight takes place in Harlem in the early 1960s with a prologue that flashes back to the 1930s and a game of craps with loaded dice that culminates with the winner, Dady Jerry, taking the money and running while leaving behind his dead wife, who has just given birth to a son. The loser, Eclipse, raises the boy, Apollotis, as his own in a life of crime, for Eclipse is the lord of a gambling enterprise about to move into the more lucrative world of dealing drugs. But Apollotis wants to convert the bar that is the enterprise's headquarters into a dance club as the first step in forming a string of dance clubs so that he can "be legit" (28) because the time is the beginning of the civil-rights movement and he has become interested in the Black Muslims. His proposal elicits scornful laughter from the others who when not playing Eclipse's gang members double as chorus members. With elements of Greek tragedy, African folk tales, and African-American music that do not fuse, the play's mode is only minimally naturalistic, jumping from street language to poetic reverie, for example.

Dominated by the Darwinian struggle for survival, the play is better integrated philosophically. In forming a string of dance clubs, Apollotis wants to exercise his "choice," only to be told by Eclipse, "You can't do nothing without me. Legit my ass!" (28) At play's end Neptune discloses that she switched the dice in the 1930s craps game so that Dady Jerry would be perceived as cheating and killed. Her explanation to Dady Jerry is "To help my man [Eclipse] reach his potential. Make you let go of all that friendship loyalty shit that would get us nowhere" (73). Reunited with his father, Apollotis wishes he had "more answers" as to his "place" in existence (60). At play's end he has an answer. Of the seven characters, excluding the eighth, who functions as the voice of the chorus, one, Neptune, is left standing. *Dancing on Moonlight* ends in a bloodbath because only in death is there salvation. Life, according to Neptune, is "doing what you have to do to survive. Regardless if you like it or not" (71).

The final play in this group of plays that speak in defense of naturalism is Horton Foote's *The Trip to Bountiful* in the Signature Theatre Company production of 2005. It is included not for a philosophical position but for its imaginative mode of production. Act 1 opens in the Houston apartment of Ludie Watts, his wife Jessie Mae, and his mother Mrs. Carrie Watts. Recovering from his illness that put them in hard times, Ludie and Jessie Mae need the older woman's government pension check to help make ends meet. She, however, has other plans for its use. Since she is determined to see her home in Bountiful before she dies from a heart condition, she needs it to pay for the trip back to the home town. E. David Cosier's set made a realistic play naturalistic. By splitting the stage in half with an invisible wall separating the halves—one side Ludie and Jessie Mae's bedroom and one side the living room that doubled as Mrs. Watts' bedroom—and by filling in the two rooms with furniture, the set created a cramped, even claustrophobic, atmosphere. It also created a bipolar atmosphere with Devon Abner's Ludie as the intermediary between the two women, who do not get along, partly because of the difficult living arrangement and partly because of their different temperaments.

The lights came up on Ludie, unable to sleep, rising from bed next to his sleeping wife, and, after disappearing in the upstage passageway behind the rooms, entering the converted living room where his mother, played by Lois Smith, sat by the window, her mind on Bountiful and desirous of talking about it with her son who, though a loving son, had no memories of it. Awakened, Hallie Foote's Jessie Mae joined them, and once awake talked for most of the two scenes in the apartment but not about Bountiful. Considerate and supportive with Ludie, Jessie Mae was nonetheless apprehensive about any discussion of Bountiful because her mother-in-law had run away before and they had to go after her to stop her before she could leave Houston. Furthermore, she suspected the check had arrived, even to examining the older woman's purse when she was out of the room, yet throwing a fit when the latter found in the bedroom's dresser a recipe that she, Jessie Mae, had asked her to find. Domineering with the older woman, she resented having to act as a warden with her when she wanted to be seeing a movie or having her hair done, shopping or having a soda with a friend in the drugstore: aspects of life that she so rambled on about that the talk contributed to the naturalistic exactitude. Smith's Mrs. Watts had to endure the oppression. She had to swallow her pride and apologize for the recipe incident; she had to lie about not receiving the check and not running away; and she had to be quick in concealing the check, particularly when Jessie Mae, having decided to go out, returned for the money she forgot and almost caught her mother-in-law endorsing it in a scene in which the spectator could feel the tension not only onstage but in the audience rooting for her to escape the repressive environment.

The production benefited from Signature's flexible stage with sections that can be wheeled about to change locations: from the Houston apartment to the Houston bus station where Mrs. Watts meets another traveler, a young woman played in the production by Meghan Andrews. Her role began slowly as a passenger in the waiting room next to whom Smith sat, periodically getting up and hurrying to the door to the street to see whether Ludie and Jessie Mae were approaching. Her nervous energy concerned Andrews' Thelma, putting her in a predicament when Abner and Foote arrived, the latter going on interminably about the problems her mother-in-law caused her. Thelma did not want to lie, and she did not when Ludie asked her about noticing his mother, but sympathizing with the older woman, she seized the opportunity to leave the waiting room and board the bus for a scene in which her role contrasts with that of Jessie Mae.

After a momentary darkness during which the sections of the bus station were wheeled away, John McKernon's lighting came up on Smith and Andrews, seated next to each other on chairs in another split focus except that this split fused into a single focus as the two women discovered each other. Age and experience disappeared. No carping tone surfaced. Sharing replaced concealment and withdrawal into the lonely self, although without each other, they had justification for being lonely. Alone in the waiting room, on the bus Andrews' Thelma could confide in her companion the reason for her dislocation, to live with her family while her husband was overseas, and her worry for him. Alone with her memories in Houston, Smith's Mrs. Watts could relive them with her companion. The scene was luminous: two women traveling together on a bus to Harrison, there to part company, Thelma to continue on to Old Gulf and Mrs. Watts to continue on to Bountiful, on a segment of a journey backward and forward in time that transformed a naturalistic stage.

The next three plays, extraordinary summational plays in the war against the naturalistic play, also transform the stage. This study has already quoted Eric Overmyer's objections to the naturalistic play. Its language is relaxed, its narrative is predictable, and its characters are circumscribed by forces such as age and ethnicity over which they have no control.[4] In short, it is uniform and univocal whereas his play, *Dark Rapture*, is polymorphous and multivocal. For clarity's sake the examination of his play that follows begins with language and proceeds to narrative and motivation, although initially with some overlapping and repetition because it is not a simple, straightforward narrative with recognizable characters speaking everyday language.

Dark Rapture opens on a night fire on a northern California hillside. One man appears followed by a second man. After acknowledging each other and the wonder of such an event, the second man, Babcock, describes another night fire he witnessed. "Big orange tongues a molten magma whatever creepin' down the hillside like some kinda hellacious glacier. Like some kinda red-hot tectonic taffy" so intense it could "melt cars. Asphalt like butter."[5] When he says about the exploding light, sound, and heat in front of them that he has "never seen nothin' like this" (261), the implication is that the previous description was not that of a real event but a surreal one—that is, one to startle and engage the other man's imagination. The other man, whom the playbill identifies as Ray, seems to be literal-minded, for he remarks that the explosions are the resins in the eucalyptus trees catching fire and that he saw many night fires in Cambodia, presumably while serving in the Vietnam War. Yet he startles and engages Babcock's attention, first by professing experience of night fires similar to the one they are witnessing and then by explaining that since a night fire's attraction is its being "out of our control," it is the source of "stories" and "love" (262).

Natasha Katz's lighting and Tony Meola's sound made the opening scene of a brilliant Second Stage Theatre production of 1995–1996 lurid and disorienting with glowing fire and howling wind, sirens and explosions. Overmyer's "charged, shaped, and heightened" language made the scene poetic theatre as opposed to geezer theatre, in Mac Wellman's terminology, dissolving naturalism's conventions of "literalness, preaching to the choir, sentiment, political correctness or polemic, easily explainable motivations or naturalistic dialogue or cliché characters."[6] The scene's prevailing image is fluidity: the description of night fires and volcanic eruptions that "melt" (261) everything in their path. With the one character exhilarated and the other voluble as they watch the spreading fire before Ray ascends the hillside to his house, the scene presents the raging of a force that the two men regard as mysterious because once released it is out of man's control. Their reaction to it and each other the theatre spectator can regard, if not as mysterious, certainly as suggestive. Babcock emerges after Ray emerges and attempts to engage him in conversation, an overture to which Ray does not immediately respond. Neither does he identify himself when Babcock volunteers his name. The latter does not lose interest, though, for he lingers to watch the homeowner ascend the hillside.

The second scene is the visual counterpart to the verbal first scene. The prevailing image is fluidity. A half-naked couple lie in bed in a hotel room in Cabo San Lucas, Mexico, "melting away" in a climate that is "hot and sticky" and under the influence of the tequila they have been drinking. Since they run out of salt, the condiment the aficionado licks from the fist as part of the ritual of tequila drinking, they alternate licking each other's body. They thereby release a force that rages out of control. Closing her eyes and clutching Danny's hair as he licks her, Julia cries out, "Oh my god. Oh fuck" (264).

Scenes 1 and 2 can be thought of as taking place in the fluid subsurface, the reality Wellman calls chaos or anarchy. Scene 3 is the verbal scene in the world of surface reality. Given the scene's opening words, the prevailing image is fixity. Two men are at the site of scene-1's night fire. "X marks the spot" (265), Lexington says to Vegas, indicating the location of what had been the home of Ray and Julia Gaines before the fire. Vegas is not sure, but based on the remaining topographical markers, Lexington is positive. The problem for them is locating Ray Gaines. They know where his wife, Julia Gaines, is. Once they say, "Cabo San Lucas" (266), they identify the woman in scene 2. Babcock's appearance to relate his hillside conversation connects the verbal scenes 1 and 3 and the characters because he identifies the exhilarated man as fitting the description of the man Lexington and Vegas wanted kept under surveillance; Babcock lost him after the fire engulfed him and the suitcases he brought from the house. With the force released in scene 1 having spent itself, the missing Ray is either a "crispy critter" (267) among the corpses emergency teams are digging out of the rubble or he is somewhere other than Cabo San Lucas, the site of his wife's, Julia's, extramarital affair. His absence is a problem because the two men do not know what he knew or knows about the contents of the suitcases. Julia too is a problem because they do not know whether they can trust her. But these are controllable problems, and they see themselves in control. Dispensing Babcock to Cabo San Lucas to keep her under surveillance, they decide to wait until all the bodies are recovered before acting. If Ray did not die in the fire, they will find him even if he changes his name. They believe that no one can change who he or she is, a truth that for them is contained in the maxim, "Wherever you go, there you are" (268).

Scene 4 is the visual counterpart to the verbal scene 3 and, in the opening references to "desalinization" (269), connected to scene 2, the Mexican bedroom scene, as scenes 1 and 3 are connected. It is set in a Los Angeles used-car lot to which two men, Tony and Ron, have come ostensibly to buy a car but actually to confront the salesman, Nizam. Identifying themselves as Armenians, they demand that he identify himself as Turkish. Nizam is reluctant to, not only because having been born in America he thinks of himself as an American of Turkish heritage, but also because he senses that they are looking for trouble. He is right. Since a card in his wallet identifies him as the Honorary Turkish Vice-Consul to Los Angeles, from their point of view he is Turkish as they are Armenian, even though the two were born in America. For them ancestry and not place of birth determines identity, and the card states that he is a representative, albeit honorary, of Turkey. They therefore demand that he acknowledge the Turkish Ottoman Empire's World War I genocide of Armenians in a holocaust resolutely denied by Turkey. They demand, in other words, that he acknowledge that "what happened happened" (273). He refuses, arguing that although he is sorry for whatever that happened, it took place before he was born and therefore "has nothing to do with" him. "That sound like an unequivocal admission of historical culpability to you?" (274), Tony asks Ron, who replies in the negative. Releasing a force he controls, Tony does not decide to wait before acting as Lexington and Vegas decide to do. He takes out his gun and kills Nizam. The gunman's earlier remark to the salesman, "History is a living wound" (274), sums up this scene and the preceding one. Just as the letters in a name or on a card fix or determine identity, so does the past fix the present. History, in the sense of real events on the surface of existence, determines identity.

At this point I want to proceed from the examination of language and its visual counterparts to narrative. With scenes that fade into one another in seemingly unrelated locations with no intervening transitions and two orders of movement, linear and non-linear, the mode of production is cinematic. A summary, introducing two characters the audience has not yet met, will establish the naturalistic plot. Lexington and Vegas are organized crime lieutenants who conspire with Julia, a woman whose trust fund enables her to live in northern California but who needs a bankroll to start a career as a Hollywood filmmaker. She does not bring into her money-raising scheme either her husband Ray, a screenwriting hopeful, or her lover Danny, a stuntman whose sole function is to satisfy her sexually. Tony and Ron are organized crime soldiers, and Julia's subpartners, who have their own agenda for raising money to finance Armenian operations. Max—short for Margaret—Ray meets in his new identity, and Babcock and Renee are characters of shifting identities. Shadowy characters, scheming women, money-laundering mobsters, and twisting, turning action in a rapid succession of scenes add up to play noir, the theatrical equivalent to film noir. One scene alone establishes the film-noir basis. In a sultry greenhouse reminiscent of Raymond Chandler's *The Big Sleep*, though with a different cast of characters, Lexington and Vegas confront Julia, demanding to know why money they advanced her to launder she left in her home, while she was in Cabo San Lucas, to be destroyed in the fire or discovered and taken by her missing husband Ray. Vegas even quotes Chandler. Vincent Canby in his review of the Second Stage Theatre production wrote, "Mr. Overmyer's script is pure film noir, which is far from being pure theater. As you watch it, you have to act as your own cameraman and film editor."[7] Canby did not have the space in which to explain the second sentence, which is that the play lacks a single, authoritative point of view.

Multiple points of view suggest another type of play, which is not unusual in Overmyer's theatre because as Mel Gussow characterized the playwright's work, "his plays are polymorphous, changing shape as they unfurl, catching the audience off guard and festooning the characters with alliteration and onomatopoeia."[8] A quotation provides a lead to this second type. As an epigraph to the afterword from which this study quoted in chapter 1, Overmyer paraphrased a sentence in André Breton's 1924 *Manifesto of Surrealism*: "Perhaps the imagination is on the verge of recovering its rights."[9]

With a strong strain of surrealism in his theatre,[10] the type of play is a surrealistic play.

Surrealism addresses a disconnection or disharmony in the human being brought about by the repression of the irrational expressed in dreams and the imagination, for instance, under the cultural enthronement of reason. Desire manifested as *l'amour fou* liberates because it does not obey rules and regulations. Released, the repressed expression interacts with governing reason to create wholeness by restoring the human being to harmony with himself/herself and the world he/she inhabits. To reveal the disconnection or disharmony and effect the fluid subsurface's release, surrealism explodes, disrupts, and subverts the fixed surface reality, but its goal is a new connection or harmony: a surreality. A surrealistic play seeks to achieve the goal of surreality by juxtaposing discordant images to startle and engage the imagination, thereby generating tension and conflict to cause interaction that initiates a quest for reconciliation in a new synthesis.

The juxtaposing of discordant images to startle and engage Ray's, and the audience's, attention occurs in the opening scene in Babcock's descriptions of "tectonic taffy," "juice" that "dessicates [sic]," and the "heard . . . hush" of "absolute silence" (261–62). I want, however, to prevent any misunderstanding. The study discussed the first four scenes in terms of the opposition of verbal and visual, fluid and fixed, yet these terms are not themselves fixed on characters or scenes; they were applied to indicate emphasis. Babcock is not always fixed or fluid, and neither is Ray; each one's identity shifts because everything in the play keeps shifting. As Gussow wrote, Overmyer's plays change "shape as they unfurl." Babcock's language in the opening scene is more figurative and therefore more poetic than Ray's, yet when the latter says that since a night fire's attraction is its being "out of our control" and therefore the source of "stories" and "love" (262), he affirms the surrealist's belief that the energy that surrealism releases from culture's encasement is the source of creativity. With its glowing fire, the verbal first scene is also visual. Julia's opening speech in the visual second scene is of poetic images beginning, "Cabo. Tequila. White light. Blue and white light" (263).

The emphasis is present, but it is only an emphasis in a particular scene and present for the purpose of establishing oppositions and antinomies, tensions and ambiguities. To the opposition of fluidity and fixity in images and forces that are out of control and kept under control can be added surrealism and naturalism. In the first two scenes, which can be called surrealistic, the language builds in intensity as each scene summons an event in front of the characters that threatens to consume their bodies, Ray's physically and Julia's and Danny's lustfully. In the second two scenes, which can be called naturalistic, the language builds in intensity as each scene summons an event in the past involving the consumption of a body or bodies about which the characters are unsure or in disagreement. And the fourth scene ends with Tony firing a bullet into Nizam's body. The opposition to Babcock's figurative description in the first, surrealistic, scene is Lexington's literal description in the third, naturalistic, scene. Whereas Julia's language as Danny licks her body in the second, surrealistic, scene is an outpouring from the depths of her nonrational, spontaneous being, Tony's language as he converses with Nizam in the fourth, naturalistic, scene is rational and calculating. Yet these oppositions are not attached to the characters for the play's duration. Lexington and Vegas try to fix the location of fluid Ray, just as Tony and Ron try to fix Nizam's position on an event that is fluid to him, but Lexington and Vegas are fluid when it comes to deciding Julia's fate in the greenhouse, just as Tony and Ron are fluid when ordered to kill Babcock.

With these oppositions and antinomies established, *Dark Rapture* develops a new antinomy that contributes to the tensions and ambiguities. Central to surrealism is the antinomy of chance or coincidence and design.[11] When in the opening scene Ray appears followed by Babcock, the latter's appearance seems to be nothing more than coincidence. His lingering to watch Ray ascend the hillside might be a bit odd but not so odd as to arouse suspicion. Only when he reports to Lexington and Vegas is it clear that he is part of a design orchestrated by the two men. That Tony and Ron stop at the used-car lot where Nizam works seems to be an instance of chance. Once they demand to see his wallet, though, they seem to be checking to verify that they have the right man. In these two cases coincidence yields to design, but these two cases are not the whole story.

Scene 5 continues to illustrate this new antinomy while reinforcing the existing opposition of fixity and fluidity. In the Second Stage production, Santo Loquasto's set split the stage into two parallel, simultaneously acted scenes. In one, in Cabo San Lucas, Babcock entered a cafe to sit and watch Danny and Julia while in the other, in Seattle, a woman, Renee, came into an espresso bar, sat, and engaged Ray in conversation. We have to wait before deciding whether chance or design is operating. What can be discussed is the simultaneity of two conceptions of time: one linear, developing from the antecedent of Lexington's ordering Babcock to Mexico, an action in support of the naturalistic plot, and one lateral that is apparently synchronic and simply visually present.

The simultaneity is the fundamental surrealist principle of juxtaposing discordant images. In Elizabeth Deeds Ermarth's analysis, the surrealist principle puts the object of perception "in crisis by radically pluralizing the context in which we perceive it, specifically by removing it from the contexts where we conventionally perceive it and placing it in surprising ones." The consequence of the object's estrangement from its normal order is that it becomes destabilized or unfixed from its "solid"—culturally fixed—"identity"[12]; it becomes fluid. The objects in multiple contexts are the naturalistic and surrealistic plots and characterizations. In the naturalistic plot, two mob lieutenants are trying to recover money, given to Julia to launder, from Ray if they can find him and if he has it; to this end Babcock pursues him. In the surrealistic plot, Ray with Max is trying to change his identity while Babcock with Renee, their identities shifting, pursues. The characters, primarily Ray and Max, Babcock and Renee—but all of the cast to a greater or lesser degree—are naturalistically determined and surrealistically liberated. Before the study can explore this last point, however, it has to introduce one more object that is simultaneously naturalistic and surrealistic. I also want to acknowledge the cast. The production opened with Scott Glenn as Ray, Marisa Tomei as Julia, Ellen McElduff as Max, Jennifer Esposito as Renee, and Dan Moran as Babcock/Nizam. When I saw the play, Casey Biggs was Ray, Pamela Gray was Julia, and Maya Thomas was Renee. The two other roles had not changed. These five actors and all of the cast were superb, playing *Dark Rapture* as a stage noir and naturalistic-surrealistic drama.

The naturalistic object yet to be discussed is the suitcases containing the millions of dollars Julia Gaines is laundering for the mob lieutenants in return for their investment in her production company. She went to Mexico to have an alibi while Ray was to take the suitcases to their destination. He did not know what the sealed contents were, but he knew she was cheating on him. Hence the fire is the chance occurrence that allows him to unseal the cases, making them the surrealistic object, the *objet trouve*:

> What is a surrealist object? One might say roughly that it is any *alienated* object, one out of its habitual context, used for purposes different from those for which it was intended, or whose purpose is unknown. Consequently, any object which seems gratuitously made, without any other purpose than the satisfaction of its maker; further, any created object that realizes the desires of the unconscious, of the dream.[13]

The suitcases realize the desires of Ray's unconscious not only because they afford him the opportunity to extricate himself from a loveless marriage but also because they stimulate his imagination to create a new identity. He explains to Max, the woman he meets in Key West, his reaction when he discovered that the fire destroyed everything he owned: "Gone. Up in flames. Like shedding an old skin. All that baggage. That history. That old life that didn't work. That I'd fucked up from day one. Melted away. I saw myself floating up from the flames like the phoenix. I could walk away from all that. Spit out the ashes. Reinvent myself" (291). Although Ray reinvents himself, he is wary about what he reveals about his identity. He is Ray Avila to Renee, the woman in Seattle with whom he is intimate and who reappears in New Orleans. He first tells Max he is Ray Gaines when he tells the story from which the preceding passage is quoted and then says that his "real name's Ray Avila" (293) and that the story did not happen to him but is a screenplay he "wanted to try . . . out" on her (293). To neither woman does he say anything about the money, but I want to say to the reader that he/she should note Ray's desire to shed "history" because history and imagination constitute the play's encompassing antinomy. History is naturalism's fixed, determining surface reality whereas imagination is surrealism's fluid, liberating subsurface reality. If we construct a spectrum with imagination at one end, history at the other end, and their union in the middle, we can see how *Dark Rapture* dramatizes their roles in the making of identity, bearing in mind, however, as we proceed from narrative to motivation that placement on the spectrum is not absolute but relative to the situation and the other character or characters.

Nizam and the two mob soldiers, Tony and Ron, form a set of juxtaposed discordant characters. The used-car salesman appears in only one scene. They appear in two and briefly in a third. In the second they are sent to kill Babcock, who trades them money and weapons for their Armenian agenda in return for his life; in the third they report back to Lexington and Vegas. Nizam is at imagination's end of the spectrum. Because the past is "ancient history" that has "nothing to do" with him (272), he feels secure in his American identity when scene 4 opens, yet his imagination has failed him. Too late he realizes he should have changed his name to "George" (271). Ray does not change his name, but Ray is common whereas Nizam is not. Furthermore, he carries a card in his wallet identifying him as Honorary Turkish Vice-Consul. And when he becomes wary, he claims that he was born in an "Armenian neighborhood" in Los Angeles (272), a claim that to Armenian descendants Tony and Ron is transparent and provocative. The two mob soldiers are at history's end of the spectrum. Lacking imagination with Nizam, they cannot perceive him as anyone other than a member of a nationality whose ancestors killed their ancestors. Since "history is a living wound" (274), they retaliate.

The next set of juxtaposed discordant characters, moving in from the spectrum's ends toward the middle, consists of Julia and Lexington and Vegas. Aside from scenes with her lover and collecting insurance money from her lawyers, she appears in scenes with them, her partners in the money-laundering scheme. She wants to create a new identity as a filmmaker, a person who films acts of the imagination. To get started in that career, she contracts with the history of organized crime's involvement in illicit activities for the bankroll she needs. Yet she does not capitulate to that history. Part of the money that the lieutenants transfer to her she invests with Tony and Ron for the high percentage of return they promise her. Her imagination is so audacious, given the risk she takes with mob money, it commands the lieutenants' respect. "I like your balls," Lexington confesses to her in the greenhouse. "I have to admire your balls" (289). He and Vegas do not want to leave the mob to create new identities, which would be impossible anyway because the mob would not let them walk away knowing what they know about its history. They contract with her because they like the idea of being associated with the industry that films acts of the imagination; the association enhances their images, their identities. As Vegas, reviewing their arrangement, says to her, "Convenient and profitable for both parties. A little glamour. Could rub off, who knows. Maybe you win an Oscar. Thank us, your acceptance speech. My good friends, colleagues" (287).

Of the four remaining principals, Ray and Max are a team on imagination's side of the spectrum while Babcock and Renee are a team on history's side, though both teams are close to the middle. Unlike Nizam, who grants that something happened but will not acknowledge its relevance to him, Ray will not grant that anything happened. Denying the history the lieutenants construct for him saves his life in a scene in a New Orleans hotel that is an obvious counterpart to the Los Angeles used-car lot. The lieutenants do not know how to interpret his denial of every statement they make about his identity as Ray Gaines. They suspect his passport identifying him as Ray Avila is forged, but if they shoot him when Lexington draws his gun, they cannot be sure they killed the right man. Of course, luck plays a role too. They would have to kill him and Renee, who is with him, somewhere other than in the hotel room, and they would have to kill Julia, whom they bring into the room but who, to save her own life, denies he is her husband.

Unlike Julia, who wants to produce creations of other people's imaginations, Ray intends to produce his own creations. Her imagination is audacious; his is unrestrained. In the passage quoted earlier, he believes that the fire set him "free" from "all that baggage. That history" (291): all the traditional determinants of identity such as place of birth and education, marital status and previous employment that one carries through life. The line that sums up his and Max's position as they head for Grenada at play's end is "From here on in we can make it up as we go along" (315). Since Max at this point knows about the money, they will need a history consistent with their new lifestyle. It will be a history they invent.

Unlike the mob soldiers, who demand an acknowledgment from Nizam, Babcock and Renee take a different tack with Ray. They too want an acknowledgment of what happened during the fire, an acknowledgment that includes the money's existence, but their strategy is to win his confidence. Renee tells him stories in the hope that he will unburden himself and confide in her about the fire and the suitcases' contents. Her stories are grounded in real events in the histories of Cuba and America—her great-grandfather working in the cigar factories in Ybor City, the "Cuban quarter of Tampa" (281), José Marti's role in the revolution for Cuba's independence, and Kennedy's assassination—not only to invest her stories with authenticity but because she and Babcock are steeped in history. If the audience accepts only a part of what the two say as truthful, that part is impressive, for he claims to be José Marti Chibas Valenzuela, whose family aligned itself with Marti in the revolution, and he was able to trade arms with the two mob soldiers for his life, which implies connections with arms merchants. Of course, not all of what they say can be believed, but even discounting his alleged role in the Kennedy assassination, they are still cloaked in mystery.

Take Renee's appearance in the Seattle espresso bar in scene 5, the split-stage scene in which she enters the bar, takes a seat, and identifying herself as Renee Valenzuela strikes up a conversation with Ray. When he later asks her about her presence there, her reply is that it was a chance meeting. Design is another possibility, confirmed by act-2's closing scene in which she and Babcock are together. The latter could have lied to Lexington and Vegas about losing Ray in the fire and smoke but instead followed him to the airport to see the flight he boarded and then sent Renee to track him down by checking Seattle hotels, even though that scenario strains credulity. What one makes of their relationship in act 1 depends on how one interprets the simultaneous staging in which she converses with Ray while Babcock observes Julia and Danny in a Cabo San Lucas cafe. Yet regardless of how the spectator interprets scene 5—as naturalistic, surrealistic, or both; as design, chance, or both—Babcock and Renee are linked, though the link develops as the plots develop.

So too is Babcock linked with Ray. In trading arms and money for his life, he "agreed to leave the country. Change my name. Cease and desist" (316). Thus with the exception of the money that Ray and Max have, his situation parallels theirs. Ray has the freedom and the imagination but needs a history for his new identity as a traveler. Long on history but short on capital, Babcock needs imagination with which to invent a new identity. The two men with the two women need each other, a need that Ray understands only naturalistically in that the mob money he has makes him a target. I realize the argument is circular. He does not understand the surrealistic plot because it is not a matter to understand. The naturalistic, linear plot is the rational, surface reality; the subsurface reality drives the surrealistic, non-linear plot. By dramatizing both, however, the play dramatizes their inseparability.

Dark Rapture opens with Ray's appearance at the hillside fire. Toward the end of act 1, he relates to Max how he felt "blessed" when he saw the fire because it freed him from the past. "I could walk away from all that. Spit out the ashes. Reinvent myself." Yet as soon as he appears, seeing in the catastrophe the opportunity to escape the "old life" (291), Babcock *"appears out of the darkness"* talking about watching a catastrophe such as the lava flow from a volcanic eruption "comin' toward you. Like sheer fuckin' inevitability. Lurchin' outa the dark rapture" (261). In the naturalistic plot, Babcock's presence is inevitable because Lexington and Vegas have him keeping Ray, the husband of the woman to whom they entrusted money, under surveillance. In the surrealistic plot, his presence is inevitable because he is Ray's shadow: the part of his life that Ray would relegate to his unconscious but that will not accept denial, that like gnome Gene in Greenberg's "The Author's Voice" demands acknowledgment.

Renee's counterpart is Max. When Ray relates to her how he saw in the fire the opportunity to shed his old life, she understands the impulse. "I've been there once or twice myself. Light out for the territory and don't look back. It's very American" (292). By equating Ray's desire to escape the past and Huck Finn's desire to escape civilization's constraints, expressed in the closing paragraph of Mark Twain's *Adventures of Huckleberry Finn*, Max makes the impulse to reinvent oneself ingrained in the American character, but ironically she also makes the impulse childish. It is so ingrained that the American Dream has come to mean the opportunity to invent or reinvent oneself. History is Old World; ancestry, for example, determines the inhabitant's identity and the role or roles to play in life reserved for that identity. Imagination is New World; the inhabitant invents or transforms his or her identity. It is also childish, however, to think that one can create himself/herself divorced from all of the determinants of identity that fall under the rubric of history.

The final scene takes place in Bequia in the Grenadines. "Retired" and "rich," Ray and Max decide to visit a few of the neighboring islands and then "winter in Grenada" (314). Their euphoria leads Max to declare, "From here on in we can make it up as we go along" (315). The words are no sooner spoken than Babcock appears, claiming "coincidence." Denying his name is Gaines but acknowledging that the three of them were momentarily together in a Key West hotel before a hurricane made landfall—by allowing him to escape, Babcock had a contract put out on him by the mob lieutenants—Ray expresses his hope as he and Max are about to leave that they "never meet again." Babcock's reply is cautionary: "Watch your back. You never know what's out there, lurchin' in the dark rapture." At the sound of the words spoken in the opening scene, Ray acknowledges that he was on the hillside watching the night fire. "Thought so," says the other man (316).

As soon as Ray and Max leave, Renee joins Babcock, now identifying himself as José Marti Chibas Valenzuela. In act 2 her link with him is established, but based on what they say to others, the relationship is that of daughter and father. Yet when she enters, she gives him a "*long kiss on the mouth*" (317), paralleling the kissing Ray and Max engaged in while planning their itinerary. Their passionate kiss notwithstanding, Babcock is not forthright with Renee. To her question about the persons with whom he was conversing prior to her entrance, he answers, "Tourists" (317), paralleling the exchange between Ray and Max, for he was not forthright with her about his identity. When she expressed her hope that someday he would tell her who he really is, he replied, "Maybe" (315).

The scene's final parallel is in the couples' destination. Babcock proposes to Renee that in the morning they leave for Grenada, and she accepts. Rather than resolving antinomies and ambiguities, the scene compounds them. In the naturalistic, linear plot, Babcock will pursue Ray because he is convinced he is Ray Gaines, Julia's husband, and not Ray Avila as he claims to be and because he is convinced he has the millions of dollars of mob money. Yet the play ends on the surrealistic, non-linear plot because no rational explanation can account for his proposal to travel to Grenada, the destination Ray proposed to Max before he arrived. The Second Stage production emphasized the surrealism. Its final image was a smiling Dan Moran's Babcock, or José Marti Chibas Valenzuela, making himself comfortable on the hotel patio as he relished the prospect of a continuing chase.

A production should end on the surrealistic plot because Ray's wish that he and Babcock "never meet again" is naive. Babcock and Renee have become part of his history that can be repressed but cannot be willed out of existence. That is, the wish invokes the control and order of existence that surrealism delights in dethroning. Two interpretations come out of the final scene, each one based on an elaboration of surrealism's original definition. In the 1924 *Manifesto of Surrealism*, André Breton defined surrealism as "psychic automatism in its pure state" in which writing, for example, is freed from the "control exercised by reason."[14] The first elaboration that this study cites as it applies to the creation of theatre is in the 1930 *Second Manifesto of Surrealism*:

> Everything tends to make us believe that there exists a certain point of the mind at which life and death, the real and the imagined, past and future, the communicable and the incommunicable, high and low, cease to be perceived as contradictions. Now, search as one may one will never find any other motivating force in the activities of the Surrealists than the hope of finding and fixing this point.[15]

The point at which the two opposing forces, the two realities—in *Dark Rapture* the naturalistic and surrealistic plots—cease to be an antinomy and become one plot, one reality, is the synthesis, the surreality. It lies in the future, after the final scene, but in Ray's acknowledgment to Babcock that he was on the hillside during the night fire, an acknowledgment he withheld when he, Max, and Babcock were together before the hurricane struck, the final scene prefigures the eventual reconciliation. In this interpretation slowly but surely the plots and the principal characters are converging.

The second elaboration that this study cites as it applies to the creation of theatre is in the 1932 *Communicating Vessels*. About surrealism Breton wrote:

> I hope it will be considered as having tried nothing better than to cast a *conduction wire* between the far too distant worlds of waking and sleep, exterior and interior reality, reason and madness, the assurance of knowledge and of love, of life for life and the revolution, and so on.[16]

Surrealism connects the two opposing forces, the two realities so that they are better appreciated as an antinomy that does not ultimately become a synthesis, a surreality. In this interpretation, which works better than the first interpretation for Overmyer's play, the naturalistic plot and the surrealistic plot, fixity and fluidity, the surface and the subsurface interact to fuel one another and the chase—the quest without which life ceases to be as fulfilling as possible—without ever converging into one plot, one reality. The naturalistic suitcases become surrealistic objects that become naturalistic objects when the mob lieutenants pop them open and find a screenplay. Images continue to form and dissolve only to form again. Identities continue to shift. Antinomies and ambiguities continue to develop. The war between the naturalistic play and the non-naturalistic play continues to be fought because it is necessary to generate the tension that theatre requires and that convergence, resolution, and peace would end.

The quest would end too, or, rather, it would reduce to a pursuit of mobster money because without the surrealistic plot, *Dark Rapture* would be an enjoyable play noir but no more than that. The presence of the two plots to challenge each other demonstrates that not only can a play mix modes and tones, genres and styles but that the mixture elevates *Dark Rapture* to a drama of national character in attitude towards identity as self-invention while still being an enjoyable play noir. Naturalism defines identity as determined by forces over which one has little control: history, for example. Surrealism liberates one from a deterministic definition, enabling him/her to imaginatively create the self. A mixture of the two conceptions creates a quest for a surreality of the two conceptions and great theatre.

A Len Jenkin play can be interpreted according to surrealist principles, but this study will not so interpret it, although the play, *Kid Twist*, opens with incongruous images in a prologue entitled "Testimony." While waiting for the house lights to go down and the actors to take their places, the audience hears over speakers excerpts from the courtroom testimony of Abe Reles about his underworld activities, the historical source for which is the 1951 record of organized crime and its enforcement arm in the 1930s.[17] In answers to the prosecutor's questions, Reles describes in graphic detail the murders that he and associates like Pittsburgh Phil committed for the Syndicate, the enforcement arm. Jenkin builds the prologue on two contrasts in verbal images. The first is in level of usage. A questioner asks Reles in standard, literal English about the particulars of his role as a gang leader for Murder, Incorporated: "Mr. Reles, did you kill a labor delegate named Seligman?" In nonstandard but figurative English, the gang leader responds: "It was an easy pop. I follow the guy into the movies. . . ."[18] The second contrast occurs within Reles' responses, in the juxtaposition of extraordinary violence committed in ordinary places. For example, he tells the jury how he took the fire-ax from the movie-house wall and while the audience was watching the screen sank it into the delegate's head or how he and his partners overpowered a victim in the living room of his, Reles', apartment, took him tied up in a ball to the garbage dumps, and torched the body.

By presenting the dialogue offstage, the dramaturgy achieves two quick objectives. The amplified sound creates a sense of another reality in life, an underworld heard but not seen, active but concealed. And dialogue spoken by disembodied voices creates a sense of forces, not characters. Reles is named in the testimony, but the audience does not necessarily know him and the prosecutor is not named. He represents law and order; his questions, which assume that human beings are capable of governing themselves according to civilization's precepts, are calculated to bring the underworld's activities to the surface. In his answers Reles describes a world in which the inhabitants drop civilization's surnames for gangland's nicknames; it is a realm in the midst of civilization unrestrained by its law and order. As he says about splitting a skull in a filled movie house and then running in the ensuing pandemonium, "It was a natural" (45). The incongruity between the conscious mind and the subconscious urge, civilization's control and savagery's frenzy, and thinking about one's behavior and acting without remorse is summed up in this exchange:

Q: Tell me, Mr. Reles. You're a human being. How did you conceivably justify your participation in so many hideous crimes?

A: I wanted to eat steak and drink champagne and go to Florida (47).

The incongruity in the prologue is the first of Jenkin's subversions of naturalistic theatre. Spectators at a naturalistic play expect a setting to reproduce as exactly as the stage permits surface reality inhabited by characters who look, speak, and act as the counterparts they represent do in everyday life. Instead, spectators encounter an absence, a space filled not with props and actors but with disembodied voices, and their frustration increases as the incongruity increases. Suddenly a white curtain without anyone in front of it occupies the space, and a single offstage voice replaces the dialogue. It is the frustration of "conventional expectations of clarification and reconciliation" in postmodernism's theatre experience with which Elinor Fuchs introduces her study of the death of character and the issues attendant upon that death. In *Kid Twist* the actor, the character as the focus of traditional theatre in that his/her acting—doing something—is the play's raison d'etre, seems to have disappeared. Still in her introduction, Fuchs asks, "What happens to the presentation of time and space when we are no longer in a theater of character, when the human figure is no longer the single, perspectival 'point' of stage performance? One answer, traceable to the symbolists and to Gertrude Stein, is the landscape stage. . . . There are, of course, human figures on these natural/conceptual landscapes, but the landscape itself is the central object of contemplation."[19]

Having subverted character, Jenkin restores it in the form of human figures who appear one by one against the curtain. Reles was a real person, and the prologue is a condensation of testimony given by him and other hoodlums combined with dialogue Jenkin wrote for the play. A mixture of research and invention, *Kid Twist* takes its inspiration from a real person who played a key role in historical events first as killer and then as witness. In March 1940 one of Murder, Inc.'s gang leaders, Abe Reles, nicknamed Kid Twist, turned state's evidence and helped to send Pittsburgh Phil and other gang members to the electric chair. He was being held in protective custody on the sixth floor of the supposedly impregnable fortress, the Half Moon Hotel on the Coney Island waterfront, when on the morning of November 12, 1941, his broken body was discovered on the roof of the hotel's kitchen extension. Two bedsheets that had been knotted together fluttered about the body. To this day his death remains a mystery, as does his life. Dead at age thirty-four, he had been arrested forty-two times, six of them for homicide, but convicted only seven times: once for assault, once for petit larceny, once for parole violation, three times for disorderly conduct, and once for juvenile delinquency. A savage animal, he was also a domesticated animal. At the time of his death, he was married with a six-year-old son. His wife was expecting their second child.

I do not mean to suggest in the above discussion that *Kid Twist* is a series of alternating scenes, one of subversion followed by one of restoration. All the while the prologue is subverting character through the absence of visual images, it is enhancing character through the presence of verbal images resonating in the absence. *Murder, Inc.*, the account of the Syndicate's rise and fall, is the document against which the critic verifies the accuracy of the events the play dramatizes. To the actual courtroom testimony that the prologue delivers, the playwright adds dialogue that he wrote to build the conflict. He also alters the testimony. Immediately after admitting to the labor delegate's murder in the movie house, the killer turned witness testifies how he and Pittsburgh Phil gunned down John the Polack. But in the testimony recorded in *Murder, Inc.*, although the gang leader went along for the ride, two gang members did the actual shooting. Furthermore, the prologue testimony purporting to be Reles' was in fact Blue Jaw Magoon's courtroom testimony of how he and Pittsburgh Phil gunned down Whitey Friedman, a man the underworld suspected of being an informer.[20] Kid Twist Reles was not the only hoodlum to testify against former gang members during the prosecution of those Syndicate members who could be put on trial. Yet the prologue implies that he was by appropriating for the character in the play with his name courtroom testimony given by others. Unseen but so heard that he dominates the testimony, the Kid is the underworld's unitary self: the self that speaks for the unconscious, the unruly, the disorderly.

With the prologue over, character's visual restoration begins with the underworld brought onstage in the persons of the actors portraying hoodlums who one at a time are put into a police lineup. Since the Kid is the only one of them to speak, the only one whose body has a voice, he solidifies the character as unified, unitary self. The scene then shifts to the Half Moon Hotel, where the unconscious force is placed under the rule or order of consciousness for the two acts of the play proper, during which the character Abe Reles is confined to a room with actors in the roles of police guards, the visible symbols of law and order. The period covered is the final three days of protective custody, following which, according to the bargain struck with the District Attorney's office, Reles will have concluded his courtroom appearances testifying against his former associates and will leave the hotel a free man. That is his expectation anyway. The audience's expectation also appears to be in line for realization, for with character restored and setting actualized, the play appears to be settling into a naturalistic drama, and on one level it is. *Kid Twist*, however, has more than one level. While in the hotel, the Kid has little to do except talk with the police officers assigned to his room, place bets with the waiter who brings him his meals and who doubles as a bookie, sleep, and sleeping, dream. Dramatized, the dreams form most of the non-naturalistic contents of the play's two acts, and their contents are for the most part the murders about which he is testifying, although unlike the testimony, his dreams reveal a rudimentary conscience in the person of a rabbi from his Jewish upbringing. Playing more active roles are the comic-book Joker; baseball's Babe Ruth, who has the same penchant for mayhem that Reles does; and Captain Pruss of the ill-fated *Hindenburg*, which burst into flames while descending into the mooring station at Lakehurst, New Jersey, in 1937. The only explanation he can offer his guards for dreaming about the airship is that he must have read about the disaster in the newspaper.

By dramatizing the dreams, the play summons the subsurface reality to the surface and in so doing simultaneously creates and subverts or dissolves character as a unitary self. Dreaming, the arrested Kid eludes law and order's control to be who he was before being taken into custody. Yet he is not in control of himself; he is not the voice that dominated the testimony. The voices of the rabbi and the Joker, Ruth and Pruss fracture into selves the unitary self that Reles claimed for his identity in the prologue and lineup because with the professional killer and the family man in him, they too speak for him. This pattern of simultaneously creating and dissolving also constitutes the interaction of history and invention. The first murder enacted onstage is that of Puggy Feinstein. While Pittsburgh Phil and the Kid struggle to pin him to the ground, Babe Ruth appears and proffers his bat. Taking it, the Kid smashes Puggy's skull. So much for the dream. The facts are very different. On Labor Day night in 1939, two teenagers came upon a burning body on a vacant lot in Brooklyn. The charred remains were identified as those of Irv (Puggy) Feinstein, a hoodlum ordered executed because his gambling operation was encroaching upon another gangster's territory. In court Reles testified to the details. Puggy was brought into Reles' house where Harry (Pittsburgh Phil) Strauss jumped him in the living room (while Reles' mother-in-law slept in the bedroom). As Reles and Buggsy Goldstein held him down, Strauss tied him in such a manner that any movement he made would tighten the noose around his neck. They took the body tied in a ball to a vacant lot where Buggsy, pouring gasoline, cremated him. As a result of testimony by Reles and others, Strauss and Goldstein were sentenced to death.[21]

These details have already been given in the play in another context. In the prologue they describe the death of Rocco Morganti. The audience, however, cannot be expected to know how in fact each hoodlum was killed; it cannot be expected to question the veracity of the Kid's dream. It does not have to. The play itself does by having someone outside the dreams comment on the acts of violence that spawn the dreams. Each of the Kid's dreams is followed by the appearance of a character identified only as the Reporter, who phones in to his newspaper the account of the latest gangland slaying. For Puggy's death he dictates to the copy editor on the other end of the line that the "local milkman discovered the body, which had multiple stab wounds in the chest" (63). Since the audience cannot know that in fact Feinstein was strangled and cremated, it must accept the reality established by the play. Yet the play establishes two incompatible realities. The audience sees the victim hit with a bat and hears stab wounds as the cause of death. With clarification frustrated, which version does it accept: the murder as enacted in a dream or reported in a newspaper?

Let us look at one more execution. In act 2 the Kid enters a room in which Jake the Painter is relaxing in a bathtub next to which sits his mistress, a blind Chinese woman preparing an opium pipe for him. After conversing with Jake for a few minutes, the Kid sends Lae-Lin out of the room and, while she is gone and with the Joker an onlooker, stabs him. The scene fades with Lae-Lin on her knees feeling for the body in the bloodied water. For the record, in September 1932 Abe Reles shot and killed Jake the Painter on the street.[22] The historical record is not being dramatized, however. The Kid's dreams are, and the suspicion caused by Babe Ruth's presence in the first dream is confirmed by the Joker's presence in the second. The Kid is exaggerating. Should the audience therefore accept the Reporter's account? As the scene with Lae-Lin fades, the lights come up on him as he phones in the details of Jacob Greenblatt's death. "In attempting to defend his premises Mr. Greenblatt, a public accountant, was shot to death by the intruders. Mr. Greenblatt's secretary, Gloria Chow, described the killers as masked Negroes in Good Humor man uniforms, who ran downstairs into a BMT station and disappeared in the crowd" (89). Once again, the record is not being dramatized; the Reporter's version of it is. The suspicion caused by his suggestion in the first report that he was present at President Roosevelt's speeches is confirmed by the second report. He too is exaggerating.

By simultaneously developing the non-naturalistic dreaming and the naturalistic reporting, the play continues the pattern of simultaneously bolstering and undercutting character. Both the Kid and the Reporter seek to create themselves as the dominant force controlling the events dramatized, only to have the other one's activity reduce his power. With the time of the play late autumn of 1941, America's entry into World War II looms in both the Reporter's coverage of Roosevelt's speech warning about the "'Nazi peril'" (57) and the Kid's conversations with the guards and the waiter. His courtroom appearances displaced by war news from the daily newspaper delivered to the room and therefore not worth reading, the Kid magnifies his role in the gangland slayings in his dreams. In an attempt to awaken the public to the implications of violence, the Reporter magnifies his role on the national and international stages in his reports. He wants to connect what is happening at home with what is happening in Europe, but because he is physically removed from the war, he can only report the domestic violence in increasing exaggeration as the warning goes unheeded. The Kid, on the other hand, can only commit the violence in increasing exaggeration to keep pace with the war news displacing him. Separating himself from the "schmucks" who get killed in wars started by gangsters like Hitler, he sees himself as a businessman who sells his service for a good price and does not get killed (71–72). Yet in his act-1 accounts of the gangland slayings, the Reporter does not even mention him.

The pattern simultaneously creates and dissolves character as a unitary self. We have already heard and seen how the Kid is and is not a unitary self and how the Reporter is a unitary self. But since every time he phones in a report, he phones a different newspaper, giving different datelines in the same report, he is a generic reporter. And since he identifies himself with different bylines such as "Seymour Scoop" (64) and "Nate Newshound" (69), many voices speak in him as they do in the Kid. Moreover, the two principals share images. After he remarks to his police guards that the sole reason he can think of for dreaming about the *Hindenburg* is that he must have read about it in the newspaper, the Kid's first act-1 dream is dramatized. Compared with subsequent ones, this one is benign, but it introduces the characters with whom he identifies. While the rabbi reads from a holy book, the Joker, Babe Ruth, and the airship's Captain Pruss horseplay with him in prison. As the cellmates disappear, the Reporter phones in his first story, a summary of speeches by Roosevelt alerting the public to the possibility that the "'Nazi peril'" could involve the United States in the war. In his second story, he follows the account of Puggy Feinstein's slaying with the news that the *Hindenburg* is scheduled to arrive shortly. Although the time is wrong, for it exploded in 1937, the association with Roosevelt's warning is right. Before its destruction, the airship symbolized National Socialist aspirations in world affairs. After the Kid's next killing, the Reporter gives the next day for the airship's arrival. As he exits the stage in act 1, the report seems to be coming true. The *Hindenburg* approaches, except that it approaches, not as a news item, but as an image in the Kid's dream, carrying among the passengers Babe Ruth and the Joker and bearing the symbolic significance the Reporter assigns to it. Captain Pruss calls attention to the "swastikas on our underbelly" that "wiggle waggle over America" (69). By merging the action in the Kid's dreams and the Reporter's stories and separating it between them, the dramaturgy subverts drama's traditional protagonist as a single character, a unitary self.

The pattern obtains throughout the dramaturgy. Dramatizing history, it distorts history. Developing the non-naturalistic subsurface and the naturalistic surface, it creates two incompatible realities of dreams and reports. The first act-2 dream is the electrocution of Pittsburgh Phil with both the Reporter and the Kid present. In rapid succession the newspaper man links the electrocution, the result of the gang leader's testimony, with the arrival of the "Nazi balloon" (80), and the informer, whose dreams manifest his deepening awareness that walking away a free man will be difficult after testifying against gang members, sees his former associate dead in the airship. Awake he is visited by his wife, who tells him that his notoriety has forced her and the two children to move, and by his mistress, who tries to knife him after he refuses her request for money so that she can get away. Asleep he dreams of killing Jake the Painter, whose killers the Reporter identifies as masked Negroes before alerting the copy desk of the *Hindenburg*'s imminent descent. Asleep again the Kid dreams of the Joker, who appears with a plan for escaping to Mars and blowing up Earth as they leave. "BOOM! It's a cinch," he says. "Wars are starting. BOOM!" (93–94) Since the diabolical funnyman double-crosses him, the Kid has to kill him in the rocket ship and return to Earth. For the killer turned informer, there is no escape.

What Jenkin is doing is twofold. He is destabilizing character and narrative, the traditional grounds of drama generally and the naturalistic play specifically, and he is creating a new type of play. We can appreciate the second part if we replace the term level with more contemporary terms. *Kid Twist* has parallel universes, multiple frames, and concurrent tracks, the most obvious instance being the presence of historical and fictional characters such as Captain Pruss and the Joker. And not only do the characters move back and forth from frame to frame, the frames interpenetrate. When the Reporter first appears, the stage directions indicate that the Kid "*does not react to his presence*" (56). The two principals do not react to each other as characters, but they do react to each other's images impinging on the dreams and reports until the reaction becomes an interaction: an interpenetration in which each one seizes the other's images. Their relationship transformed, their initially incompatible realities—their universes, frames, tracks—become compatible.

The informer is drugged by his guards, who have been paid to silence him. As they are about to push him out the hotel window on November 12, 1941, the *Hindenburg*, which burst into flames on May 6, 1937, enters and explodes, incinerating those aboard. The Kid and the Reporter witnessed Pittsburgh Phil's electrocution in the act's opening dream, but now, for the first time, they see the event before them as catastrophic. That those aboard the flaming airship blame the Kid for the explosion that blows up the world signals the outbreak of a global conflagration; that they blame him for the explosion that kills them completes his realization that his violent behavior has consequences beyond gangland. As he sinks into death, the moral cretin cries from the extinction of self-consciousness, "Momma, momma. I don't wanna go down. Keep me up . . . keep me floating. . . . Up into the *light*." As he witnesses the airship explode, the Reporter cries, "My God! It's in flames. . . . Oh, the humanity, and all the passengers!" (99–100), speaking words actually broadcast at the 1937 site.[23] For the first time, he drops his wise-cracking newspaper lingo to respond to the violent extinction of life; he realizes that innocent people are the victims of violence. In one blazing illumination, the two principals synthesize, enlarge perceptions, and sunder. The Reporter exits after acknowledging Roosevelt's condolence to Hitler for the *Hindenburg* disaster, and the Kid falls while a chorus chants a Kaddish.

The play is not over, and Jenkin is not finished dissolving a naturalistic play's boundaries separating it from the audience while maintaining a naturalistic play's plot. When the prologue ends, a police sergeant appears onstage to call forth hoodlums being detained until charged with specific crimes. One by one, Sarge summons four to parade across the stage before exiting: Puggy Feinstein, Big Sid, Jake the Painter, and Abe (Kid Twist) Reles. As each arrives onstage, he pauses in front of a brightly lit white curtain marked with lines for height measurement. The image is that of a lineup. As each pauses, Sarge calls upon the audience to "Look 'em over. Next man. See the man who robbed you? See the man who murdered you? See anything you like? See anything you remember?" (49) The assumption is that the audience can identify the criminals if it has a mind to it. The reason behind the assumption is found in the play's mirroring images because just as the Kid and the Reporter mirror each other, so do they mirror the audience.

The lineup concluded, the stage becomes a room in the Half Moon Hotel overlooking the beach, amusement rides, and sea. *"The room has no walls."* It has a window *"created in the space . . . clearly defined, though not a physical 'window.' When someone on stage looks out this 'window,' he is facing the audience"* (50). From time to time, the Kid goes to the window, looks at the sea below, and muses on the creatures swimming in the ocean's depth. Supposedly looking at the sea, he is actually looking at the audience, for the audience represents the America in which he originated and in which he flourished in his short life. Brought forth from the underworld at prologue's end, the Kid is returned whence he came at play's end with the guards' explanation that if not silenced, he will continue to expose society's complicity, a complicity made evident by the audience's silence during the lineup. Pushed out the window, the man who reveled in killing gets his foot caught, and he hangs upside down in the position of the Hanged Man in the Tarot cards while Sarge gives the audience a second chance to become involved by repeating his lineup exhortation: "Look him over. Look him over. Look him over" (101).

By dissolving the fourth wall, suspending a resolution, and inviting the audience to participate in the play's creation, the dramaturgy makes the audience the protagonist representing the larger society that reflects the onstage division between the Kid and the Reporter, a society that glamorizes violence in its entertainment industry at the same time that its civic and religious groups expose its corrosive effects. Interpreted this way, the resolution must come from within the audience from the imaginatively engaged spectators. No matter how interpreted, though, *Kid Twist* achieves what Jenkin said a theatre experience has to have to hold his interest: "There needs to be a continuing sense of *wonder*, as powerful as that in fairy tales, moonlight, or dreams."[24]

The final work could be analyzed for the different genres it interacts or for the mystery it recovers. Instead, it will be analyzed for two primary ways in which it subverts the naturalistic play while maintaining two primary elements of the naturalistic play. The work is Quincy Long's *The Joy of Going Somewhere Definite*, given a dazzling production by the Atlantic Theater Company in the 1997 season. The two primary elements are costume and language. The play is set in the Northwoods. The three men who undertake the quest are loggers dressed in outdoor garb: caps and fur-lined jackets over flannel shirts and jeans. Their language is replete with the Uh's and stammerings, the repetitions and incomplete thoughts synonymous with naturalistic language. They therefore would seem to be fulfilling Zola's dictum in his 1873 preface to the stage adaptation of *Thérèse Raquin* that the "time has come to produce plays of reality."[25] Reality, however, is not what it appears to be.

The play's script includes in the cast a Foley Artist/Musician, whose role the settings, or stage directions, describe: "An onstage FOLEY ARTIST/MUSICIAN creates aural scenery with sound effects, while various arrangements of tables and chairs serve to suggest a roadhouse, a truck. . . . Coin tossing, beer drinking, rifle shooting, cigarette smoking, letter reading, etc. is all mimed by the actors and supported with sound effects."[26] A Foley Artist is normally associated with film and television production; working on a Foley stage, he/she is the person who creates the sound effects on the soundtrack. If his/her services are utilized in theatre, he/she is out of the audience's sight. In place of the term Foley Artist, the Atlantic Theater playbill credited Daniel Barnhill with creating the sound effects and being a musician along with another musician, Louis Tucci. These two played the musical interludes that the cast performed in a work that for reviewer Peter Marks is "almost, but not quite, a musical; characters repeatedly burst into song in a score imbued with a country twanginess by the talented Joshua Rosenblum. (The musical interludes are so good, in fact, that the play could support another number or two.)"[27] But while supporting the argument that the play is polymorphous, its almost being a musical is not one of the two subversions of naturalism.

The first subversion is in the combination of Barnhill's sound effects, Kyle Chepulis' bare-bones stage design, and Howard Werner's lighting. Naturalism's strength is creating as faithful as possible a reproduction of everyday surface reality. In showing what theatre in the closing quarter of the 19th century had to do to become naturalistic, Zola wrote, "Most of all we would need to intensify the illusion in reconstructing the environments, less for their picturesque quality than for dramatic utility. The environment must determine the character. When a set is planned so as to give the lively impression of a description by Balzac; when, as the curtain rises, one catches the first glimpse of the characters, their personalities and behaviour, if only to see the actual locale in which they move, the importance of exact reproduction in the decor will be appreciated."[28] *The Joy of Going Somewhere Definite* destroys the illusion. What the audience sees and hears is not accuracy of detail but artifice, as we shall see and hear as the second subversion is established.

Act 1 opens on three drunken loggers enjoying themselves in a Northwoods barroom. The set does not resemble a barroom; it does not resemble anything because it consists of only a few chairs and a table. The imaginatively engaged spectator taking cues from the actors' language, the sound effects, and the lighting makes the environment a barroom. The clothes the three are wearing indicate a cold climate; seated at the table in the relaxed postures of men who have been drinking, they are raucous; a woman mimes bartending; and music plays as if coming from a jukebox. The language is the second subversion because although the words are naturalistic in that they are appropriate for the occupation and the situation, the effect is anything but naturalistic. Raymond, the loudest of the three, speaks first: "And I say I say I say I say I say I say." By repeating the subject and predicate five times, he withholds the direct object, suspending the sentence and the audience until he surprises by following the sixth "I say" with "No." After the second logger, Merle, counterpoints with "Yeah," Raymond continues with a battery of negatives declaring that he will not "take that no / Not from nobody don't limb trees," eliciting the third logger's, Junior's, "No way" (5).

When finally identified, the object is a "nobody" (5). Raymond, the logging-crew leader, had a fight with someone not a logger who he feels insulted him. The nobody does not appear onstage so that once the men relive the fight, they respond to other stimuli in the skeletal set, the sound effects, and the language. So too does the audience respond to the cues as an audience does at any performance, as anyone does listening to language being spoken. Yet the strategy of having a gap between the crew leader's intent to name an object and his deferring of it creates multiple possibilities in the listeners awaiting the sentence completion and therefore confusion and error. How many imaginatively engaged spectators drawn into the gap would expect "No" to be the object of "I say"?

Another of Long's strategies for subverting naturalistic language as a medium for communication is having loggers who have been drinking speak it in a noisy barroom. As Raymond relates his story, although he hit the nobody as hard as he could, he felt no shock because his "whole hand" is numb from years of maneuvering a vibrating chain saw. Misunderstanding, Junior hears "holy land." A riff on "whole hand" and "holy land" (7) ensues until Merle clarifies each partner's confusion to the other. A more revealing exchange occurs—this one involving the barmaid, who is asked to lower the blaring sound of the jukebox music—over the misunderstanding of protecting the ears from deafness caused by the relentless noise of a vibrating chain saw. Junior, who interprets the conversation as referring to safe sex, claims not to need protection because he has a "wife" (9). Raymond, who has an attitude toward women, baits his younger partner with remarks about women and marriage. The baiting prompts Junior to rise unsteadily, the sound effects creating the sounds of a chair being moved and beer cans falling, and challenge Raymond: "My wife is a woman" (10).

As soon as Junior injects his wife into the conversation, Raymond, who must be in control of every situation, reminds him that he is more qualified to speak about wives and marriage because of his "fifteen years of it" (9). Sensitive to his probationary status on the crew and consequently defensive and aggressive, the youngest of the three challenges until the leader motions him to "siddown Junior" (10). In instances such as this one, language connects the men. With the confusion clarified and tempers mollified, they join in song with affect and animation bewailing a man's life "WITHOUT HIS WOMAN" (10). Yet disconnection is inevitable, for the cast speak naturalistic language, which the play demonstrates is an inadequate medium for communication. Taken individually the naturalistic sounds the men make, and most of them are monosyllabic in the opening moments, should not be confusing, but when strung together the sentences they form create ambiguity and multivocality that keep subverting the literal, univocal naturalism so much so that *The Joy of Going Somewhere Definite* could be called a poststructuralist play because basic to poststructuralism is the argument that language generates expectations that it subverts while fulfilling them. That is, language never fully reveals the object (the signified or concept); it merely reveals more language (more signifiers or symbols such as sounds and words that name the signified). When Raymond finally identifies the withheld object and thereby closes the gap he opened by repeating the subject and predicate five times, the object itself keeps the gap open, for he is an unnamed "nobody."

The subversion of the language begins slowly with each scene adding to the confusion and error and always in conjunction with the subversion the sound effects create while creating the set. With the barmaid giving last call, the loggers become aware of someone else in the barroom. Standing at the bar, wearing a hat and crumpled suit (both black as I remember from the 1997 Atlantic Theater Company production), he arouses the loggers' interest by not removing his hat or acknowledging Raymond's calling to him. When the crew leader asks the barmaid for a quarter, she refuses without giving a reason, though the audience assumes that she does not want the men to start an activity such as playing the jukebox that will delay the barroom's closing. When Raymond asks Merle, he gives a reason for refusing, and it confirms the assumption about the crew leader's reason for asking because Merle says that he is tired of listening to the same song. Junior, however, offers a quarter without being asked.

Over the barmaid's objection, Raymond initiates a visual pattern that repeats the verbal pattern he initiated in the play's opening moments. When he mimes throwing the coin at the stranger, he surprises his crew, the barmaid, and the audience, all of whom thought he wanted the quarter for the jukebox, and he indicates the object. Because the stranger is bent over staring at the floor, he is literally in suspension, his hat falling off only when he lifts his head at the noise of the coins and ashtray the sound effects create as the loggers mime throwing at him in an effort to knock his hat off. Because he does not speak, except for "Uhhhhhhhhh" (15) before falling down despite their overture of camaraderie by offering to buy him a drink, he is the visual counterpart to the verbal "nobody" whose presence mystifies because no vehicle is parked outside the roadhouse that might yield a clue to his identity.

At the barmaid's urging, the revelers take him with them when the bar closes. Her rearranging the chairs to form the seats in a truck's cab in front of the table indicates a change of scene, which takes place only in the spectator's imagination because nothing else changed in the Atlantic Theater's stage design. The three pick him up and lay him on the table, which becomes their pickup truck that they mime driving, while singing, to a friend's ice-fishing shack on a frozen lake in a part of the state that borders Canada. They plan to resume drinking while looking at pictures of "naked women" (19) the friend has there, but with the sound effects supplying various sounds for actions not physically occurring, they crash into the shack, and when they attempt to reverse the truck, a tire breaks through the ice. Stuck, they renew their interest in their silent passenger.

Having aroused the loggers' curiosity, the stranger engages their imagination in a game that joins the verbal pattern with the visual action and the aural images. While Raymond gets a washtub from a nearby shack, he tells the two crew members to get the passenger and some empty beer bottles from the truck. "What's he got in mind you think?" (28), Junior asks Merle. Since Raymond continues to defer the object, giving instructions for setting up the activity without identifying it, he creates a gap between what he has in mind and what his audience anticipates, and when he fills in the gap, he surprises both his onstage audience of crew members and his offstage audience of theatre spectators. He tells Merle and Junior to stand the stranger up on the overturned tub, extend his arms, and put a bottle in each hand. With the crew leader going first and the other two following, the three mime firing a rifle at each target and mime replacing with fresh empties the hits the sounds of which the sound effects actualize. Between the time that Junior, who has never fired a rifle, misses and Raymond can reload and fire for a second go-round, they discover the stranger has fallen off the tub, ending the game.

The loggers' curiosity aroused and their imagination engaged, Raymond now begins to interpret as a distinct activity, but I do not mean to imply that interpreting replaces other activities. The loggers are speakers and listeners, actors in some onstage occurrences and audience for other onstage occurrences, transmitters of signals and interpreters of them. When they go to pick up the stranger after he falls off the washtub, Raymond asks the other two, "Whata you make of this this?" After listening to them express their feelings about "him" (33), the deferred object that Merle supplies, the leader speaks. Interpreting the stranger's "demeanor / Way he's so inward" as evidence of his suffering, Raymond appeals to him to "repent / Say we're sorry / Promise never to do it no more" (34–35).

The loggers have to interpret what they see and hear because the stranger cannot be ignored. His presence in the roadhouse and his acquiescence in the game-playing are visual images so piquant that they invite a reading of his demeanor. And when he finally speaks words as opposed to the earlier "Uhhh-hhhhhh," he does what speakers do. He transmits equally piquant verbal images, and he defers the object: "I don't believe I" (36). Raymond in turn does what an audience does; he expects an object that is not forthcoming. Hearing the verb "believe" as intransitive, he has confirmation for his interpretation of the stranger as a sinner lapsed from grace: "Well well / There it is" (36). Since the stranger does not add an object to the verb "believe," the crew leader interprets the words as forming a complete sentence: an admission of lapsed faith. He has the two loggers get an axe, mime cutting open the fishing hole inside the shack, formed by Junior rearranging the chairs as the barmaid formed a truck by rearranging them, and mime dipping the sinner in the baptismal water. The three proceed to sing a song of salvation and dance in celebration of bringing a soul to redemption.

Though the stranger does not resist the game-playing or the baptismal rite, he resists reduction to a unitary meaning. Generating expectations, he also subverts them. Not only does he fall off the washtub ending the game, as the loggers sing and dance, he *"slips beneath the surface"* of the ice (38), and they have to mime reaching into the water and pulling him out. He is unstable and elusive, for as soon as they have him connected to an interpretation, he becomes disconnected. He is a presence in their midst and in his silence an anti-presence. Yet Raymond is determined to assign a meaning to him based on a letter found on him.

If we substitute meaning for object-signified-concept, we have poststructuralism's defining characteristic, which holds that just as a signifier leads to a signified, which leads to another signifier, so is meaning deferred, elusive, suspended. If we combine this characteristic with a defining characteristic of performance, we can better understand why meaning is deferred. By changing inflection when they speak and coordinating the words with body language, for example, actors create characters, each one of whom has his or her perspective on the action or, in the case of *The Joy of Going Somewhere Definite*, the stranger. Performing their lines from different perspectives—Raymond's or Junior's or the barmaid's—they create gaps in a unified, coherent picture, gaps that spectators not only instinctively fill but in postmodern theatre are invited, even stimulated, to fill. Audience members try to anticipate the suspended object or meaning, they align themselves with perspectives characters have established in the performance, or they take their own perspective. Just as the cast participate in creating the set as an ongoing activity, so the imaginatively engaged spectator participates in creating the play, the elements of which in postmodern theatre are fluid and multivocal.

Raymond's interpreting is the exception. He brings to the postmodern, poststructuralist play the mindset of a naturalistic character for whom the stranger's meaning is fixed and unequivocal. When the loggers pull him from the water, Merle discovers a letter in his hat in which Marie informs Claude that she "CAN'T GO IT ANYMORE" with him but is safe in "HIS BIG ARMS" and "KEEPING THE CAR." There is no ambiguity in the letter for Raymond; words mean what they say they mean. "She took him for his automobile and some stranger with big arms / Says it right here / Does it or does it not?" (41–42), he demands of the others, eliciting Merle's concurrence. His interpretation yields a unified, coherent picture of the puzzle that is the stranger, identified as Claude: the absence of a vehicle at the roadhouse, the face of suffering, and the silence of inwardness.

What Raymond does not realize is that the picture he frames is that of himself, the pieces of which are his sexist remarks and his references to Junior's wife and marriage. In the barroom he alluded to "fifteen years of it" (9). At the lake he admits that he is not married but can empathize with Claude presumably because his wife left him. From his perspective women have been betraying men ever since the Garden of Eden:

> Adam and Eve
> Standing up
> Front of God and everybody
> . . . .
> And then this snake and his love cabin (47–48).

Although men cannot "hold" women when they want to leave or make them feel "love" when they do not, they "sure as hell can punish 'em" (44) when they transgress, he concludes one of his tirades. The additional discovery, that the stranger has a bullet wound, only solidifies his interpretation and resolution. Noting the envelope address in Canada, Raymond marshals his crew for the drive there to punish the wife and the "BIG ARMS" (41) referred to in the letter. Act 1 ends with the singing loggers—Guy Boyd as Raymond, J.R. Horne as Merle, and Jordan Lage as Junior in the Atlantic Theater production—advancing toward the audience: "LOOK OUT MISTER BIG ARM / IT'S GONNA BE A WAR" (56).

When the loggers left the roadhouse, they put the stranger in the back of the pickup truck. Bound for Canada with "PURPOSE SHININ'" (56) at the close of act 1, they put him in the cab with them because for Raymond the situation has changed. He believes that he has closed the gap between himself as subject and the stranger as object and will close it between the stranger, Claude, as subject and Claude's wife as object. Identifying with Claude, he has fixed into meaning all of the ambiguity in which the stranger is suspended, despite the latter's persistent elusiveness and not only in falling off the washtub or slipping under the ice. When Raymond and Merle jack up the truck to get the tire out of the water, Junior, alone with him, insists that he did not shoot him, but the wounded man neither blames the logger nor offers an explanation for the wound. He does not "remember that so well" (50), he says. What he does remember, though the telling is more rambling than coherent narrative, is walking in water with his wife and a boy who despite their holding "him up . . . died." All that Junior can manage is "Oh" (52–53) before the other two loggers return.

Had Raymond overheard the talk, he would not revise his interpretation but would fit the allusions to wife, boy, and death in the water into his grand narrative in which the wounded man is the symbol of betrayed and suffering mankind. Yet just as the play dramatizes fluidity while the crew leader is solidifying meaning and dramatizes multivocality while he is imposing univocality, so the play deconstructs binary oppositions such as male and female, subject and object while he is constructing them. Claude is the surrogate center of Raymond's grand narrative, but act-1's drama is in the loggers interacting among themselves and with the stranger, the deferring of objects and the playing of games, and the contrasting of Raymond's high-toned purpose and the self-ironizing song lyrics such as the rhyming of "TREES" and "SNEEZE" (20) and revelations such as Raymond's confession of loneliness to Junior: "Oh I could take and be my own woman sure / Put on the bra and panties and pretend." But, he quickly adds, "I don't do that / Won't do that" (44).

A fourth set of antinomies to go with fixed and fluid, univocal and multi-vocal, centered and dispersed involves direction. The loggers' "PURPOSE SHININ" propels them linearly to a showdown in Canada with Marie and the "MISTER BIG ARM" who supplanted Claude in her affection. The play's images, however, are those of circularity. The aural image is that of wheels spinning on the tractionless ice. The visual image is that of revelers dancing by the shack. The verbal image is that of sentences that go round and round and digressions that subvert linearity. When, for example, Raymond and Merle return from jacking up the truck, the former orders the stranger in the cab and Junior in the open back. The latter protests that whenever cab space is limited he is the one relegated to the back, prompting Merle to explain the logging crew's hierarchical order. The newest member nevertheless refuses to leave until the leader allows him in the cab with Claude on his lap, but then Raymond refuses to leave until Junior agrees with him. Multivocal "Uh huh" and "Yeah" are unacceptable. Junior must repeat Raymond's univocal "RIGHT" (55).

Although *The Joy* was performed with an intermission between acts 1 and 2, a production would not need one to set the stage for the Canadian site. The table and chairs are simply reconfigured. The performers establish the scene by their language and activity supported by the sound effects and lighting. Act 2 opens with Marie, Felicity Huffman in the production directed by William H. Macy, explaining to another woman, played by Dale Soules, who doubled as the barmaid and the waitress in a forthcoming scene, why she came to the house where they apparently reside, since the time is night and they are wearing bathrobes. The old life, the life she fled, was centered in her relationship with a man she first refers to as "he" (57) and then as "Claude" (59). His being "sent away for robbing" caused her "behavior problems" (57) as a teenager. Though they were subsequently married, his violent temper so frightens her that she has had court orders protecting her. But as she has come to understand herself, the legal system cannot save her; only God can. God is the new life, the new "core" of her "behavior." Only He can heal her "past" and make her "whole" (58–59) before she "goes down the drain again" (61). They also sing, and their lyrics repeat some of the images in the men's number that closes act 1, particularly in the advance in a combat mode on "MISTER BIG ARM" (56): for Raymond, the man with whom Marie betrayed Claude. In the women's song, "HIS BIG ARMS" are God's that "SOOTHE YOUR FEARS AWAY" (62). By the time they sing, the confusion in language that creates certain expectations is being dispelled for the audience but not for the loggers, who have yet to arrive on their quest.

As Marie talks, she is presented sympathetically, more a victim than a victimizer, and given her characterization of Claude as a "psycho" (58) so vulnerable that the house seems to be a shelter for battered women until the surprises begin. The house is a domicile for a religious community that has granted Marie probationary status, although she came hoping for full membership. The other woman, a directress, surprises when she assures the novice that she will not be shocked by any revelations about her life: "Well it's not like I've never been fucked you know." The novice in turn surprises by rejecting the older woman's "stupid advice about . . . fucking" (61). This examination of *The Joy* began with two ways in which it subverts the naturalistic play while maintaining two elements of the naturalistic play, but act 1 does not exhaust the naturalism or the surprises. The interaction of naturalistic and non-naturalistic modes is the play's dynamic, its generating force, causing the simultaneous fulfilling and subverting in scene after scene.

The surprise in which Marie rejects the directress' advice reveals another side to the novice. Tough-minded, she is determined to change for the reasons given above and encapsulated in her resolve to get "control" (58) of her life by surrendering it to God. Yet other reasons obtain too. In this opening scene of act 2, she does what Raymond did in the opening scene of act 1. She defers the object or complement in a passage such as the following: "Oh don't be don't be don't be don't be / Don't you understand" (60). In another passage, spoken in response to the older woman's "fucked" statement, she withholds the anticipated object, "sex," and instead says, "God": "I'm not talking about / God" (61). She knows that her head is filled with thoughts "that go round and around," and she wants religion's instruction "to dispel them" (60–61). In other words, she wants no more behavior problems or surprises, no more suspended sentences or ambiguity. She seeks the order and the direction that a fixed, univocal, centered, linear life offers.

Since these principles motivate Raymond, she and the crew leader, who arrives with his fellow loggers, should be able to talk to each other after the men get over their surprise at realizing that the Mister Big Arm in her letter is God and after Raymond inveighs against organized religion. He does convince her to come to the motel where the men are staying to tell Claude that she intends to leave him for the cloistered life in a scene that in naturalistic theatre would be the climax leading to unraveling, reconciliation of some sort, and resolution. Like the play's language, the scene fulfills those expectations while subverting them. Propped up on the table, now a bed in a motel room, in the presence of the author of the letter to Claude found on his person, the figure completes the quest for the stranger's identity and meaning. He also subverts the quest by not being who the loggers assume he is. Marie does not recognize the figure because "it isn't" Claude (82).

To the men, the figure is Claude, played by the Atlantic Theater Company's artistic director Neil Pepe, because the hat he is wearing contains a letter addressed to that person. The word "Claude" is a sign, yet the only agreement between the signifier "Claude" and the signified concept it refers to is one of convention, which dictates that the letter's recipient be the addressee. Since signs are arbitrary, no essential meaning inheres in the name "Claude." Raymond, however, perceives the stranger as Claude because for traditionalist Raymond the signifier leads directly and unequivocally to the signified. In his conception of reality with its linguistic system, when the signifier connects with the signified, meaning becomes fixed and univocal. The irony, of course, is that when he speaks, he subverts the traditional system as in the play's opening moments when he deferred the object, disconnecting and dispersing it.

His perception changes, but before continuing with the crew leader, we should examine how for the stranger and Marie the motel scene fulfills and subverts naturalistic theatre's climactic scene. Seeing Marie in the room, the stranger calls her to his bedside to confess to her, his nurse, that with another man named Mike he killed a man in the snow and "took his hat" (94). He closes the story of Claude, but he keeps open his own story. Although the confession recalls his rambling at the lake about himself with a wife and a boy who died, he dies before clarifying whether he has a wife, who he and Mike are, and why they killed Claude. His confession is his reconciliation with his past, yet by deferring meaning, he subverts context. He slips away again from himself and the others.

Marie, on the other hand, craves meaning. The motel experience reinforces her resolution to enter the religious community. Accepting the fact that the stranger is not Claude and that Marie therefore is not the betrayer he thought she was, Raymond attempts to seduce her. She does not resist, but since she is not in the mood, she cannot close her eyes because as she explains, "When I close my eyes I see things that they bother me" (90). Since Raymond cannot perform if his partner has her eyes open, he storms out of the room. This incident is followed immediately by the one in which the stranger confesses to her and dies. She does not clarify what "things . . . bother" her when she closes her eyes, but they have to do with her past, from which she wants to be healed—made whole.

After praying for the stranger's soul and Claude's too, Marie sings a song praising the "ONLY LOVER" her "SOUL CRAVES." That lover is God or Christ, Whose coming will "RELEASE" her "FROM DESIRE" (95). She probably would accept Raymond's narrative of mankind's fall. She probably would acknowledge woman's guilt in the fallen state. She, however, takes the narrative to its logical conclusion, as Raymond does not, as the Western world's metanarrative: a continuum progressing linearly from the past to a future that is outside of life. Since she must have a "core" that integrates her and since she wants to study the "spirit and how it fits together" (58–59) her impulses, she renounces life with its "RESTLESS YEARNING" and "DESIRE" for transcendence. The lover's coming is "FOREVER" (95).

Neither Marie nor the stranger changes as a result of their encounter. She remains fixed in her resolve; though dead, he remains fluid in suspension on the table onstage for the rest of the play. The cast do not move him when they reconfigure the chairs for the restaurant scene that follows the motel scene, though they do not acknowledge him. He is simply present in all his mystery. Her narrative connects with a larger design; his, disconnected, is self-contained. In *The Cultural Turn*, Fredric Jameson contrasts fragments in modernism and postmodernism. In the latter "each former fragment of a narrative, that was once incomprehensible without the narrative context as a whole, has now become capable of emitting a complete narrative message in its own right. It has become autonomous. . . ."[29] Eliot's *The Waste Land* exemplifies the modern conception. The modern world may be a "heap of broken images,"[30] but if they are connected into a narrative context, they reveal a salvific design; for the reader who does not know how to shore them against his/her ruins, the poem supplies notes. Within the boundaries of these distinctions, Marie's narrative is modern whereas the stranger's is postmodern. It is an autonomous narrative disconnected from the loggers' "PURPOSE SHININ" that brought them to Canada and Marie's "RELEASE . . . FROM DESIRE" for the "GLORY" of transcendence.

Earlier I called Raymond a naturalistic character in a postmodern, poststructuralist play. Were he not so funny, and played with such exuberance by Guy Boyd, criticisms leveled at Zola's characters could be leveled at him. To crude, gross, scatological, vulgar, and obscene could be added sexist, salacious, sacrilegious, domineering, opinionated, and obstinate. Reading into the letter Claude's betrayal by Marie, he proclaims:

> How much of it is a man supposed to take
> Is it fair for her to just run off and take his car in the boot
> Fuck's sake
> I can't think of a thing on her side in this (42).

When Junior complains that by hitting him, the crew leader knocked a tooth out, he replies, "Well now you can play for the [Detroit] Redwings [in the National Hockey League]" (53). Learning that Marie has taken refuge in a religious community, he gives his perception of such places: "Kind of a place they teach you to deny your own name and your husband's name and your children's names and kiss old Jesus' ass everytime you want to go 't the toilet" (69).

Yet Raymond changes. He does not become refined, but he changes in act 2. At the lake the stranger had to be Claude because the letter identified him as Claude, and, as he believed then, identity is fixed. Accepting the fact that the stranger is not Claude, he realizes that identity is not fixed, that signifiers are arbitrary. To avoid identification should they encounter resistance at Mister Big Arm's address, the loggers adopt aliases in Canada. Junior is Doug, Merle is Pete, and Raymond is supposed to be Frank except that he balks at the notion of an assumed identity. "My name is Raymond" (66), he asserts; "I don't want to be Frank" (71). Yet while maneuvering into position to seduce Marie, he answers to the name of Frank, and he becomes Claude by wearing the stranger's hat when he and his logging team leave the motel and the stranger who they think is sleeping and who, now that he is not Claude, no longer interests them. He even gains respect for Junior for standing up to him when he stormed out of the room after the abortive attempt to seduce Marie and into the bathroom where the crew's youngest member, attempting to sleep, hit him: "Goddamn Junior / Goddamnit you're all right" (96).

The team members also realize that experience is multivocal. Marie could not close her eyes with Raymond because she was not in the mood for sex. Stopping at a restaurant after they leave the motel, Raymond asks the waitress, with whom the loggers have been kidding around, whether she closes her eyes when she is with her partner. She replies in the affirmative, prompting Raymond's rejoinder that closing the eyes is the "normal course." But now it is the waitress' turn. "Unless it's love," she rejoins, her admission that a situation has different meanings for different participants, silencing the three men for a "*long pause*" (99). They have a spiritual dimension to them in that they can be touched by love. Junior knows he has been touched, for he excuses himself to phone his wife. And since they are not victims of forces over which they have no control, they are not naturalistic characters in a naturalistic play.

The loggers' confirmation that they are free to make choices about their lives leads to the play's closing musical number. With the stranger sitting up behind the three and though unacknowledged by them adding his voice, the four men sing a song that replies to Marie's song in that by repeating key words, it opposes her goal of transcendence. Although it is understandable that people seek "PEACE" and "RELEASE" from travail, the truth is that in life "PEACE" is transitory: a "DAYDREAM" that "COMES AND THEN GOES." Since peace cannot be held, the best thing to do is "GO ON HOME" (101). When Marie assured the religious community's directress that she would be safe following the loggers to the motel, she used the traditional metaphor of staying on the "path" (78) through the world, a metaphor that implies linear direction and journey's goal. The men's decision to "GO ON

HOME" changes the linear direction to circular and replaces the journey's completion with recursiveness, for once the men are home, they can begin a new adventure.

> Circularity is a characteristic of poststructuralism: If you want to know the meaning (or signified) of a signifier, you can look it up in the dictionary; but all you will find will be yet more signifiers, whose signifieds you can in turn look up, and so on. The process we are discussing is not only in theory infinite but somehow circular: signifiers keep transforming into signifieds and vice versa, and you will never arrive at a final signified which is not a signifier in itself. If structuralism divided the sign from the referent, this kind of thinking—often known as 'post-structuralism'—goes a step further: it divides the signifier from the signified.[31]

"GO ON HOME" applies to theatre as performance. The lyrics advise the spectators to go home because the performance is over for that evening. With naturalistic theatre's resolution deferred, meaning is deferred for the loggers. The spectator who craves meaning has to supply his or her own or accept Marie's resolution. *The Joy of Going Somewhere Definite* is naturalistic theatre for Marie but postmodern theatre for the men, and as postmodern theatre it goes home until the next time it is performed.

Finally, by going home, the loggers can prepare for the next adventure. It will be going somewhere definite, for there is a joy in questing for a single reality that answers all questions: be it meaning, resolution, or transcendence. The adventure will also be filled with unexpected discoveries, for they are the source of realizations about themselves and the quest that stimulate adventurers to continue questing indefinitely and joyfully as the most challenging way to live life. In terms of theatre, the definite quest in a fixed, univocal, surface reality is the naturalistic play while the indefinite quest in a fluid, multivocal, subsurface reality is the non-naturalistic play. The joy the imaginatively engaged spectator can experience is participating in the tension and the creating that the interaction of the two warring realities generates. The image that summarizes is that of Raymond, Merle, and Junior advancing toward the audience in an act-1 showstopping number, singing, "IT'S GONNA BE A WAR," to which I say, "I hope so," as the conclusion will summarize.

NOTES

1. Émile Zola, "From *Naturalism in the Theatre*," trans. Albert Bermel, in *The Theory of the Modern Stage: An Introduction to Modern Theatre and Drama*, ed. Eric Bentley (Harmondsworth: Penguin, 1976), 368–69.

2. Kia Corthron, *Breath, Boom* (New York: Dramatists Play Service, 2002), 5. Hereafter to be cited parenthetically.

3. Keith Glover, *Dancing on Moonlight* (New York: Dramatists Play Service, 1996), 55. Hereafter to be cited parenthetically.

4. See chapter one, note 12, and chapter two, notes 2 and 14.

5. Eric Overmyer, *Dark Rapture*, in *Collected Plays* (Newbury, VT: Smith and Kraus, 1993), 261. Hereafter to be cited parenthetically.

6. In the preface to *Collected Plays* xii, Overmyer states what he is for and against in theatre.

7. Vincent Canby, "Film-Noir Culprits, Pursuing the Loot," *New York Times*, 24 May 1996, C1.

8. Mel Gussow, "Always on the Verge of Dramatic Adventure," *New York Times*, 30 Nov. 1994, C13.

9. Overmyer, "The Hole in the Ozone," 448. See André Breton, *Manifestoes of Surrealism*, trans. Richard Seaver and Helen R. Lane (Ann Arbor: U of Michigan P, 1972), 10.

10. For an analysis of Overmyer's adaptation of Heinrich von Kleist's *Amphitryon*, see Andreach, *Drawing Upon the Past*, 192–202.

11. It is so central that Roger Shattuck singles it out in his introduction to Maurice Nadeau, *The History of Surrealism*, trans. Richard Howard (1965; Cambridge, MA: Harvard UP, 1989), 18–22.

12. Elizabeth Deeds Ermarth, *Sequel to History: Postmodernism and the Crisis of Representational Time* (Princeton: Princeton UP, 1992), 93–94.

13. Nadeau, 185.

14. Breton, *Manifestoes of Surrealism*, 26.

15. Breton, 123–24.

16. André Breton, *Communicating Vessels*, trans. Mary Ann Caws and Geoffrey T. Harris (Lincoln: U of Nebraska P, 1997), 86.

17. Burton B. Turkus and Sid Feder, *Murder, Inc.: The Story of the "Syndicate"* (London: Victor Gollancz, 1952).

18. Len Jenkin, *Kid Twist*, in *7 Different Plays*, 45. Hereafter to be cited parenthetically.

19. Elinor Fuchs, *The Death of Character: Perspectives on Theater after Modernism* (Bloomington: Indiana UP, 1996) 6, 12.

20. For the killing of John the Polack, see Turkus and Feder, 60–61; for the killing of Whitey Friedman, see 138.

21. Turkus and Feder, 197–214.

22. Turkus and Feder, 44–45.

23. The words were spoken by Herbert Morrison for station WLS in Chicago. See Michael Macdonald Mooney, *The Hindenburg* (New York: Dodd, Mead, 1972), 239.

24. Len Jenkin, "Some Notes on Theatre," in *7 Different Plays*, 435.

25. Émile Zola, preface to *Thérèse Raquin*, trans. Kathleen Boutall, in *Theatre/Theory/Theatre: The Major Critical Texts from Aristotle and Zeami to Soyinka and Havel*, ed. Daniel Gerould (New York: Applause, 2000), 354.

26. Quincy Long, *The Joy of Going Somewhere Definite* (New York: Dramatists Play Service, 1999), 4. Hereafter to be cited parenthetically.

27. Peter Marks, "Three Fools Gear Up for a Letdown," *New York Times*, 11 Apr. 1997, C3.

28. Zola, "From *Naturalism in the Theatre*," 369.

29. Fredric Jameson, *The Cultural Turn: Selected Writings on the Postmodern 1983–1998* (New York: Verso, 1998), 160.

30. Eliot, *The Waste Land*, 53.

31. Terry Eagleton, *Literary Theory: An Introduction*, 2nd ed. (Minneapolis: U of Minnesota P, 1996), 111.

Conclusion: The War at the Opening of the 21st Century

This book opened with John Guare's preface to a collection of some of his plays published in the 20th-century's closing decade. In the 1996 preface, Guare looks back on the century as a war against the reigning dramaturgical-theatrical form: the naturalistic play. Reviewing a new book in 2006, co-editor of *The Brooklyn Rail* and playwright Jason Grote looks back on the "past decade or so" as a "watershed moment" for theatre. He explains: "There may be more multivalent, creative theater being created today than in any other time in U.S. history. Whereas theatrical movements of the recent past have privileged spectacle over text or collage over narrative, or have involved a re-assertion of traditional forms, much contemporary work exists comfortably in multiple theatrical traditions, or in no tradition at all." The implication is that non-naturalistic plays must have gained strength by century's end. That implication is certainly present in Grote's review of a collection of plays entitled *New Downtown Now*, for only in referring to one of them does he use the term naturalistic play, and after highlighting some of the plays' exciting moments, he concludes that the collection is a "vital work, a necessary addition to the library of anyone who cares about contemporary theater."[1]

New Downtown Now has a preface by the editors and playwrights Mac Wellman and Young Jean Lee, but it is the introduction by playwright Jeffrey M. Jones that I want to acknowledge. Had it not been included in the collection, it deserved to be published separately, for without convoluted theory, it takes the reader through a subject disorienting and incoherent to many who would like to experience new theatre but do not know how. Beginning with a discussion of how one reads and/or watches conventional plays, he takes the reader through discussions of concepts such as displacement and framing, character and pattern that he applies, where applicable, to conventional plays and then to the collection's plays to illuminate the concepts, thereby affording

165

access to the plays and contemporary theatre. Incidentally, he does not use the term naturalistic play, preferring the terms conventional theatre and realistic play. Under framing, for example, he discusses how conventional theatre sets a frame for the action. The classic frame that I would suggest is the kitchen with sink contained within the stage's four walls, one of which is invisible. Jones goes on to show how the new theatre has multiframes or "multithreaded narratives—each narrative running in its own frame or window, with the action (and often characters) moving between concurrent narratives and frames."[2]

Paul C. Castagno's study was published separately as the book *New Playwriting Strategies*. He too cites the 20th-century's final decade as pivotal. In 1990 he attended a seminar on New Directions in American Theater, where he became interested in the dramaturgical practices of a group of playwrights, some of whose work he had been familiar with in isolation, as collectively forming a new approach to playwriting. The book is an outgrowth of that seminar; its goal is to "clarify and codify these practices into a coherent, working aesthetic for playwrights."[3] In addition to the pivotal decade, the book connects with *New Downtown Now* and Grote's review of the latter book and not merely because Grote mentions Castagno's book in his review. As Grote points out, he knows the two editors of the collection and many of the playwrights whose plays are collected as "friend, colleague, former student, or some combination thereof" (64). In an article written in 1990, the *New York Times* critic Mel Gussow linked Mac Wellman, Eric Overmyer, and Len Jenkin, among others, as playwrights who put words at center stage.[4] With others—Jeffrey M. Jones, for one—they teach playwriting at major universities. Wellman's co-editor of *New Downtown Now*, for instance, enrolled in his program after a futile search for challenging theatre. Thus the playwrights whose plays are collected in the volume those two edited can be thought of as younger than the group of which Wellman and Overmyer, Jenkin and Jones are members.

Another way of putting the matter is that the collected playwrights have been learning the new aesthetic from the group's plays and actualizing it in their own plays. What Castagno does is extract the practices that constitute the new aesthetic from the works of Wellman and Overmyer, Jenkin and Jones, and others. His first chapter includes a list of terms in the aesthetic; reading them, one keeps encountering the names of the four playwrights and others in whose writings the terms can be found or whose writings illustrate the terms. Since the playwrights whose works Castagno studies are language based, a cluster of terms will serve as an example. Multivocality refers to the variety of voices or speech patterns within a character, a principle that violates the naturalistic principle, though Castagno uses traditional rather than naturalistic, that a character can speak only language consistent with his or her socioeconomic status. Polyvocality refers to the variety of voices that can go into the making of the play, a principle that violates the traditional principle that a play can have only a single or dominant point of view. The hybrid play therefore is a "literary and theatrical crossbreed, a blending of genres and disparate sources both textual and performative" (35).

Castagno uses a term that leads to this book's closing statement: "Dialogic clash occurs when language levels, speech genres, or discourses collide in the play's script" (9). Jones begins his explanation of how his concepts or terms work through the example of tweaking "the [standard] model [of conventional theatre] by introducing an element that 'does not belong,' thus establishing a tension between it and the model that eventually warps and changes the 'reality'" (x). In a separate review of the plays of Elana Greenfield, one of the playwrights represented in the *New Downtown Now* collection, Grote found that the "emotional life . . . is, like every other space in her writing, a place where opposites collide."[5] "Clash," "collide," and "tension" are the key words in these passages, and they apply as well to Guare's plays. The Signature Theatre Company devotes each season to the works of a contemporary American playwright. Commenting on the choice of Guare for the 1999 season, James Houghton, the company's artistic director, said, "'He crosses into every territory: realism, surrealism, naturalism, and doesn't sit in any particular time or style.'"[6] This book's argument is that the purpose of the clash, collision, and tension—the war—between naturalism and non-naturalism, traditional or conventional theatre and innovative theatre is not to rout the enemy but to interact the opposing forces. The interaction of various realities not only makes possible the crossing in Guare's plays, it is the contemporary American theatre in its most creative mode.

NOTES

1. Jason Grote, "Revolution at the Gates: Mac Wellman and Young Jean Lee's *New Downtown Now*," *The Brooklyn Rail* Sept. 2006, 64. Hereafter to be cited parenthetically.

2. Jeffrey M. Jones, "How to Read a Curious Play," introduction, *New Downtown Now: An Anthology of New Theater from Downtown New York*, ed. Mac Wellman and Young Jean Lee (Minneapolis: U of Minnesota P, 2006), xiii. Hereafter to be cited parenthetically.

3. Paul C. Castagno, *New Playwriting Strategies: A Language-Based Approach to Playwriting* (New York: Routledge, 2001), xi. Hereafter to be cited parenthetically.

4. Mel Gussow, "Playwrights Who Put Words at Center Stage," *New York Times*, 11 Feb. 1990, sec. 2, 5.

5. Jason Grote, "There Are No Words for Certain Things: Elana Greenfield," *The Brooklyn Rail* July/August 2005, 32.

6. Steven Drukman, "In Guare's Art, Zero Degrees of Separation," *New York Times*, 11 Apr. 1999, sec. 2, 7.

Index

Weber, Bruce, 62
Wellman, Mac, 37, 165, 166
Werner, Howard, 150
West, Cheryl L., 7–8
Wever, Merritt, 31
What Did He See? (Foreman), 75
What Then (Groff), 29–34
whirlwind as energy, 78
Wilson, Edwin, 6

Winiarski, Jo, 29
Women's Project production, 81–82
The Working Theatre, 123

Y, discussion of, 42–44, 46–47

Zinoman, Jason, 33
Zola, Émile, 2, 6, 10–13, 19, 123, 150–51